EMINENT
EDWARDIANS

BY THE SAME AUTHOR

Hurrell Froude and the Oxford Movement
Hawker of Morwenstow
(Editor) Cornish Ballads and Other Poems,
by Robert Stephen Hawker

EMINENT EDWARDIANS

Piers Brendon

SECKER & WARBURG
LONDON

First published in England 1979 by
Martin Secker & Warburg Limited
54 Poland Street, London WIV 3DF

SBN: 436 06810 9

Printed and bound in Great Britain
by W & J Mackay Limited, Chatham

To
TOM AND NANCY
under whose hospitable roof
this book was conceived

Contents

Acknowledgements   ix
List of Illustrations   xi
Introduction   xiii

LORD NORTHCLIFFE   1
ARTHUR BALFOUR   65
MRS PANKHURST   131
GENERAL BADEN-POWELL   195

Acknowledgements

I would like to express my warmest thanks to all who have helped me with this book. I have received assistance from many librarians and archivists and I am particularly indebted to Victoria Moger of the London Museum, to Gordon Phillips of *The Times* and to Peter Cooke at Baden-Powell House. I am grateful to Betty Wood for showing me round the Girton College archive and to Michael Holroyd for supplying me with a key reference. I have benefited greatly from the criticisms of Rex Bloomstein, Paul McHugh, Michael Murphy and Michael Woodhouse, all of whom have read sections of the book. P. N. Furbank has perused the entire manuscript and, as always, his comments were unerringly perceptive and enormously valuable, as were those of David Farrer. I have received much advice and support from Andrew Best. Tom Rosenthal has given me constant aid, generous encouragement and splendid hospitality. The forbearance of my wife and children during the long period when they lived not only with me but with – successively – Lord Northcliffe, Arthur Balfour, Mrs Pankhurst and General Baden-Powell, is beyond praise and thanks.

*   *   *

The photograph *Shooting party at Blenheim, 1896* is reproduced by gracious permission of Her Majesty the Queen.

ix

The author and publisher also wish to thank the following for their help in locating photographs and permission to reproduce them:

Fawcett Library, City of London Polytechnic (*Mrs Pankhurst, the Suffragette Queen*); Sir Geoffrey Harmsworth (photographs of Lord Northcliffe); The Museum of London (*Mrs Pankhurst and Christabel in prison uniform, Mrs Pankhurst travels First Class, Mrs Pankhurst being arrested near Buckingham Palace in 1914, Mrs Pankhurst, Nurse Pine and detectives*); Radio Times Hulton Picture Library (*Blériot, accompanied by Lord Northcliffe, The Philosopher-Statesman, Lord Balfour with Chaim Weizmann, Lord Balfour with Lloyd George, Mrs Pankhurst in about 1904, Mrs Pankhurst in New York, The submission of King Prempeh*); Public Relations Department, The Scout Association (*The hero of Mafeking, Mafficking*).

Illustrations

Between pages 16 and 17
Alfred Harmsworth, creator of the popular press
Alfred the marathon bicyclist
Alfred aged thirty

Between pages 48 and 49
Lord Northcliffe and Arthur Balfour pulling the Wright
brothers' flying machine at Pau, 1908
Lord Northcliffe and Winston Churchill, Versailles 1918
Northcliffe with his mother in 1921
Blériot, accompanied by Northcliffe, Victoria station, 1909

Between pages 80 and 81
Arthur Balfour, the Prime Minister, in 1903
Arthur Balfour aged nine
The Philosopher-Statesman

Between pages 112 and 113
Lord Balfour with Chaim Weizmann in Jerusalem, 1925
Lord Balfour with Lloyd George at a garden party, 1922
Shooting party at Blenheim, 1896

Between pages 144 and 145
Mrs Pankhurst, the Suffragette Queen
Mrs Pankhurst travels First Class
Mrs Pankhurst and Christabel in prison uniform

xi

ILLUSTRATIONS

Between pages 176 and 177
Mrs Pankhurst in about 1904
Mrs Pankhurst being arrested near Buckingham Palace,
1914
Mrs Pankhurst, Nurse Pine and detectives
Mrs Pankhurst in New York, 1913

Between pages 208 and 209
Lord Baden-Powell, Chief Scout of the world, aged eighty
Stephe at Charterhouse
Captain Baden-Powell, aged twenty-six
B-P on stage

Between pages 240 and 241
The submission of King Prempeh
B-P overwhelming an Ashanti warrior
The hero of Mafeking
Mafficking
B-P tells a campfire yarn, 1908

Introduction

Of all the details which scandalized respectable readers of Lytton Strachey's *Eminent Victorians* possibly the most infamous related to the venerable figure of Dr Arnold. The eminence of the celebrated Headmaster of Rugby School was surely beyond question. When his own son, William Arnold, first set eyes on the awesome vastness of the Himalayas he was irresistibly 'reminded of Papa'. Yet Strachey attempted to cut the Doctor down to size not just metaphorically but literally: 'his legs, perhaps, were shorter than they should have been.' Challenged, the biographer could produce no evidence for this slur. And Strachey later mischievously acknowledged that he had made Arnold's legs shorter because he thought they should have been. In more serious vein, however, he claimed to have somewhere read an account which confirmed his diminution of the Doctor. In fact, though he relied entirely on published works, Strachey's research had been surprisingly wide-ranging and it seems likely that he misappropriated the scurrilous detail from another imposing Victorian Headmaster, E. W. Benson, later Archbishop of Canterbury, whose legs really were somewhat stunted.

Be this as it may, Strachey clearly saw himself as one of

the 'apish, impish creatures' who dogged the footsteps of Clio, pompous and self-important Muse of History, 'tittering, pulling long noses, threatening to trip the good lady up, and even sometimes whisking to one side the corner of her drapery and revealing her undergarments in a most indecorous manner'. Witness his travesty of the Victorian era, an era when

> all the outlines were tremendous, all the details sordid; when gas jets struggled feebly through circumambient fog, when the hour of dinner might be at any moment between two and six, when the doses of rhubarb were periodic and gigantic, when pet dogs threw themselves out of upper storey windows, when cooks reeled drunk in areas, when one sat for hours with one's feet in dirty straw dragged along the streets by horses, when an antimacassar was on every chair, and the baths were minute tin circles, and the beds were full of bugs and disasters.

Strachey was a partisan who renounced the aloof detachment with which historians had been wont to judge the past. He was an ironist who eschewed the solemn reverence with which biographers had been accustomed to treat the dead.

He was also a miniaturist who recognized that the vast accumulation of knowledge about our immediate forebears is actually an impediment to understanding them. And he appreciated that a compact biography could be the distillation of innumerable histories. This is not to say that Strachey's four subjects are justly represented. They are distorted, exaggerated, idiosyncratic figures, etched with a satirical, polemical and at times malicious, pen. Yet, like Dickens, Strachey transcended the limitations of caricature. With pellucid style, with meticulous detail, with remorseless wit, Strachey created characters more vital than creatures of flesh and blood. They were inspired fictions no doubt. But they revealed the souls of their subjects, and evoked the spirit of their age, more vividly than interminable facts retailed by dull historians. Place Strachey's scintillating miniatures beside the prosaic studies of photographer-biographers and it becomes plain at once that objectivity is a chimera. The camera's lens reflects verisimilitude whereas the prism of the artist's imagination refracts truth.

Despite the hostility of certain critics (none more virulent than Dr F. R. Leavis, who was fond of telling his Cambridge pupils that Lytton Strachey was responsible for the outbreak of the Second World War − apparently his malign influence on Keynes and his economic theories was somehow to blame) *Eminent Victorians* has been recognized as a classic ever since its publication sixty years ago. The author of a modern work which invited comparison with it, especially in terms of literary merit, would be very foolish or very arrogant indeed. On the other hand, Strachey's *method* − the irradiation of an epoch by means of sharp biographical vignettes − still has much to recommend it. This is particularly so where the Edwardian era is concerned. The history of those callow years which inaugurated the present century has been written − is being written − over and over again, in bewildering detail. Huge biographies (representing a revival of the nineteenth-century tradition against which *Eminent Victorians* was a reaction) threaten to smother the leading figures of that time. The opaque monographs of sociologists and economists, of 'psychohistorians' and 'cliometricians', make their predictable contribution to the murk. Television programmes, which focus nostalgically on the imperial power and the social glory that was Britain before the lamps went out, obscure the picture still further. Amid the encircling gloom, however, there are a number of beacons and the student of the period must seek light where he may.

This book draws on many sources, dim and bright, printed and manuscript. Otherwise it follows Strachey's pattern and attempts to unlock an age by means of a few key figures. Its subjects were chosen because each has a unique fascination and each flourished during, and is in some way representative of, the Edwardian era. Moreover, their eminence was global. Lord Northcliffe created the popular press; Arthur Balfour gave his name to the Declaration which led to the birth of the state of Israel; Mrs Pankhurst was leader of the militant women's movement; General Baden-Powell founded the largest youth organization in history. Each of these characters invited an essay that might aim at once to illuminate and to entertain, for each stamped the imprint of a monstrous personality on the modern world.

Lord Northcliffe

I

When, shortly before his death in 1922, Lord Northcliffe attacked one of his male nurses with a poker, his enemies might have been forgiven for regarding it as an appropriate consummation to his career. After all, the man congratulated by Lord Beaverbrook as being 'the foremost figure in journalism in the whole world history of the profession' was notoriously a megalomaniac prone to bouts of violence. What press magnate was not? The Prime Minister himself, Lloyd George, had referred in Parliament to Northcliffe's 'diseased vanity', tapping his forehead suggestively at the words. Then there was the testimony of Fleet Street, which Northcliffe was said – predictably – to bestride like a Colossus. At Printing House Square, home of *The Times*, he had long been subject to 'brainstorms', 'lunatic rages' and fits of demonic vituperation. At Carmelite House, headquarters of the *Daily Mail*, he had habitually bullied and occasionally assaulted members of his staff, who were in consequence terrified of him. From office-boy to editor they trembled and sweated at his approach. One journalist instinctively raised his hat and bowed when speaking to Northcliffe on the telephone.

3

Another answered, 'Yes, O Lord.' 'He thinks I'm God,' said Northcliffe. 'Perhaps I am . . .'

A multi-millionaire who had risen from nothing to control the largest publishing business in the world, Northcliffe was constantly being told (not least by his own journals) that he was the most powerful man in the British Empire. He was the moulder of minds. He was the wrecker of governments. He was the winner of wars. He was the 'reincarnation of Napoleon'. Increasingly Northcliffe began to believe it. His vaunting faith was endorsed by both sycophants and revilers. J. L. Garvin, editor of the *Observer*, called him 'Jove' and urged him to be a 'dictator in dead earnest like Roosevelt' and thus satisfy Democracy, 'a woman which is always wanting a man'. A. G. Gardiner, editor of the *Daily News*, depicted him as 'a poisoner of the streams of human intercourse', an 'unscrupulous enemy of human society' and a corrupter of the soul of journalism. The Aga Khan assured him that he was a great cosmic force for good. Oswald Spengler denounced him as a 'master-nature' who had driven the nations towards war. The merest jokes seemed to inflate Northcliffe's ego. Lloyd George remarked, 'Even the Almighty formed a Trinity. Northcliffe is a Unitarian.' It was put about that the ministry had collapsed and Lord Northcliffe had sent for the King. The King himself, George V, condemned Northcliffe's 'dictatorial assumptions' which seemed to dwarf even those of his American counterpart, William Randolph Hearst. President Wilson's *éminence grise*, Colonel House, noted in 1917 that Northcliffe 'handles himself just as if he were Dictator of England, and, in a way, he is, for the Government are afraid of him'.

Northcliffe, then, appeared to be the apotheosis of power, capricious and unbridled. And if there was something abnormal, even pathological, about his exercise of so much power the explanation surely lay in the whispered rumour that Lord Northcliffe was the victim of what his newspapers referred to as 'the hidden plague' – syphilis. Not that there was any obvious sign of it. In fact, with his steely blue eyes, his golden Napoleonic forelock, his pale, clear skin and his flagrantly handsome face, Northcliffe was the picture of Dorian Gray undefiled. Nor did the metaphors which were most often employed to characterize Northcliffe suggest any infirmity. Rather they testified to him as a titanic natural force – an erupting volcano, a typhoon, an earthquake. With monstrous geniality, Northcliffe preferred to dramatize himself as 'Lord Vigour and Venom' or 'the Ogre of Printing House Square'. Usually, after the American fashion, he liked to be known as 'the Chief' – even his wife called him that. Once, staying at a health resort in southern France, he described himself as 'the crouching tiger of Pau' who would shortly spring on the 'swell-headed' inmates of Carmelite House. This feline image gives a hint of the real Northcliffe for; behind the public sound and the private fury there lurked, indeed, a newspaper tiger.

Northcliffe's power awed his contemporaries almost as much as it did himself because the popular press was a new creation, his creation. In the absence of other forms of mass communication its influence seemed to be boundless. It was not. Even Northcliffe's most trivial crusades were failures. He tried to convert his compatriots to 'standard' bread made from wholesome wholemeal; to this day they prefer the cotton-wool variety. He attempted to encourage English aviation by sponsoring events and offering prizes; they were won by Frenchmen. In 1920 he announced at Carmelite House,

It is about time men had a new hat. Why not offer £100 for the best design for a new hat? There is at present only the silk hat, the pot-hat or bowler (what in America is called a Derby), the straw hat, the felt hat of various shapes (usually referred to as the Trilby – I do not know why) and the universal cap. A new-hat-for-men competition would be most amusing . . . Let reference be made to hat monotony.

Despite vigorous propaganda and the largest circulation on earth, the *Daily Mail* could persuade no one except Winston Churchill, a handful of eccentrics and a few obsequious reporters to wear the new headgear. Readers were amused by the stunt. They enjoyed the flim-flam patter. But they could not be induced by Lord Northcliffe to change their hats, habits or minds. If he could not convince them in small matters still less could he do so in great. They would neither vote nor go to war at his behest. Thus Northcliffe's power was little more than a kind of wide-awake fantasy. It was epitomized in the visit to Fontainebleau where he tried on Napoleon's hat. With superstitious delight he exclaimed, 'It fits!'

The truth is that Northcliffe's journals did not so much direct as reflect their reader's views. Northcliffe himself was 'the common man to an uncommon degree'. As he acknowledged, 'most of the ordinary man's prejudices are my prejudices . . . and are therefore the prejudices of my newspaper.' Northcliffe's success was largely built on his receptiveness to, and his mirroring of, public opinion. He was always reluctant to insult his readers gratuitously by telling them what they did not want to know. They did want to know about hats – 'Terrors of Top Hat Wearing' was a favoured early headline – and about skirts –'The Battle of the Skirts: Long *v.* Short': 'What a great talking point,' said Northcliffe. They wanted to know about first-class murders and highly-spiced scandals, decorously presented of course – Northcliffe's private sexual habits may have resembled Mussolini's but his public attitudes, like those of most Edwardians, were products of the fertile union between Mr Podsnap and Mrs Grundy. They wanted to know about baby-farming and ill-health, about sport and money, about rumours of wars and royalty, about scientific marvels and the strange things found in tunnels. In short, they wanted entertainment disguised as information.

This Northcliffe was eminently fitted to provide. For the essential bent of his mind was towards acquiring useless knowledge for its own sake, knowledge of the kind provided by *Notes and Queries, Believe It Or Not, Reader's Digest* and his own *Answers*. He had an unfailing, if also undiscriminating, eye for fascinating journalistic tit-bits, some valuable, some meretricious, all shiny and bright. He aspired to be an eagle; in reality he was a jackdaw. He longed to be hailed, as he reckoned Hearst was in the United States, as a man of 'super-Cabinet rank'. Instead he found himself snapping up unconsidered trifles and playing second fiddle to politicians whom he despised. He yearned to conduct the music of the spheres; he became the victim of lunatic crotchets. A visiting American newsdaperman was astonished to hear him raging at *The Times* on the telephone, 'What have you done with the moon? I said the moon – the *moon*. Someone has moved the moon! . . . Well, if it's moved again whoever does it is fired!' It turned out that the weather report was not on its usual page. H. G. Wells said that Northcliffe's 'skull held together, in a delusive unity, a score of flying fragments of purpose'. At last, under intolerable pressure, Northcliffe's mind splintered crazily. It was as though the tangential, the inconsequential and the irrelevant had finally gained their just ascendancy.

Yet Northcliffe and Northcliffe's career cannot be dismissed that easily. His complex nature, an unplumbed pool where charm and sadism, benevolence and malignity struggled bloodily for dominance, was one of the strangest to emerge from his own or from any other era. The boyish young man, who loved his mother to the point of obsession, kept an aquarium divided into two compartments, one containing goldfish, the other pike; when the spirit moved him he would lift the partition between them. The campaigner against the use of birds' feathers to decorate women's hats once wantonly struck down a seagull with his stick and beat it to death on the sand. In other respects, however, Northcliffe was a symbolic figure. He was the average man writ large, a Pooter who became a Ponderevo. He was the personification and the amplifier of so many typical Edwardian attitudes – chauvinism, imperialism, conservatism, snobbery, vulgarity, prudery – that he still commands attention. Even his powerlessness is instructive. For, though the politicians feared him, he did little more than confirm his contemporaries in their preference for glittering, frippery preoccupations instead of dull, serious ones. Yet, with that insight which was the converse of his intellectual obliquity, Northcliffe had, at the zenith of British global power, a vision of the long afternoon of British decadence. He foresaw the rise of 'commercial America' – where he was in some ways more prominent and in most ways better appreciated than was the case at home – 'aided and abetted in its plans by a pathetic, worn out, vitiated commercial England'. It was ironical that the nearest Northcliffe came to exercising the power he craved was as purveyor to the British masses of standard bread and aerial circuses.

II

Lord Northcliffe was born, plain Alfred Charles William Harmsworth, at Chapelizod near Dublin on 15 July 1865 —astrologers were to conjure much with the fact that he shared Napoleon's zodiacal sign, Cancer. Alfred was the eldest of fourteen children produced in twenty years by Geraldine, *née* Maffet, herself the daughter of a Protestant land agent of Scottish extraction. Geraldine was as formidable a Victorian matriarch as this prodigious feat of generation suggests. She did not, in fact, like children and even as grown men her doting sons quailed before her. In 1908, at the age of seventy, she observed that Alfred must be ill because for the first time in his life he had contradicted her. It happened seldom, if ever, again. The Ogre of Printing House Square meekly obeyed her when she ordered him from the room and duly modified the policy of *The Times* to conform to her views. These were old-fashioned and inflexible. On a visit to America with her 'Firstborn' (as Alfred insistently signed himself in letters to his mother) she refused to visit Washington's house at Mount Vernon because she 'would not pay tribute to a rebel'. Geraldine's Tartar quality was well caught in 1918 by Alfred's brother, Lord Rothermere, who suggested that she would make an excellent member of the War Cabinet. However, she was always to be the first woman in Alfred's life: he called her 'darling'; he called his wife 'dear'. In those golden days, when Oedipus was a king rather than a complex, everyone considered that Alfred's most exquisite characteristic was his passionate devotion to his mother.

Alfred's father was, except in the field of procreation, an inadequate parent. 'Harmie', as Alfred Harmsworth senior was known to his cronies, came from English peasant stock though, in his cups, he claimed to be 'descended from Kings' – through his mother, whose origins cannot be traced. His marriage certificate also bore witness to a wishful imagination. It gave his occupation as 'Gentleman'; he was actually a schoolmaster. He met Geraldine on a park bench, impressed her with his laugh, his looks and his Micawberish aspirations. He was also suitably malleable. She married him in 1864 and quickly pushed him into qualifying as a barrister in England. Unfortunately Harmie's grandiloquence was less suited to the legal than to the saloon bar and his diary is full of entries like,

9

'Made a fool of myself last evening. No more drink . . .'
and 'Very seedy, my own fault, too much drink.' Occasionally he would obtain a small brief. But in general his growing family lived precariously, flitting from house to house
in now more, now less, genteel districts of north London.
Geraldine struggled to keep up appearances but at times
there was not enough to eat and for want of blankets the
children were wrapped in . . . newspapers. Whether her
Firstborn's assertive adoration was his attempt to supplant
Harmie in her affections Freud only knows. But it is
clear that from an early age Alfred loathed the taint of
poverty and nursed ambitions to replace his father's
fantasies about royal roots by a real kingdom made with
his own hands.

One witness remarked that the juvenile Alfred dwelt
'in a world of his own, of which he was chief and king and
sole possessor'. But uneasy lay the head that pretended to
wear the crown. Alfred's head was unusually large and it
was the source of some trouble to him from his infancy upwards. At different times Harmie's diary recorded, 'Baby
Alf very unwell with his head . . . ailing in his head . . . Dr
says congestion of the brain.' His parents were the more
worried about what they called 'little Alfred's fits' because
he was such an abnormally silent child. Later in life he
was prone to headaches and he always preferred to work
lying down; the contradictory explanations were offered
that otherwise he suffered from 'flushings of blood to the
head' and that when he was horizontal 'the blood doesn't
have to make the effort of running uphill to the brain'. The
mature Alfred was as interested in heads as he was in hats,
though he was apt to judge men more by the shape and
size than by the contents of their skulls. 'Pinheads' he
dismissed. Kitchener was damned as 'a tall man with a
narrow forehead'. Haig, on the other hand, must be a
great general because he looked like one – though this was
a common English fallacy. Northcliffe was particularly

impressed by Edison's 'magnificent head'. However, Lloyd George (himself a keen amateur phrenologist) was distrusted by Northcliffe not just because he was 'oblique, evasive and Welsh' but because, 'It's his big head on a little body that I don't like.' Where outward appearances were concerned, of course, Alfred's own majestic head stood out above all the rest. As he strode purposefully on youthful business in Hampstead or St John's Wood other heads turned to look at his. He reminded observers of a Greek god. Those who examined him more closely noticed a single blemish. Alfred bit his fingernails until the blood ran.

What notions were germinating behind his noble brow? Whatever their nature, it is certain that they were not formed by thorough schooling. Alfred's education, determined by his father's finances and his own temperament, was erratic. He taught himself to read by means of a toy printing set, the gift of a neighbour, George Jealous, who was editor of the *Hampstead & Highgate Express*. He became fond of the racier English novelists, Defoe, Smollett and, above all, Dickens. Aged eleven, Alfred was sent away to Stamford Grammar School in Lincolnshire where he was caned three times a week for two years and was miserable. Then, until he was sixteen, he attended Henley House School in St John's Wood, at that time under the sympathetic headmastership of John Vane Milne – whose son, A. A. Milne, was to coin the well-known aphorism that 'Harmsworth killed the penny dreadful by the simple process of producing a halfpenny dreadfuller.' H. G. Wells later taught at Henley House and he penned a barely disguised account, in *The New Machiavelli*, of Alfred's only notable achievement there, his founding of the school magazine.

He went over us as a motor-car goes over a dog. There was a sort of energy about him, a new sort of energy to us; we had never realized that anything of the sort existed in the world . . . Almost instantly he had developed a clear and detailed vision of a magazine made up of everything that was most acceptable in the magazines that flourished in the adult world about us, and had determined to make it a success. He had by a kind of instinct, as it were, plagiarized every successful magazine and breathed into this dusty mixture the breath of life . . . [He] conducted the magazine so successfully and brilliantly that he even got a whole back page of advertisements from the big sports shop in Holborn, and made the printers pay at the same rate for a notice of certain books of their own which they said had been inserted by inadvertency to fill up space.

Wells here captured the essential Alfred – the dynamic huckster, the inspired counterfeiter, the unscrupulous mountebank. Not for nothing was Alfred's schoolboy nickname 'Dodger'. It was appropriate that his first adolescent attempt to make a fortune should consist of the manufacture and sale of an elixir described as a 'silk hat reviver'. This was not a success. His next venture, a patent remedy made largely from kitchen soap, was an expression of his attitude towards doctors, whom he called 'quacktitioners'. Its bottles bore the legend 'Tonks's Pills – Cure All Ills', but it too failed to seduce the public.

Alfred's personal allure, however, was irresistible. And between his commercial operations and his marathon bicycle rides he found time to succeed at one of the age's most popular (though least discussed) indoor sports – inveigling the parlour-maid into bed. Her name was Louisa Jane Smith; she had an illegitimate child, who, sustained and encouraged but not publicly acknowledged by Alfred, proved to be a disappointment and was eventually dispatched to Australia where, between the wars, he died of drink in an asylum. Immediately Geraldine became aware of the outrage committed under her roof, the sixteen-year-old Alfred and Louisa were packed off – but he temporarily and only to the Continent, as companion to a young aristocrat on grand tour. It was explained that Alfred was travelling for his health. On his return the Firstborn apparently found his mother rigid in her determination that he should do nothing further to aggravate the servant problem. He was obliged to move into lodgings and find a smart answer to the question of how to support himself. An accomplished vamper, he composed the 'Ellen Terry Waltz' and toyed with the idea of soaring to wealth and fame on wings of song. But what with his experience on the *Henley House Magazine* and the holiday work he had done for George Jealous's local paper, it was obvious that his vocation lay in journalism. With Alfred's push, charm, flair and looks – he always tried to impress editors by dressing immaculately – he could surely sell words. They were commodities like any other and they were less trouble to produce than Tonks's Pills or silk hat rivivers. Each 'quacktitioner' to his cure – Alfred just *knew* how to provide what people wanted to read. Soon he was earning three guineas a week as a free lance.

One of the journals to which he contributed was called *Tit-Bits*, started in 1881 by George Newnes. It was a cheap compendium of miscellaneous scraps, jokes, stories, curiosities and out-of-the-way facts. *Punch* guyed its 'giblets journalism', offering as a satirical tit-bit the information that British mills, working double shifts for twenty-five years, eight months and three weeks, could manufacture enough blotting paper to soak up the Pacific. But *Punch* could not rival the appeal of *Tit-Bits*. Its circulation surged upwards as the masses, pouring from the elementary schools established by the 1870 Education Act, sought light, palatable reading matter on which to cut their intellectual teeth. Alfred earned a guinea a column by writing on subjects like 'How Some Fortunes are Made' and 'Organ Grinders and their Earnings'. It did not take him long to appreciate the fact that Newnes was revolutionizing popular journalism. Gone were the solid tombstones of print, the grave political debates, the dusty moral homilies. In their place were short, lively, peptonized paragraphs, rich in every kind of 'human interest'. The new approach was summed up by the Northcliffean hero of W. L. George's novel *Caliban*. 'Who the hell wants to read about . . . the rights of small states? What the public wants is half a column on how Kruger stole Joe Chamberlain's top hat.' Alfred was not yet suitably placed to give the public what it wanted wholesale, to play Napoleon to Newnes's Mirabeau. But he made a stride in that direction in 1886 when he secured the editorship of the Coventry journal *Bicycling News*. There he earned the sobriquet 'Yellow-headed Worm' from contributors whose articles he cankered. He also outraged their susceptibilities by employing a female correspondent – ladies did not move on bicycles. But though he raised the circulation of *Bicycling News* he regarded Coventry as 'too middling – you are not quite down, but you are by no means up . . . I must be up!' He soon returned to London. There in 1888 he raised the capital (through some friends of Geraldine's) to start a weekly rival to *Tit-Bits* and he married his pretty childhood sweetheart Mary (usually called Molly) Milner. Within four years Molly was taking lovers and Alfred's publications had the largest circulation in the world.

III

Like most innovators Alfred did little that was new. He simply appropriated the *Tit-Bits* formula, but instead of providing his own miscellany he encouraged his readers to do it for him. He gambled on the voracious curiosity of the superficially educated who would surely, if given the chance, write and ask for the tit-bit they fancied. Hence the title of his journal, *Answers to Correspondents*, quickly shortened to *Answers*. The system was economical and it enabled him to gauge his market to perfection. The initial problem, of course, was that without *Answers* there were no questions. Alfred seems to have solved it by starting with issue No. 3. Certainly he posed the first questions himself and continued to do so when the supply of authentic ones failed, plagiarizing on a large scale, especially from American sources – Hearst was at that time satisfying his countrymen's hunger for information about whether sea-serpents were real and what it felt like to be a murderer. Alfred answered endless inquiries of that kind. 'Can Monkeys Smoke?' 'How to Cure Freckles.' 'Why Jews Don't Ride Bicycles.' 'How Madmen Write.' 'What the Queen Eats.' 'Can Insects Feel Pain?' *Answers'* headlines were striking: 'A Terrible Time with a Tiger', 'Mysteries of a Hashish House', 'Horseflesh as Food', 'An Electrical Flying Machine', 'Mr Answers Under Gas', 'Narrow Escapes from Burial Alive'. The jokes were simple: 'The sculptor is the most likely of all men to cut a figure in the world.' The anecdotes were piquant: The Prince of Wales is known as 'Tum-tum' to his friends because of his 'graceful rotundity of person'. The competitions and insurance schemes were enticing. The serial stories were cliff-hangers. Hoardings blazoned forth what Alfred called the greatest words ('Tennyson couldn't have written them') in English literature:

'When you travel by train
Stick to *Answers* might and main.'

But for the first few nail-biting months Alfred could not make *Answers* pay. London, suffused by pea-soup fogs, was preoccupied with an inimitable serial of its own–the exploits of Jack the Ripper.

Also, *Answers* was competing against two hundred other new publications founded in 1888. But none of their editors could match Alfred when it came to devising promotional stunts. He effervesced with the excitement and energy of a born barnumizer. He was the master of market-stall mummery and fair-booth rattle, of baiting hooks for readers and 'figuring out angles'. Thus his chance encounter with an ex-convict gave him the idea for the first really successful *Answers* serial, 'Confessions of a Ticket-Of-Leave Man'. A visiting American entrepreneur suggested a 'novelty' known as 'Pigs in Clover'. It was a glass-topped box containing seven coloured balls which, rolled into the correct holes, spelled out *Answers*. Alfred sold the 'Pigs' for threepence. But they were so popular that he could not satisfy the demand and they fetched a shilling on the black market. Other *Answers* products followed, a prize dog, a fountain pen, a toothache cure—Alfred swore it was 'efficacious' – and patent treatments were advertised to stop blushing, remedy baldness, increase height and eclipse red noses. But the turning point for *Answers*, increasing its circulation to over 200,000 copies a week, occured as a result of Alfred's meeting a tramp on the Thames embankment. (Alfred was always interested in human derelicts and it later became his practice to pick them up in his motor-car, treat them to a bath and a suit of dress clothes, introduce them, under assumed names, to polite company and regale them with champagne and truffles – before sending them about their mendicant business.) Anyway, the embankment tramp revealed that his vision of prosperity consisted of 'a pound a week for life'. This became the prize of the next *Answers* competition, the object being to guess the total value of the gold and silver in the Bank of England on a specified day. The winner got within two pounds of the correct sum and Alfred, by requiring five independent witnesses to sign each of the 718,218 entries, put *Answers* in touch with over three and a half million potential readers. It really was, as Alfred's sandwich-board men had asserted, 'The Most Gigantic Competition The World Has Ever Seen' and it laid the foundation for his 'Schemo Magnifico'.

Alfred Harmsworth, creator of the popular press

Alfred the marathon bicyclist – on the extreme right

Alfred aged thirty

This was the ambitious plan to use *Answers* as a base from which to establish a great confederacy of new publications. A vital preliminary step was to wrest full financial control of *Answers* itself from subscribers of the original capital. Alfred soon accomplished this, though the episode is one of the murkiest in his career. He threatened to sell his own shares and start a rival journal. And he seems to have hinted that he would expose one major stockholder as a homosexual if he did not cooperate. In complete command, Alfred placed his brothers in subordinate posts, the vital office of financial controller being ruthlessly filled by Harold Harmsworth. Harold cared only about 'grabbing' money and 'knifing' anything that did not pay, and he annoyed Alfred by referring to their proliferating periodicals as 'rags'. Alfred was sensitive about what came to be known (to his fury) as the 'hooligan department' of his empire. The historian of *The Times* might dismiss *Comic Cuts* and *Illustrated Chips*, both begun in 1890, as 'comicalities for errand boys'. Alfred was proud of them. They made him laugh, just as gramophone records of sneezing and snoring made him laugh. What is more, they were 'Amusing without being Vulgar' – vulgar, that is, in the sense of being unsuitable to the most genteel domestic circle. Alfred hated low vulgarity and, apart from his compulsion to explain to visitors that Pau was pronounced po, he always eschewed it. He aspired instead to that artificial refinement which was, as it happened, the most ineffable form of Edwardian vulgarity. Pooterism, the English obsession with class distinctions and the nuances of snobbery, was perhaps Alfred's chief legacy from his father. Despite increasing poverty towards the end, Harmie believed as keenly as Geraldine in shunning the common and the plebeian. He once admonished his son Cecil to economize with the paradoxical utterance, 'Do not demean yourself to the vulgarity of a tramcar unless absolutely necessary.' Unhappily cirrhosis of the liver sent Harmie to join his ancestors, royal or not, before Alfred came into his proper kingdom.

There was even less reason for Alfred to be ashamed of the women's magazines, such as *Home-Sweet-Home*, which followed *Cuts* and *Chips*. *The Times* olympian might disparage *Forget-Me-Not* as containing 'novelettes for the kitchen'. Alfred's opinion was probably best summed up in his slogan for *Home Chat*: 'The Daintiest Little Magazine in the World'. Whether on the subject of 'Confessions of a Wallflower' or 'How to Kiss and When to Kiss' or 'Are Flirts Always Heartless' or 'Diary of a Professional Beauty', his women's journals did not so much pander as grovel to the proprieties. In their pages correct etiquette was the burning issue and women were ornamental and unemancipated, so abjectly the softer sex that female prisoners were referred to as 'lady convicts'. (Alfred disliked masculine, trouser-wearing women: they might interfere with the birthrate.) As for the boys' periodicals, *The Wonder*, *The Marvel*, *Union Jack*, *Boy's Friend*, *Pluck Library*, there was nothing in the least bit dreadful about them. On the contrary, they were wholesome, patriotic, respectable and pure. As were profitable volumes such as the *Harmsworth Self-Educator*. And the most *risqué* stunt attempted by his religious journals was the *Sunday Companion*'s importation of water from the river Jordan. Apart from propriety, Alfred's publications had one other thing in common – their immense popularity. By 1894 they had a combined sale of over a million a week and Alfred had made a fortune. One of his first purchases was a country house called Elmwood, in Kent, which he furnished with princely extravagance and scrupulous bad taste. Clearly, though, when it came to judging the taste of the public he was well-nigh infallible. His growing retinue called him Alfred the Great.

Seeking new worlds to conquer, Alfred crossed the Atlantic for the first time in 1894. His arrival in the United

States went unheralded and he claimed to be unimpressed by America. There was 'mud in the streets' of New York. But, with his sharp counterfeiter's eye, he observed that money was being coined on the sidewalks. Joseph Pulitzer's newspapers (not seriously challenged until Hearst bought the *Journal* in the following year) were selling in their hundreds of thousands. Pulitzer's success inspired Alfred. So perhaps did his personality. Theodore Dreiser described Pulitzer as 'a disease-demonized soul, who could scarcely control himself in anything, a man who was fighting an almost insane battle with life itself, trying to be omnipotent and what not else, and never to die'. Pulitzer's methods, it was true, could not be applied wholesale in the staid 'Old Country'. Not that Pulitzer was, as is often claimed, the inventor of yellow journalism, with its melodramatic typography and its sulphurous compound of sex, sin and violence; as early as 1875, for example, the virulently jaundiced *Chicago Times* announced the hanging of four repentant murderers with the headline 'Jerked to Jesus'. But Pulitzer did employ many of the techniques of sensationalism, he engaged in furious crusades and he had a weakness for alliterative headlines such as 'Baptized in Blood' and 'Mangled by Mongrels'. Still, the founder of *Answers* could not but admire an editor who sent out his minions on a quest for news that was 'original, distinctive, dramatic, romantic, thrilling, unique, curious, quaint, humorous, odd, apt to be talked about'. Alfred saw that English conditions matched those favouring the expansion of the popular press in America – the intellectual awakening of the inhabitants of bursting industrial cities, their increasing wealth, leisure and interest in sport, even their habit of travelling to work by train. Cheap paper, freedom from government imposition, novel modes of communication such as the electric telegraph, the telephone, the typewriter and the linotype machine (Alfred was fascinated by American 'gadgets'), all meant that the new market could be supplied. Moreover, Alfred's home market, because it was more compact, was much larger than the American one. Pulitzer's *World* only reached New Yorkers: Alfred envisaged a journal that would be distributed throughout Britain. As his friend Max Pemberton put it, Alfred's realization that the 'morning newspaper which does not reach the breakfast-table is born dead' was his 'Columbus Egg'.

When involved in secret business negotiations Alfred chose as his code name 'Atlantic'. Pulitzer's pseudonymous title was 'Andes'. There is no doubt that in the creation of mass journalism the mountain spake unto the deep. But it is not clear precisely what message Alfred received or how far he consciously modelled himself on Pulitzer. Of course they shared uncannily similar traits. Dreiser ascribed the fact that the *World*'s reporters 'had a kind of nervous, resentful terror in their eyes, as have animals when they are tortured', to the blind Pulitzer's 'vital, aggressive, restless, working mood, and his vaulting ambition', which made 'a veritable hell of his paper and the lives of those who worked for him'. It would have been an apt description of Alfred and the *Daily Mail*. It seems, though, that the characters of newspaper proprietors are set inexorably in the same type – Gothic. Hearst and Northcliffe, for example, in spite of the former's starting life with so many millions that he could ask his mother to buy him the Louvre, were brothers under the skin, Citizen Kane and Citizen Able. Both had Napoleonic fixations, ruthlessly sought supreme political power, were violent Jingoes abroad and at home tempered their reactionary views with radical sympathies, alternated between bouts of energy and lethargy, disliked coarseness but shared the popular taste in entertainment, took a cruel delight in appointing two men to the same job and watching them fight for survival (Pulitzer did that too), and earned the abiding mistrust of their respective countrymen. Thus, although Alfred may have aped Pulitzer he also resembled him. And on his first trip to the United States he was fired generally by American vim and enterprise, as he was to be on so many later visits. Subsequently Alfred appropriated Pulitzer's 'eyes', his gifted and irreplaceable confidential secretary, earning himself the rebuke, 'I always knew you were a hard man, but I didn't think you would steal a dog from a blind man.' But the incontrovertible trophy that Alfred brought back from his first transatlantic trip was Pulitzer's 'ears'. These were the little boxes on each side of the title of the *World*, and Alfred purloined them to advertise the peculiar virtues of his first daily paper, the *Evening News*, which he bought shortly after his return.

IV

The tone of Alfred's introductory leader in the *Evening News*, on 31 August 1894, was sober, measured and eminently respectable.

> Freed from fad and prejudice, the *Evening News* will preach the gospel of loyalty to the Empire and faith in the combined efforts of the peoples united under the British flag. While strongly and unfalteringly Conservative and Unionist in Imperial politics, the *Evening News* will occupy an advanced democratic platform on all social matters. It will be progressive in municipal reform; non-sectarian in all questions affecting the religious beliefs of the community, sympathetic towards labour and friendly to every phase of communal advancement.

In spite of this the *News*'s editor, Kennedy Jones, had grounds for his suspicion that Alfred was 'going to turn the paper into an evening *Answers*'. Leaders were cut down. Paragraphs were shortened. Style was simplified and foreign words were banished. A short story and a women's page appeared. Sport and crime featured largely. Alfred went round the office saying, 'Maps, maps, maps!' There was a rash of articles on such familiar *Answers* topics as 'Baby Farming in Belgium' and 'Secrets of the Dissecting Room'. Kennedy Jones, one of the most hated figures in Fleet Street, was fond of instructing his reporters to apply a glove-stretcher to their minds. But Jones's own consciousness of the possibilities of popular journalism expanded under Alfred's pressure. The figures spoke for themselves. The *Evening News*, like most of the nine London evening newspapers, had been losing money before Alfred bought it – he had referred to it as a 'gold brick'. But in the first week of his ownership it began to show a profit and he recovered the entire £25,000 which the *News* had cost him within three years. By 1898 it was selling 800,000 copies a day and making £50,000 a year. Alfred proved how potent the *Answers* seed was, especially when stimulated by fertile applications of American sensationalism. He reflected the spirit of the age by covering his newspapers' thrusting fecundity with a cloak of decency and decorum.

Exactly the same techniques were applied to the *Daily Mail*, which Alfred launched in 1896. This operation, the outcome of which, as he remarked, could have been 'Bankruptcy or Berkeley Square', was the most meticulously planned in his career. Its success was his greatest achievement and signalled a new epoch in the history of the press. When the first edition sold nearly 400,000 copies Alfred declared, 'We've struck a goldmine.' The *Mail*'s 'ears', which proclaimed it 'The Busy Man's Daily Journal' and 'A Penny Newspaper for one Halfpenny', gave an indication of the commercial, commuting audience it had won. It appealed preeminently to the growing white-collared lower-middle class. Just as Northcliffe's *Daily Mirror*, it was later unkindly said, was designed for those who could not read, so his *Mail* was designed for those who could not think. But whatever their intellectual capacities, it was the attitudes of the lower-middle class, refracted through the prism of Alfred's personality, which set the *Mail*'s discordant, polychromatic tone. Alfred believed that his customers, especially the female ones, liked 'to read papers which seem intended for persons of superior social standing'. It was doubtless with this in mind that he later pronounced, 'All *Daily Mail* correspondents are supposed to travel with a valet.' And it was for this reason that the *Mail* paid servile attention to the doings of the monarchy and the aristocracy. On the other hand, for the *Mail* not to have professed its faith in the common man would have been an insult to its proprietor as well as its purchasers. Thus the paper's social position fluctuated uneasily between snobbery and egalitarianism. The *Mail*'s political opinions were equally ambivalent, though the paper did consistently reflect the anti-German and pro-Imperial mood of the time. A. G. Gardiner maintained that Northcliffe

has no loyalties to anything ... When Mr Chamberlain opened his protection campaign, he came out against it ... He went to Chamberlain's Glasgow meeting, saw the vast audience ... believed it spelled victory, and next morning came out in the *Daily Mail* a sort of St Paul of the new gospel – only to desert it again directly the gospel began to wane.

Gardiner was not quite right. Alfred did have loyalties, but only temporary ones. He could no more sustain them than he could sustain a coherent argument. He jumped straight to a conclusion, reiterated it dogmatically ... and then changed his mind. H. W. Massingham, editor of the *Nation*, was nearer the mark when he said that the *Mail* 'has no views and all views'.

Of course, the *Mail* was read for its news rather than its

views. It was here that Alfred excelled. He was probably justified in boasting that he could go on a penny ride in an omnibus and come back with a story that any newspaper would be pleased to print. He had a craving as well as a nose for news: it was not just for fun that he incessantly telephoned the *Mail*'s news editor, W. G. Fish, with the enquiry, 'Anything fresh, Fish?' Alfred's mind pulsated with ideas about news. He discharged them like electric sparks, shocking his staff into activity. His prime victim was Thomas Marlowe, who was said to have secured his place in the *Mail*'s editorial chair against a rival, also appointed by Alfred, through the abnormal strength of his bladder. Alfred urged Marlowe to print news about 'Coronation socks', about the Wallaceites, 'who do not seem to be vegetarians in the strict sense of the word', about 'Standard bread on the Lusitania'. He complained that 'interesting pieces of news are being cut. Take, for example, Girl killed by a Whirlwind. Surely that is a very strange piece of news; it is buried on page five.' He made transparent protestations: 'I am not fond of flaring headlines, but they are getting more and more deadly. Try "London Street Noises" and "Ugly and Bad Stamps".' And, 'If we had wanted sensationalism (personally I don't like it) there was a splendid story of the old-fashioned melodramatic kind in the murder case tried at the Bordeaux Assizes – an innkeeper and his wife who murdered the guests, with a deaf and dumb man as the chief witness.' Eventually Alfred's communiqués, praising, vilifying, exhorting, threatening, became regular features in the daily lives of his subordinates. Their quicksilver quality was well represented by W. L. George:

Why were the Bishop of London's remarks on the rise of immorality dropped out of the second edition? The make-up is bad. It is no use advertising ladies' underclothes on the financial page. I can't make out what the

picture of Dollie Johnson on the back page is. It looks
like a gasometer. Or Westminster Abbey by moonlight.
Mem. Keep up the agitation against wood pigeons.

News was not news for Alfred unless it was interesting;
anything sufficiently interesting was news.
If there was no news he created it. He campaigned for
daylight saving, small-holdings, aviation, motoring, sweet
peas. He even crusaded, Pulitzer-like, against the Lever
'Soap Trust'. But the English libel laws were (and are)
more stringent than the American and he was successfully
sued for £150,000. Anyway serious muckraking was as
indelicate as it was hazardous. It was better to stick to
'talking points'. 'Each day we must have a feature . . .
something different . . . a surprise.' They turned out to be
the *Answers* mixture as before: 'The Truth about Night
Clubs', 'Do We Eat too Much?', 'The Riddle of Spiritualism'. (Alfred thought there was 'nothing in spiritualism':
all the same, he had an uneasy feeling that the 'Unseen
Hand' was keeping an eye on him.) Occasionally a
genuinely important talking point was aired, such as
Belgian atrocities in the Congo. But it was important only
for as long as it held readers' attention, then it was discarded like any old hat. A member of his staff noticed with
astonished dismay that at one moment Alfred would focus
the entire force of his concentration on the subject of the
vital necessity of improving Anglo-American relations.
The next he would switch, with equal vigour, to arranging
details of the *Daily Mail* 'Golden Slipper' competition, to
be won by the actress with the smallest foot. It was hardly
surprising that Alfred took to repeating Kennedy Jones's
catchphrase, 'Everything counts, nothing matters'. Northcliffe's methods made the *Mail* the most successful newspaper hitherto seen in the history of journalism. But by
confusing gewgaws with pearls, by selecting the paltry at
the expense of the significant, by confirming atavistic

prejudice, by over-simplifying the complex, by dramatizing the humdrum, by presenting stories as entertainment and by blurring the difference between news and views, Northcliffe titillated, if he did not debauch, the public mind; he polluted, if he did not poison, the wells of knowledge.

Not that any of this was the result of deliberate policy: Alfred was in every sense the man of mercury. Unstable, he took the line of least resistance; perverse, he sometimes doubled back on his course. Like the flea and the grasshopper to which Lloyd George compared him, Alfred kept 'jumping from one idea to another. If a thing does not "catch on" at the moment he drops it and tries something else.' As with stunts, so with newspapers. Some links in his growing chain broke and had to be reforged or replaced. In 1903, for example, Alfred founded the *Daily Mirror* as a journal written for women by women. Unfortunately the ladies in charge turned out to be as helpless and innocent as their contemporary stereotype. The coarse Kennedy Jones found himself in the unaccustomed role of censor: headlines such as 'Our French Letter' had to be altered to 'Yesterday in Paris'. Alfred quickly dismissed the women – it was 'like drowning kittens' – and changed the *Mirror* into an illustrated 'tabloid' for both sexes, pioneering in the process a technique for printing photographs which soon made line drawings obsolete. The new *Mirror*, reflecting as it did the views of the working class, won an ever-increasing audience, though it was never popular with Alfred. It was brazen. In this it resembled the moribund *Weekly Dispatch* which he purchased from George Newnes and flogged back into life. Alfred complained about the 'common-looking babies' in its beautiful baby competition and wanted to eliminate its new-found vulgarity by employing 'a supervising sub-editor of education and refinement'. He indulged his capricious temper to the full with underlings in such rude outposts of his empire. In 1909, for instance, he played Caligula on the telephone: 'Who is that?' 'Editor, *Weekly Dispatch*, Chief.' 'You *were* the Editor.' Alfred became predictable only in his arbitrariness, though sometimes employees of greater repute were treated with greater respect. One such was J. L. Garvin whom he appointed to edit the ailing but influential *Observer*, bought in 1905. Alfred probably valued Garvin less for the political mentorship he proffered than for his ability to 'froth at the mouth in prose'. Alfred was too wayward to endure prolonged guidance from any-one except his mother and he sold the *Observer* (by then profitable) after six years rather than follow Garvin's line in politics or dismiss him outright. Thus Alfred made a virtue out of volatility. Journalism, after all, was dedicated to novelties and ephemera, and success in the profession went to the dodger with the most art.

Alfred's nimblest stratagem in 1905 was to invest £50,000 in the *Manchester Courier* in an endeavour to make it 'the leading Conservative organ in the North'. It so happened that this sum was about the going rate for a barony and that Arthur Balfour, the Prime Minister, was Member of Parliament for a Manchester constituency. Alfred had always maintained that 'When I want a peerage I will pay for it like an honest man' and this, in effect, was what he did. At the end of the year, just before he lost his seat in the Liberal landslide, Balfour promoted Harms-worth to Northcliffe. Alfred adopted the name from a part of the Kent coast near Elmwood, but he incorporated Bonapartist bees into his coat of arms and he soon took to signing himself with the single Napoleonic N. However, Northcliffe did not, at the age of forty, become one of the youngest peers ever created simply in return for political services rendered. He reached his Edwardian eminence because he had built an empire. True it was an empire without a Napoleonic Code, a moral void dominated by Alfred's despotic will and governed by the changes and chances of his fleeting mind. But it was an empire without precedent and it had taken a new type of man to construct it. As W. L. George wrote, talking to Northcliffe

> was like sitting for thirty-six hours in a second-class railway carriage coming up from Surbiton. But he's got something that they haven't, something terrific, intensity of interest, intensity of will. He knows desperately what he wants. He may catch flies but he's got the mind of a lion. Somehow, shrilly, coarsely, stupidly, by energy, by occasional generosity, by courage

he had revolutionized the fourth estate and made a singular impact on his age. Alfred's peerage, in short, was an acknowledgement that the fusion of so many teeming littlenesses had produced a kind of greatness.

V

Once, when walking down Fleet Street, Northcliffe observed that a chimney at the *Daily Mail* building had caught fire. It was obviously a symbolic conflagration and he turned to his companion excitedly: 'Look,' he cried, 'the smoke of their brains!' Northcliffe loved the *Mail* with the hot passion of youth. His love was really a form of narcissism, for the paper was a printed expression of his own personality — ardent, hectic, incandescent. The *Mail* had also blasted him to international fame. When he visited the United States in 1901, for example, he had a private audience with the President. And Pulitzer invited him to edit the *World* on the first day of the new century. For this special occasion all its staff (except one recalcitrant, whom Northcliffe later employed on the *Mail*) wore evening dress in the Englishman's honour. He transformed the paper into a 'tabloid' with the motto 'All the news in sixty seconds.' The stunt caused nation-wide interest and it began to establish Alfred in American eyes as 'the liveliest and most vital entity in England'. He wrote to his 'darling Mum', 'People say that no young man's coming has ever stirred up the United States so much before.' In fact, Alfred's brave new *World* was generally criticized, though Hearst was hostile largely because his own *Journal* was temporarily eclipsed. Hearst wrote,

Would you like to look at Mr Harmsworth? Imagine a face that presents a mixture of Napoleon, Edison and the left hand cherub leaning over the frame of Raphael's 'Sistine Madonna' ... Harmsworth is trying to buy the London *Times*. He wants to own 'a great paper, the greatest paper'. Therefore he knows that he owns no such paper now. May he get *The Times*; and when he gets it, may he show us the real Harmsworth editing a real newspaper.

Hearst was right. Alfred Harmsworth had created the *Daily Mail* and the *Daily Mail* had created Lord Northcliffe. But, though he had no intention of ending his early liaison, he had long sought a more respectable connexion. He had, in truth, been casting wanton, parvenu eyes in the direction of the Old Lady of Printing House Square.

The Times, indignantly smoothing down her ruffled drapery, rebuffed his first advances. She might be impoverished but by breeding and nurture she was impeccably correct. By 1908, though, her situation had become desperate. Circulation was falling. Past prestige could hardly avert present bankruptcy. Victorian methods were not appropriate to Edwardian circumstances. *The Times*'s chief proprietor was capable of remarking on the most extraordinary coincidence in its annual balance sheet: 'the totals on each side exactly correspond'. Perhaps after all it was extraordinary, for the general manager, Moberly Bell, kept the newspaper's accounts in a penny notebook. Some reporters at Printing House Square were, like Gladstone,

vague about the difference between a phonograph and a
telephone. Others refused to employ the latter instrument
and most shunned the typewriter in favour of the quill pen.
The editor, G. E. Buckle, opened letters with his thumb.
It all reduced Northcliffe to despair. He too believed in
observing the proprieties but such hidebound reverence
for Dickensian traditions infuriated him, especially where
news-gathering was concerned. He expostulated,

> Did you know there was a sub-editor on *The Times* who
> once spiked an elephant? Yes, an elephant escaped from
> a circus in South London and went careering about the
> streets. When this sub-editor received an account of the
> incident, he stuck it on the waste-file with other
> rejected copy. It was too interesting!

Paradoxically, such aloof disdain for his own journalistic
values increased *The Times*'s allure for Northcliffe. His
determination to be master at Printing House Square became almost a frenzy when a new wooer, Arthur Pearson,
who had imitated *Tit-Bits* and *Answers* with *Pearson's
Weekly*, entered the field. With the 'rat-like cunning'
which, it has recently been said, is the *sine qua non* of
journalistic success, Northcliffe ostensibly pressed Pearson's suit while actually damaging it beyond repair. In an
article in the *Observer* he described his rival as 'a hustler'.
The Old Lady of Printing House Square wanted to
establish an alliance with a hustler about as much as Lady
Bracknell wished to form an association with a handbag.
But it was plain that her survival depended on submission
to some fate worse than death. So it was that, like a ripe fig,
The Times fell into the hands of Lord Northcliffe.

A marriage of convenience, it was grossly unsatisfactory
from the start. There were, for example, basic flaws in the
settlement. Obviously a swap of lucre for prestige implied
obligations on both sides. Northcliffe promised to love,
honour and cherish *The Times* and to preserve it as a great

independent institution like, he said ironically, the British Museum. Under these conditions Moberly Bell promised to obey Lord Northcliffe's 'absolute instructions'. But what if Lord Northcliffe required changes of the kind which might improve the Old Lady's performance at the expense of her character? While not expecting life with Northcliffe to be 'a bed of roses', *The Times*'s manager was so apprehensive about Pearson's 'bed of thorns' that he did not insist on a clear answer to this question. Perhaps Bell thought that the sage and distinguished figures at Printing House Square could control their crass, ill-educated new overlord. The German generals cherished as visionary a hope about Hitler. Northcliffe referred to Bell, Buckle and the rest as the 'Old Gang', as 'Black Friars', as 'giant tortoises'. He wrote to them in mock medieval about their 'screeds' not being 'of great interest to ye publique'. They produced a soporific Establishment Gazette which the journalist in him loathed and despised. As a news-sheet its main function was to act as a shroud for inert men in London clubs, or as 'a piece of respectable furniture in the dentist's waiting room'. *The Times* was 'the rest-cure' where the *Mail* was 'the dog-fight'. *The Times*'s mottoes were '"Abandon scope all ye who enter here" and "News, like wine, improves by keeping".' Northcliffe once discovered, in 'that vast and gloomy labyrinth hidden away near St Paul's', a room full of old muskets and spears, souvenirs of some long-forgotten campaign. What were they doing there? he asked. Then quickly, 'I know, they're to arm the staff with, if anyone brings you a piece of news.' *The Times* was 'a barnacle-covered whale', 'a giant sloth', 'a cross between a government office and a Cathedral'. For her own good as well as for their mutual satisfaction, Northcliffe was determined to 'galvanize' the Old Lady 'into a semblance of life'.

How could this be done? Northcliffe wielded the electrodes with skill and vigour. But the torpid denizens of

Printing House Square were well insulated by the cara-
paces of their caste. Ill-adapted to moving at all, the giant
tortoises could hardly be induced to scuttle. Northcliffe
used every means to impress on them that 'there was to be
one master' at *The Times*. He employed office spies,
'ferrets' he called them, to discover their most vulnerable
spots. He invited selected victims into his presence, spoke
to them in his most inaudible voice, and then accused them
of being deaf and a danger to his business. He punished
one member of staff by telephoning him at home every
half hour for an entire evening. He was indiscriminately
'ratty and dissatisfied', spasmodically insulting and abusive
(though he avoided coarse 'expletives'), and he sometimes
went on the rampage, issuing vehement, contradictory
instructions by telephone, telegram and in person. 'A devil
of a day with Northcliffe,' wrote Geoffrey Dawson, Buckle's
successor as editor, in his 1908 diary, and it was the first
and mildest of many such entries. Eventually the nagging
took its toll. In 1910, the better to streamline himself for
the fray, Bell shaved off his moustache. The following year,
worn out by Northcliffe's constant goading, he died. Also
in 1911 the foreign editor resigned, as did Buckle – in
order to preserve his health and his self-respect. In spite
of these victories Northcliffe had been defeated. He could
not even prevail upon *The Times* to print the letters on the
same page each day. Circulation had increased a little, to
47,000, but in most respects the paper was still the supine,
loss-making, nineteenth-century leviathan of Northcliffe's
nightmares.

The *History of 'The Times'*,* truly a mammoth monument to the barnacle-covered whale, argues that Lord
Northcliffe's plan, followed 'consistently until his death',

---

* Wickham Steed, who became editor of *The Times* after Dawson,
in 1919, considered that the third volume of its history was
'magnificent' but rather 'blind' to some of Northcliffe's 'glaring
defects'. Lord Beaverbrook agreed with this view.

was to master the newspaper by 'mastering its principal members'. This is implausible. Northcliffe was incapable of following any subtle, consistent plan. As Geoffrey Dawson said, 'there has never been a less far-sighted schemer . . . in the history of the world.' Northcliffe's savage treatment of *The Times* staff was essentially the product of frustration. When thwarted he took action, any action. He once responded to the inadequacy of the *Mail*'s picture page by lining up all involved in its production and putting the tallest man in charge – despite his Napoleonic conviction that 'very tall men are rarely good organizers . . . it is the small men who have the brains'. Oddly enough the picture page did improve. An absurd change was clearly better than none at all. The root of Northcliffe's frustration with *The Times* was that change its staff as he would he could not change its nature. If he turned *The Times*, as his enemies accused him of doing, into 'the *édition de luxe* of the *Daily Mail*', he would destroy its unique prestige and influence. Northcliffe appreciated this only too well and in, for example, his insistence on the use of 'pure' English – 'motor house' for garage – he was more pedantic than the most ardent Timesian: 'American is very amusing to talk,' he said, 'but it should not be allowed to be printed in *The Times*.' When someone suggested that he should 'popularize' the paper Northcliffe retorted scathingly that it would be putting 'a Punch and Judy show in Westminster Abbey'. He was caught in the trap set by his own ambition. If Northcliffe the journalist debased the Old Lady he would violate the very distinction which was the source of her original fascination for North-cliffe the power broker. Thus the marriage of convenience was never consummated.

Yet Northcliffe did have a wholly unexpected form of success with *The Times*. For a few years he achieved the seemingly impossible. He gave the paper a mass reader-ship without sacrificing either its virgin integrity or its élite status. He simply lowered the price. He wrote to Dawson in mocking triumph:

> I hear that the old lady of Printing House Square gathered up her skirts and shrieked as at the sight of a man under the bed in the face of a real increase in demand for *The Times* for the first time since her middle age.

In March 1914 *The Times* became a penny newspaper and tripled its readership. Five months later the Great War created an enormous new demand for authoritative news and over a quarter of a million people bought *The Times*. Before 1914 no one had emphasized the German menace more vehemently than Northcliffe: 'Germany,' he wrote (with an interesting choice of adjectives), 'is new, masterful, alive, brutal and horribly *nouveau riche*.' But Lord Northcliffe did not start the war, as his opponents claimed, in order to increase the circulation of his newspapers by providing them with a sensational daily serial. Nevertheless Northcliffe and the war combined to make the present *Times*.

VI

This is to anticipate: here is the place to attempt an impressionistic portrait of Lord Northcliffe before the war, during his Edwardian heyday. His magnificent head has been depicted. It was borne, rather forward, on a thick neck, tending to grossness. In his later years, when he began to resemble an out-of-condition prize-fighter, Northcliffe kept a record of his fluctuating weight, inscribed, 'A Fat Man's Gallant Fight Against Fate'. At his heaviest he reached fourteen stone, on which he commented, 'Horrible'. He spoke quietly – too quietly to sway voters on the only occasion he stood for parliament, as a Conservative in 1895 – but the 'lowest murmur' of his

voice 'had colour and life in it'. (In 1919 he had an operation to remove a gland from his throat: before and after it
he talked with Carlylean volubility about his vital need,
stressed by the 'quacktitioners', to remain silent.) Northcliffe had 'square-tipped fingers and capable podgy hands',
and he liked to doodle with thick soft pencils, writing
'calligraphic puzzles' rather than letters. His senses were
unusually acute; according to J. L. Garvin he could detect
buried coins and flick them out of the ground with his
stick. Northcliffe moved silently and quickly on small,
splayed feet; there was a touch of flatness about them which
seemed, some thought, at odds with his agile brain. He
wore comfortable dark blue suits, soft collars and red silk
ties with white spots. His braces were always too loose and
his trousers sagged at the knees. When the mood was on
him he could be an exhilarating companion. He possessed a
'charming smile' and winning ways. But even his bantering
geniality had intimidating overtones. He inspired love as
well as fear, but it is difficult to tell whether the adoration
expressed by his acolytes was genuine or the hypocritical
devotion of the slave for his master, the victim for the
terrorist. During Northcliffe's 'brainstorms', observers
noted, his eyes became 'feral'. He was perhaps a better
subject for a Fauvist than an Impressionist.

Yet 'boyish' was the word most frequently used to
describe Northcliffe. H. G. Wells said that he never lost
'the gleam of the ineradicable schoolboy'. For the *Mail*
journalist, Hannen Swaffer, the Chief was 'the impish,
inspiring, all-compelling, boyish, magnetic, humorous
comrade, who shared our sorrows (the ones at least that he
did not create) and treated us all as kids – office-boys and
directors alike'. Actually the Chief frowned on Swaffer,
who was a drunken bohemian and coined the aphorism
that 'Freedom of the Press in Britain means freedom to
print such of the proprietor's prejudices as the advertisers
don't object to.' But Swaffer was forgiven much on account

of his name. Northcliffe had a youthful penchant for out-landish names and relished the sight of memorable by-lines, such as Twells Brex, in his newspapers. It amused him to invent pseudonyms like 'January Mortimer' for his reporters or to corrupt their real names in print; at his insistence C. Robert Mackenzie was transformed into Crobert Mackenzie and William Pollock became Pollock Pollock. Practical jokes and puerile puns always appealed to him: he nicknamed the *Daily Telegraph* the 'Bellow-graph'. More obviously immature enthusiasms were in evidence at Elmwood where Northcliffe played with model trains and arranged shooting contests with toy pistols. He enjoyed listening to popular songs on the gramophone and acquiring new mechanical inventions. He returned from the United States with a safety razor and declaimed, 'America has solved problems about which we have hardly begun to think.' He was thrilled by driving at speed in his motor cars – it was 'like being massaged in a high wind' – and he once refuted the suggestion that he was in danger of a collision with the memorable argument, 'Collision! – nonsense! . . . look at our size.' He wrote expertly about these shiny new playthings of the Edwardian rich, assert-ing incidentally that 'the perfect motor servant should be a combination of gentleman and engineer.' Northcliffe was also a fervid partisan of the Wright brothers and he was contemptuous about the sluggish attitude of his own countrymen towards aviation: as late as 1907 Lord Haldane, Secretary of State for War, had pronounced that 'aeroplanes would never fly'. In 1911, at his mother's bidding, Northcliffe promised that he himself would never fly. His feet remained on the ground. But his imagination continued to soar in a juvenile empyrean inhabited by ghouls, cannibals, sharks, snakes, torture, cruelty, disease and death. He was intrigued by such subjects as the possi-bility that heads remained conscious for a few seconds after decapitation. He slavered at the mention of wolves:

'his lips appeared to caress it as he lingered over the first vowel' of the word.

Lord Northcliffe's boyishness was a less amiable and more sinister quality than it seemed. Tom Clarke, sometime news editor on the *Mail*, reckoned that the essence of the Chief's nature was 'boyish egotism and pride of power'. This rightly implied that the core of Northcliffe's personality was unformed, molten, a mass of inchoate passions seeking channels of gratification. Lord Northcliffe was lavishly open-handed with money, but his charity was bestowed as randomly as his spite. Generosity became a weapon in his hands, all the more potent for being so undiscriminating. At a Carmelite House farewell conference in 1921 the Chief snapped, 'What was the best story in this morning's *Daily Mail*?' Taking his job in his hands a sub-editor replied, 'Viscount Northcliffe is leaving tomorrow on a world tour and will be away from England for several months.' There was a frozen silence before Northcliffe turned to his secretary, 'See that that man gets a hundred pound bonus.' Northcliffe was a bounteous host, and, though unhappy in the company of his social and intellectual superiors, he entertained in fine style at the beautiful Elizabethan mansion, Sutton Place, in Surrey, which he rented for that purpose. But he could not resist drawing guests' attention to his lack of ostentation in running the house (which later became the residence of Paul Getty) with so few servants. Nor could he break what his wife called the 'old habit of abusing his friends at his own table if they venture to disagree with him'. Actually Northcliffe was always ill at ease in social gatherings. He had a particular aversion to eating at public dinners (though he was once seen in Oxford Street devouring plums out of a paper bag). Polite society diminished Northcliffe. It was a milieu in which his waywardness was restrained by artificial conventions. He increasingly ignored them as his success grew. He did not try to conceal his boredom and impatience in any company he could not dominate. He developed an abrupt manner. He spoke in short sentences, rapped out defiantly as though he expected contradiction. Then he would fall into portentous silences. A nervous sub-editor filled one such mealtime lull with the information that he had been shipwrecked three times. 'Four times,' purred Northcliffe. 'Three times, my Lord.' 'Four times,' insisted Northcliffe menacingly. 'Three times, sir,' repeated the man in desperation. 'Four times,' stated Lord Northcliffe, dismissing both the subject and the sub-editor. Northcliffe's moods were fickle but in all of them there was 'the suggestion of power stored up, ready for instant use'. R. D. Blumenfeld, editor of the *Daily Express*, described Northcliffe as a 'cyclone of emotional contradictions'.

Yet there was the familiar discrepancy between the power of Northcliffe's delivery and the feebleness of the resulting utterance, the strength of the medium and the triviality of the message. He made his pronouncements 'incisively, with a sharp drawing back of the lower lip on the teeth, as if he meant to inoculate his words into you'. But the words themselves were callow. They were the trite, trumpery maxims of the crackerbarrel newspaperman. 'Better be damned than mentioned not at all.' 'A journalist's wife is a lump under the bedclothes.' Northcliffe did not so much talk as mouth 'talking points'. He did not deliberate, his mind pullulated with headlines, paragraphs, slogans. 'Our tons of ink make millions think.' 'Telephones multiply the man.' 'The rotary press is more powerful than the portfolio.' H. G. Wells commented on the 'blank inadequacy' of Northcliffe's education 'for anything better than a career of push and acquisition'. And nowhere was the jejune quality of the Chief's intellect more apparent than in his harping on what he was pleased to regard as the inferiority of other races. 'The Welsh, who are Orientals, do not understand fair play.' 'You must be a

Jew, you have such a Scottish-sounding name.' The
Germans 'are a nation of valets'. 'Bolshevism is the hand-
maiden of the servant races; our race, thank God, is not a
servant race.' Americans were 'white Chinese', yet those
of English descent he liked: 'it is the Negroid, Slav, Irish,
Teuton, Semitic, Italian, Scandinavian Amalgam, stimulated by a vibrant climate, money hunger and ignorant
contempt of European and the Ancient cultures, that is so
abhorrent.' Few eminent Edwardians expressed such
assumptions with such crudity. Even then it was not quite
respectable to do so, as Northcliffe implicitly acknowledged
when he claimed to be 'Judaphil'. But most members of
his own imperial race shared his views – a logical extension
of class discrimination – though they might have looked
askance at his taking legal steps to force a Jewish shop-
keeper called Harmsworth to change his name. As on so
many issues, Northcliffe followed, he did not lead, the
public mind. He was an intellectual vampire living off
popular prejudice and superstition. It was an anaemic
diet.

Northcliffe's energy sometimes exhausted itself and his
temperamental compass veered unsteadily towards dull
lassitude. His internal dynamo raced from five thirty in
the morning until ten o'clock at night for days, weeks,
months on end. Sitting in his pink chair surrounded by
telephones, or lying on a chaise-longue buried in newspapers, he was incessantly active, scribbling, instructing,
dictating, giving audiences. At times, he complained, he
had so many callers that he could not obey the calls of
nature. Eventually his natural force abated. His batteries
ran flat. He would collapse, drift, go off on lengthy,
extravagant holidays, thus 'filling up my mental accumu-
lators with energy'. Northcliffe was often ill and he charted
the state of his own and everyone else's health with
valetudinarian care. He could joke with the 'quacktitioner'
who warned about his blood pressure: 'My circulation is

in my newspapers.' But he was always nervous about over-working. And he was deeply superstitious about his own well-being, refusing to dine with thirteen present, turning silver coins when he saw the new moon, paying elaborate homage to Lady Luck. He also attempted to relax and slim by taking up golf, that great new Edwardian craze. He soon became addicted to the game. A. J. Balfour, another enthusiast, (who had once, according to a North-cliffe journal, been 'presented with a set of silver-headed caddies') came down to open his private links at Sutton Place. The Northcliffe press quickly learnt to take a more professional interest in the game, which helped to make it less exclusively patrician. The Chief himself was amused by the *Chicago Tribune*'s headline which announced, 'Northcliffe's Golf Not as Bad as Expected.' He played as he generally lived, with instinctive vigour and venom, always aiming to 'hole in one'.

Northcliffe seems to have regarded sexual recreation in much the same light as golf. He was apparently an impulsive, pouncing kind of amorist. *The Times*'s historian delicately termed him 'a strong man of vigorous appetite'. 'One made love as one brought out a newspaper,' mused W. L. George's 'Caliban', 'life being one damn exciting thing after another.' Northcliffe acquired a set of mistresses, the most permanent of whom bore him two more illegiti-mate children. She was a mysterious *femme fatale* called Mrs Wrohan, whose ripe sense of humour perhaps con-firmed the whisper that she had once been a society courtesan: she remarked to Northcliffe's lawyer that no man could serve two masters though sometimes he tried to serve two mistresses. Meanwhile Northcliffe and his childless wife maintained a respectable façade. Molly acted as his society hostess. She performed the role expertly, being decorative, agreeable and vacuous – C. P. Scott, editor of the *Manchester Guardian*, called her 'a silly little woman'. But for the most part Alfred and Molly went their separate ways. He lacked the impulse towards profound attachments and throughout his life established only one relationship of real intimacy. This, of course, was with his mother and it was his form of idolatry. Northcliffe was religious, but only in a meaningless Church-of-England way. He admired Lourdes as 'the greatest piece of show-manship in the world'. Journalists at Carmelite House never referred to the deity in print: as a sub-editor observed, 'there isn't room for two gods here.' Apart from news-papers, in fact, only one matter engaged Northcliffe's wholehearted attention throughout the Edwardian period – 'the coming German peril'. His fears were common-place: Lord Charles Beresford's invariable greeting was, 'Good morning, one day nearer the German war.' But no one disseminated belligerent propaganda on the scale of Northcliffe. Martial headlines sprang fully armed from his Jove-like head. It was no wonder that liberal contempor-aries damned him as a 'pyromaniac bent on seeing the world go up in flames'. The Great War, when it came, seemed to justify his obsession. Moreover the conflict opened up an entirely fresh field for Northcliffe's restless exertions. It at once fed and whetted his voracious appetite for power. E. V. Lucas wrote, 'August 4, 1914. – War declared. Lord Northcliffe has his teeth sharpened.'

VII

The Great War, it has been claimed, liberated the great man in Lord Northcliffe. It gave him a disinterested motive, a consistent purpose and scope for effective action. In pursuit of victory he strengthened national morale and weakened the 'fatuously optimistic' censorship. He exposed Kitchener's 'tragic blunder' in failing to provide enough shells in 1915. He shook and at last toppled Asquith's effete ministry by means of 'a Press campaign of unbridled ferocity'. He sustained the soldiers, especially Haig, against ignorant interference from the politicians, on one occasion bursting into the War Office and roaring at Lloyd George's secretary, 'I don't want to see him – you can tell him from me that I hear he has been interfering with strategy and that if it goes on I will break him.' Finally, Northcliffe participated in the government himself. In 1917 he was leader of the British War Mission to the United States where, according to Lord Beaverbrook, he 'moved from triumph to triumph'. In 1918 he became Director of Propaganda in Enemy Countries, creating for himself a deadly new role in which, according to Ludendorff, he shattered German confidence and willingness to fight. This, at any rate, is the potent myth, fabricated by Northcliffe and others, of what he did in the war. The myth resembles the high-explosive shell which Northcliffe once brought back from the Western Front. He transported it to Carmelite House in a taxi and positioned it in the basement, immediately underneath the desk of that 'rough, capable Aberdonian' journalist, Andrew Caird. 'See where it points,' chortled Northcliffe, 'What will happen to you when it goes off?' On examination it turned out to be an imitation of the real thing, made from fragments of detonated shells. It was a dud.

The truth is that the war, with its new opportunities for dictatorial control, did not so much stimulate Northcliffe's magnanimity as aggravate his megalomania. Geoffrey Dawson declared that Northcliffe was ambitious to enjoy 'the absolutely unfettered, independent exercise of personal power'. Witness Northcliffe's wistful solution to the food shortage in 1916: 'One strong man who would order the people to eat less would effect the desired result.' Nor did the conflict with Germany impose a new coherence on Northcliffe's always fissile mind. Indeed, his ideas, his moods, his direction changed more rapidly under the novel stimulus. As Winston Churchill wrote, he was 'a swaying force, uncertain, capricious, essentially personal'. 'Northcliffe may do anything,' said another politician in despair. Thus on 5 August 1914 Northcliffe stated that the French could defend themselves and 'not a soldier of ours shall leave these shores'. By 6 August he was reconciled to the Expeditionary Force. In 1914 he supported Kitchener as Secretary for War, but he soon began to assert that 'K of Chaos' was 'the Cabinet's old man of the sea' and a 'national great white elephant'. Northcliffe denounced Asquith's elegantly forensic conduct of hostilities: 'We are not at law with Germany, we are at war with her.' But he was quickly at odds with Asquith's successor, Lloyd George, whom he dubbed 'a shirt-sleeve politician'. Northcliffe favoured Haig as Commander-in-Chief: 'Lithe and alert, Sir Douglas is known for his distinguished bearing and good looks. He has blue eyes and an unusual facial angle, delicately-chiselled features, and a chin to be reckoned with.' But before long the tycoon was sending the general 'ferocious' letters and complaining about his 'dullness and pig-headedness' and his 'incredible blunders'. 'Is it believable that some men would send masses of metal weighing thirty tons (Tanks) into the mud at Ypres?' Armageddon caused Lord Northcliffe to charge his batteries with lyddite. But his targets were as various and his aim as erratic as ever.

Northcliffe's infirmity of purpose was most evident in his failure to decide whether he wished to exercise influence by controlling the press or power by holding government office. To be King-maker, 'Mentor of Ministers' and 'Breaker of Cabinets' in the words of two American headlines, had obvious charms. It tickled his self-conceit to answer Lloyd George's invitation on 8 December 1916 (the day after he took up residence in 10 Downing Street), 'Lord Northcliffe sees no advantage in any interview between himself and the Prime Minister at this juncture.' It was an overweening piece of vainglory to reply downrightly and publicly, through the press, to Lloyd George's tentative and private offer of the Air Ministry, 'I can do better work if I maintain my independence and am not gagged by a loyalty that I do not feel towards the whole of your administration.' Northcliffe loved to explain that he despised 'political jellyfish' and 'dumb Parliaments', that he had refused 'several' Cabinet posts. But he yearned to wield direct authority and found specious reasons for accepting the offices he did. He professed to disdain the baubles of rank but he obtained all possible honours for himself, his entourage, and, especially, his kin. Two of his brothers became peers and two knights. After one promotion his sister Geraldine wrote, 'In view of the paper shortage, I think the family ought to issue printed forms like Field Service postcards, viz: Many congratulations on your being made Archbishop of Canterbury/Pope/Duke/Viscount/Knight, etc.' Northcliffe insisted, with transparent emphasis, that the War Cabinet needed in it 'one or two men of inflexible determination and untiring energy'. He longed to prove in practical terms that he was what the *New York Herald* called him, 'The British Empire's greatest single human force'. Lord Beaverbrook, who admired Northcliffe as 'a man of brilliant creative talents, touched by the hand of genius', said that he 'saw himself as a Man of Destiny'. Northcliffe's 'idea was to be a kind of Clemenceau'.

'The Premiership itself was not beyond his grasp,' continued Lord Beaverbrook. This was an unwarrantable claim, inspired perhaps by the consideration that Northcliffe controlled over half the newspapers in London, whereas Beaverbrook himself never controlled more than a fifth. 'As regards abuse,' Northcliffe once remarked, 'I am a pachyderm.' He was also a political pachyderm, short-sighted, thick-skinned, bad-tempered. In his chargings, trumpetings and manoeuvrings he was stubbornly elephantine. He had a long memory but if he forgot nothing he also learnt nothing. Though unpredictable, he remained clumsy and the suave ring-masters at Westminster soon devised ways to manipulate him. Thus in 1909 Lloyd George, 'after big game', revealed his Budget proposals to Northcliffe before submitting them to Parliament. Northcliffe was 'delighted' by this 'splendid imprudence' and briefly muted the *Daily Mail*'s opposition to the Liberals, a faltering out of which the Chancellor made great political capital. Again, in 1917, Lloyd George neutralized the Northcliffe press by the simple expedient of offering its proprietor an important freebooting role in the United States. As the Prime Minister explained, 'it was essential to get rid of him. He had become so "jumpy" as to be really a public danger and it was necessary to "harness" him in order to find occupation for his superfluous energies.' After the war, with his assault on Northcliffe's 'diseased vanity', Lloyd George vanquished the press lord almost as decisively as Baldwin was later to vanquish Rothermere and Beaverbrook with his famous remark that they aimed at 'power without responsibility – the prerogative of the harlot throughout the ages'. Northcliffe could not be ignored. As Lord Milner said, 'I believe myself that he is only a scarecrow, but still the fact remains that most public men are in terror of him.' Northcliffe could not be tamed. He could not be trained. But he could be managed. In spite of his redoubtable appearance and refractory nature there was no question of his being allowed to dominate the political circus.

Northcliffe may have been cumbersome as a political animal but he was not always ineffective. Earl Grey remarked that 'Asquith's government has never acted except in response to public opinion and I am most grateful to *The Times* and *Daily Mail* for kicking it into action on many occasions.' Thus Northcliffe stiffened the Liberals' resolution over controls and conscription, though perhaps in these, as in so many other instances, he was merely anticipating the inevitable. One Cabinet Minister grumbled that Northcliffe 'gets word of something that is going to happen, writes it up and then claims that he did it'. Sometimes Northcliffe overcharged his blunderbuss and it back-fired. For example, the *Mail*'s insistence that poison gas should be used on the Germans provided them with both a propaganda victory and an excuse to employ the new weapon themselves. Northcliffe's iconoclastic attack on Kitchener (who regarded journalists as 'drunken swabs') produced a violent public reaction in the Field Marshal's favour. Copies of *The Times* and the *Daily Mail* were burnt on the London Stock Exchange and Northcliffe received five thousand abusive letters a day. He took measures to ensure his personal safety and the government, much against its will, rallied to Kitchener's defence. The fact is that it suited everyone, including Northcliffe himself, to exaggerate his power. It gratified him to give the impression that Elmwood was constantly being bombarded by the Germans and to explain to Haig that he would overthrow not only the English but the French government if it did not mend its ways. Asquith and his Liberals had a vested interest in claiming that their downfall had been caused by a malevolent press. Actually their own flaccidity had induced the national mood of dissatisfaction, exacerbated indeed by Northcliffe, which led to the political intrigue of December 1916. Northcliffe the propagandist, 'Great Master' of the 'Science of Lying', was a handy scapegoat for the German generals. It was easier for them to admit they had lost the paper war than the real war. Lloyd George, a Prime Minister without a party, found it convenient to blame his difficulties with the soldiers on Northcliffe, 'the mere kettledrum of Sir Douglas Haig and the mouth-organ of Sir William Robertson'. There was even some justification for this. Robertson, whose one sleepless night of the war was occasioned by the thought that the British armies were going to be put under French command, was obtuse and obstinate even by military standards. Yet Lloyd George would not dismiss 'Wully', as he was called, until he had safely corralled Northcliffe in the government. There was no press protest at Robertson's departure in 1918, but by this time Northcliffe had told Haig that he regarded 'Wully' as 'Woolly'. The generals, incidentally, were as baffled as the politicians by Northcliffe. In 1916, for example, Sir Henry Wilson called at Printing House Square and found his host nonsensical, self-contradictory and 'disposed to deduce impending collapse in Germany from an unprecedented rise in the price of eels'.

Lloyd George's anxiety to rid the Old World of Northcliffe was understandable. Equally understandable was the reluctance of the New World to welcome him. Some regarded the sending of such an 'unscrupulous intriguer' as 'a gratuitous insult to the Americans'. Woodrow Wilson objected to Northcliffe as the English Hearst and relished neither his advisers' information that he was the 'most powerful man' in Britain nor the press opinion that 'if he lived in America he would be a President-maker'. Colonel House, to whom Northcliffe had previously vouchsafed 'much misinformation' about the state of the Kaiser's health, toyed with the pleasant notion of allowing the press lord to 'run amok' in the United States. The British ambassador, Spring Rice, failed to organize an official reception, which provoked in Northcliffe 'one of the most formidable explosions of temper' *The Times*'s Washington correspondent had ever witnessed. Northcliffe despised Spring Rice as 'an all-covered-with orders kind of person'. The ambassador loathed Northcliffe as an *arriviste*. When they met at the embassy he greeted his guest with the words, 'You are my enemy . . . you inserted four years ago an anonymous attack in *The Times* which nearly killed me; *and Lady Spring Rice declines to receive you on that account.*' Northcliffe turned to go but the ambassador restrained him, insisting that they would have to work together. Northcliffe told Lloyd George, 'Sir Cecil Spring Rice is either overwrought by the strain of war, or is not quite right in the head.' Oddly enough Colonel House sided with Northcliffe, informing the Foreign Office that the ambassador was 'temperamentally unfitted to cope with such complex and disturbed conditions'. Notwithstanding Spring Rice's protestations he was, said House, 'unwilling to work cordially with his new colleague' and consequently 'Northcliffe's coming precipitated an impossible situation'.

Despite this inauspicious beginning, Northcliffe's War Mission was surprisingly successful and marked the apogee of his political career. His purpose was to devise the best means of cooperation between Britain and the United States, especially where the division of allied resources was concerned, in order to 'Kan the Kaiser'. Northcliffe quickly won the confidence of the American government. His phrases were vital and he did not have to be told anything twice. House actually came to like this 'dominating man with boundless energy . . . there must be more to him than his critics see, for how could he have the success he has? I confess he is a puzzle to me.' In effect it became Northcliffe's task 'literally to *beg* for assistance of all kinds and in colossal quantities' thus, to his intense chagrin, pawning the British Empire to the United States. He 'worked like a titan'. He raised essential loans. He paid out two million dollars a day for war supplies, earning himself the newspaper title 'Greatest Spendthrift in History'. He did much to counteract the 'damnable' propaganda of Hearst and to inform Americans of the huge sacrifices of blood and treasure that the British had already made. Northcliffe flattered, cajoled and conciliated the industrial moguls, who were delighted by his American forthrightness. He may have been over-loquacious, but his audiences warmed to a public figure who was so much the reverse of the traditional British 'stuffed shirt'. It was said that North-

Lord Northcliffe and Arthur Balfour pulling the Wright brothers' flying machine
at Pau, 1908

Lord Northcliffe and Winston
Churchill, Versailles 1918

Northcliffe with his mother in
1921

Blériot, accompanied by Northcliffe, arrives at Victoria station on July 25, 1909, having just flown the Channel and won the *Daily Mail* Prize.

cliffe's 'methods were pyrotechnical and the fuses did not always go off; he relied on the inspiration of the moment rather than upon preparation'. But this was usually enough. Even the hostile Henry Ford, who had been flayed by the *Mail* as a pacifist and thought Northcliffe a Jew, was persuaded to supply six thousand tractors at cost price. Northcliffe wrote that his work

> exceeds anything I have ever done in my life. It requires labour, tact, versatility and the digestion of an ostrich. Business is conducted here entirely at golf clubs, restaurants and houses. Everything here is personal . . . Much as I delight in these people – and they are a splendid people – they are the greatest nation of time-wasters on God's earth. Life here . . . is a combination of ridiculous rush and waste of time.

Northcliffe was a better publicist than he was organizer or financier and some considered his American venture a 'big coup for his own glorification' which turned out to be 'a complete failure'. Northcliffe attracted, as he radiated, hyperboles. Lord Beaverbrook said that he came back to England after his five-month exile 'like Napoleon returning from Elba'.

In fact Northcliffe wanted to be close to his mother. He was exhausted and she was now in her eightieth year. He also had a fretful feeling that Lloyd George had gulled him into the sidelines. He would show the Prime Minister, that 'dishevelled conjuror', that he could not be spirited away by political prestidigitation. Again, however, the Welsh wizard was a match for the Fleet Street impresario. With practised sleight of hand he wafted into being the one office Northcliffe's vanity would not allow him to refuse, Director of Propaganda in Enemy Countries. Northcliffe was thus induced to devote his energies to undermining the German rather than the British government. With considerable help from a brilliant team, including H.G. Wells, Northcliffe created a remarkable new weapon of war. The Germans compared it to poison gas. This was an apt analogy for the propaganda had less effect than was claimed and it was liable to blow back in the faces of its disseminators. For example, in trying to demonstrate the reasonableness of Allied war aims, Northcliffe inadvertently committed the government to supporting the League of Nations and the cause of national self-determination (for places outside the British Empire). This was all very well, but such a rational policy scarcely accorded with the hysterical 'anti-Hun' message of Northcliffe's newspapers. Wells protested about the discrepancy and complained of the 'incoherent pogrom spirit' being stirred up by *The Times*, the *Mail* and the *Evening News*. When Northcliffe rejected this criticism Wells (shortly before his resignation) wrote, 'I am sorry that you insist on being two people when God has made you only one.' That he was a victim of political schizophrenia the press lord did not attempt to deny.

Northcliffe expended almost as much energy as Horatio Bottomley, charlatan editor of *John Bull*, in fanning the flames of racial hatred during the war. The *Mail* revelled in atrocity stories, such as the German use of Belgian nuns as clappers in church bells. It led a witch-hunt against prominent 'Germans' in high places, Prince Louis of Battenberg, Lord Haldane and even Lord Milner, denounced by Northcliffe as a 'semi-German' and an 'alien-fancier'. The *Mail* condemned Quakers who looked after German children as 'Hun coddlers'. It virtually instigated the destruction of shops whose owners bore German names. About this Sir John Simon remarked bitterly that it 'must be a great satisfaction to [Northcliffe] to feel that he has sold his country for $\frac{1}{2}$d'. Sir Ian Hamilton referred to him as 'that reptile Harmsworth'. 'Every knock's a boost,' said Northcliffe cheerfully. Anyway he had seen with his own eyes evidence of enemy barbarism – 'the terrible spiked maces habitually used by the Austrians to break the skulls of the wounded'.

But how influential was Northcliffe between 1914 and 1918? Were his newspapers really a 'tremendous force' for 'mass thought-control'? Or were they just a lurid reflection of his countrymen's war-time xenophobia? Sir Norman Angell considered that at such a period of crisis, when the public mind was unusually credulous, Northcliffe's power in governing national opinion was 'decisive'. This is doubtful. Though he rampaged against the censorship Northcliffe himself acknowledged, 'The power of the press is very great, but not so great as the power of suppress.' The view of Geoffrey Dawson, who was in a unique position to judge, is persuasive. Dawson said that people read Northcliffe's papers not for their editorial opinions but because they were '*readable*'. Northcliffe's

> strongest characteristic and the secret of his success, is that he is extraordinarily sensitive to the mood of the moment. No one was ever less like a Machiavelli. What he really is, is a master of publicity, and that enables him to associate himself, and to be associated by others, with political movements and events with which in nine cases out of ten he has hardly the remotest connection.

Northcliffe was always concerned about style before content. At the end of the war his propaganda team drew up an important manifesto setting out desirable peace terms. It was read through to him but he did not hear the words. His 'mind was fully occupied with distribution and means of attaining publicity'.

VIII

Northcliffe was as eager to dictate the peace as he had been to prosecute the war and he was 'visibly astonished and upset' when Lloyd George refused to include him in the British delegation to Versailles. But Northcliffe's pacific policies were as inconsistent as his bellicose ones. He acknowledged that 'reparation in any full sense of the word is beyond human power.' Nevertheless retribution must be exacted, the Huns must be made to pay (to the uttermost farthing), the Kaiser must be tried (and hanged). Vengeance was more in tune with the national mood than reconciliation. Two minutes' hate every morning was good for the circulation. Lloyd George was so harried during Northcliffe's peace crusade that he actually specified a figure of £24 thousand million which he promised to search out of German pockets. At the same time he sent Northcliffe a telegram: 'Don't be always making mischief.' Predictably the man who won the war found it easy enough to out-manoeuvre Northcliffe in peace-time. By insisting that the Prime Minister should reveal the membership of his future Cabinet in return for his support, Northcliffe over-reached himself – as the huge Coalition victory proved. And by putting further pressure on Lloyd George during the Versailles negotiations he laid himself open to the parliamentary riposte by which the premier at once discredited him and diverted attention from the question of how much Germany was going to be squeezed. Northcliffe could burst out of the Cabinet room 'like an erupting volcano' when Lloyd George told him to 'go to Hades', but the only effective outlet for his frustration was his newspapers.

In them he carried out a vendetta against the Coalition and he vented his rage on his subordinates. One member of *The Times* staff, who had himself 'never had a word of unfair criticism from Northcliffe', acknowledged that the Chief could be 'brutal in a curiously under-hand, sly way. He didn't have it out. He pin-pricked and tormented.' Geoffrey Dawson, with his pro-government loyalties and his dinner-table indiscretions about Northcliffe, became his new target. The Chief assailed him with telegraphed complaints and 'megalomaniac' diatribes on the telephone. Northcliffe's moods became 'evil and petulant'. 'What a man!' exclaimed the editor after one 'storm' from his 'unbalanced' employer. Dawson's friends sympathized. One wrote, at the end of 1918,

> Isn't Northcliffe now just a little bit – what shall we say? affected in the cerebellum. I saw a note of his today . . . quite in the Kaiser vein – 'God and I'; 'and the Ghost can-go-to-hell' kind of thing. He is a poor turnip.

Dawson eventually resigned in February 1919. He was replaced by Wickham Steed, the eminent foreign editor, who told Northcliffe that he would regard himself 'as your trustee as far as the policy of *The Times* was concerned'.

In spite of such docility Wickham Steed was ridden as hard as his predecessor. But though Northcliffe was merciless in applying whip and spurs he also gave his new editor freer rein. For the Chief's bouts of activity were becoming more manic and more concentrated. His energy ebbed quickly and each effort left him increasingly prostrate. Moreover Northcliffe, for the first time, began to feel himself 'an old-fashioned man, belonging as I do now to an age that is passing'. He feared revolution. His memory became unreliable. He still kept abreast of fashion, insisting, for example, that films should be reviewed in his papers with the same prominence as plays. But often the new modes shocked him; the film *Honeypot* was 'a scandalous production . . . that holds up our gentlefolk to the ridicule of the mob, which is always bad'. When the fit was on him Northcliffe himself seemed to behave like the jerky flickering figures on the cinematograph screen. He became frantic about the creaking floors at Elmwood. He quizzed one of his employees, 'You belong to the Jewish persuasion, don't you Falk . . . Who persuaded you?' He instructed Steed to spell out all numbers in *The*

Times – the idea was abandoned when the editor mentioned stock exchange prices. Northcliffe sprang at the paper's advertising director 'like a tiger', raved 'for twenty minutes without a stop' and then became as 'gentle and forgiving as a woman'. On the twenty-fifth anniversary of the founding of the *Mail* Northcliffe entertained 7,000 of his employees at Olympia. (The presiding clergyman prayed for 'Thy servant Alfred' and the *Morning Post* understood that Northcliffe had hired Salisbury Plain in order 'to give a summer picnic to those who *have been* in his employ'.) In 1921 the Chief decided to take a long rest. He went round the world.

'Wire mother's health and circulation figures.' That cable sums up Northcliffe's main preoccupations as he circumnavigated the globe. He thought of his mother 'wherever you may be – of your rooms and of your movements'. And he hurled thunderbolts from afar at his editors. He also chafed about 'my awful obesity' – 'I shall never be able to look a weighing machine in the face again' – and dieted obsessively. Otherwise he contemplated the world with the candid, eager curiosity of the seeker after answers. He was struck by the lack of chimney-pots, motor-bicycles and public clocks in New York. He was disappointed by the equator. He found New Zealand

> inconceivably interesting. I call it topsy-turveydom – parlour-maids in summertime earn seven pounds a week; tops of mountains are blown away sixty miles, your money in your pocket turns black with the sulphur in the air; there are wingless birds, forty-pound trout and caterpillars with trees growing out of their heads; and there are ferns as tall as Printing House Square.

In Tasmania carrots were 'two feet long . . . one man in twenty is a giant . . . watercress develops so rapidly that it blocks rivers'. As for Australian kangaroos, 'My! how they can hop!' 'The Japanese are very impassive, but they are not so impassive as the Chinese' – 'four hundred millions of them! I never get that out of my mind.' 'Hundreds of thousands of square miles of China are covered by tombs.' 'Tigers can be shot at night by anyone who dazzles them by an electric light carried on his hat . . . the tiger is the most ingenious, far-seeing, cunning, planning animal of all.' 'Oriental cockroaches are as big as large prawns.' Northcliffe was amused by a Japanese advertisement for a Chinese cure featuring 'a man wearing a Napoleonic hat'. In the Malay States he found 'moths as big as swallows' and king cobras which chased men on motor-bicycles (the men, not the snakes, rode the motor-bicycles). In India he discovered that 'strong tea is excellent to shave with' but that it is dangerous to smoke under a mosquito net unless your valet is standing by with a bucket of water. The pyramids were very disappointing. Rats could live in the refrigerators of ships where they grew 'fur like a bear'.

The 'Pilgrim of Printing House Square', as Lloyd George dubbed Northcliffe, found it ironical that he was pursued round the world by a monster partly of his own creating, the popular press. Wherever he went he was greeted as 'the Chief' and the Chinese newspapers called him 'King of all the editors in the world'. It was an understandable kow-tow. He was a famous man in an empire which had just reached its furthest territorial limits. Northcliffe met an American who made a point of telling every Englishman 'what I think of his little ant-heap'. But even he had found travelling in the Far East 'a revelation as to British greatness'; 'our vast possessions make Uncle Sam "sit up and take notice," as he says.' Yet with his acute journalistic prescience Northcliffe seemed to detect that Britain had outgrown her strength and that the sun was about to set on the empire. He suspected that the British were a 'decaying race'. The United States was 'a potential enemy with a semi-hostile population of a hundred and ten millions, who have absorbed an immense share of the world's gold'. Northcliffe regarded it as the most important task in his life to prevent the Irish canker from eating into the rose of the alliance, to teach the Americans by British experience and advice, to restrain them from out-building the British navy, to preserve a united English-speaking front against the yellow peril. Admittedly, 'it takes at least three Japs to do the work of one European' and all their silk-weaving machinery was made in Britain. But they were a brutal race bent on world domination and they were quick to learn and to copy. Similarly, India was threatened by   .

> the swaggering, boastful, whisky-and-soda drinking, horn-spectacled, and fountain-pen-wearing Babu, who likes to think that because he has the imitative and blotting-paper mind that enables him to pass examinations, he is the equal of the Anglo-Saxon, and, *knowing* his own inferiority, is bitter and dangerous.

Perhaps Northcliffe was uneasy because he perceived in the British Empire a paradigm of his own condition, still outwardly indomitable but afflicted by internal decrepitude. The signs were unmistakable. Northcliffe's psychological cycle – from energy to lassitude and back – was accelerating its pace. On one occasion he dictated to his secretary (whom he had earlier knocked down) for six hours without stopping. He would not read the typed result. Before landing at Marseilles in February 1922 he concluded his journal:

> Every ship has its odd characters. Among those of the *Egypt* is a former fat man, now in skeleton class, who beginning life as a reporter at sixteen, is now said to have more papers than he can count and more money than brains. Is finishing whirl round world and ready for another tomorrow.

For all their irony and bombast Northcliffe's words hinted morbidly at what was apparent to his relations and employees. The Chief had returned a sick man. High society buzzed with malicious gossip about the nature of his illness. One apocryphal story, repeated by Asquith among others, related that Northcliffe had cabled the King, 'I am turning Roman Catholic,' to which George V was supposed to have replied, 'I cannot help it.' High society was right in one respect. Northcliffe's behaviour had been bizarre. His humour had been grotesque. His mind had been loose in its socket. Now it seemed to be quite unhinged. He appeared no longer to be eccentric but, at times, to be mad. The reign of inconsequentiality was at hand. Northcliffe himself telephoned the *Mail*, 'Someone has been saying I'm off my head . . .' He wanted the best reporter put on to the story.

IX

Like a strip-cartoon of Bedlam, the last few months of Lord Northcliffe's life combined tragedy and farce. In his demented, moribund state Northcliffe became a caricature of his former self, his features distorted, his idiosyncrasies exaggerated. He was more affectionate, more sensitive, more teasing, more savage, more erratic than ever before. On his return he rushed to be re-united with his 'darling Mother'. He waxed sentimental about old associations and old friends, telling one that he had consulted thirty-two specialists and was going to die. His nerves were so highly strung that the slightest noise startled him as though it had been a pistol shot. He appointed the commissionaire at Carmelite House to censor the 'coarse, abominable and offensive' advertisements in the *Mail*. He insisted that the 'squandermaniacs', 'nepotists' and 'troglodytes' of *The Times* needed 'kicking' by their 'Chief Mule', and he exploded what he called a 'stink-bomb' of vilification at Printing House Square. He drove some of his staff at Elmwood to hand in their notice. He expelled a printers' trade union leader from his office with the point of his toe and the words, 'You're damned ungrateful swine.' He mounted a bitter attack on millionaire newspaper owners, men who did not know the difference between a rotary press and a rotarian, for 'grinding down' their workers. Life had become a hell for Northcliffe and he seemed bent on making it one for others.

By the spring of 1922 he was suffering from delusions and persecution mania. He was found interminably scribbling the rune, 'Maily Dail – Million Sale'. He called an acquaintance out to his balcony and pointed to the sky. 'How many moons do you see?' he asked. 'One.' 'I thought so,' replied Northcliffe, 'but I see two.' The Chief wrote pathetically to *The Times*:

> there are outside my window two queer-looking people who have been standing there for more than a week – one of them has been discharged from *The Times*. I do not know whether it is the man or the woman of the two. They are apparently quite harmless, they simply stand and stare. They take various positions. One goes into Lord Curzon's portico, and the other takes a point of vantage in the road which divides the Carlton from the Reform Club. It is impossible for me to approach my house except by using the back door – a long way round. If I mention exactly where it is, someone who reads this communiqué will get round by the back door I expect. As it is I defy anyone to find it for I can hardly find it myself.

Northcliffe's condition confused witnesses because it fluctuated so rapidly. He behaved, as one journalist said, 'like an out-of-control clock'. He might be cool, kind and lucid. Then, without warning, he would become violent, venomous and incoherent. Northcliffe was anyway larger than life and it was at first impossible to distinguish the crazy new caricature from the aberrant old character.

At the end of May Northcliffe travelled 'incognito' to Germany, sending 'a secret messenger' ahead to make arrangements for his reception. His British hosts would recognize the messenger by his 'grey Tyrolese hat'. Anticipating assassination, Northcliffe carried a loaded Colt revolver. 'I am not afraid for my life,' he remarked, 'I shoot from the hip.' In Germany he inveighed against the women for having 'the ugliest legs in the world' and asserted both that he had been poisoned by ice cream and had contracted 'Indian jungle fever'. On 4 June he sent a telegram to his wife's lover, Sir Robert Hudson, asking him to obtain the best medical

> opinion as to my sanity . . . I do not know but I think I am going mad. Please wire me at once to relieve my suspicions. I dreamt the other night that I had run off with Princess Mary and had started a boarding house at Blackpool, and she said to me: 'Thank you, we are doing very well.'

A rash of telegrams seemed almost symptomatic of Northcliffe's malady. He sent several accusing one of his secretaries of disloyalty and conspiracy. He rebuked the day editor of *The Times* for swaggering down Fleet Street in a top hat – 'tall hats are now for undertakers.' He instructed the female staff at Carmelite House, 'Now girls be good. I shall be back in a few weeks to find out whether you have been very good.' A few days later Northcliffe arrived in Paris. His speech was a gabble. His tongue was black. He mistook the shadow cast by his dressing-gown for an intruder and aimed his pistol at it. 'His left eye had a strange squint in an upward diagonal direction' which convinced Wickham Steed that the Chief was suffering from general paralysis of the insane. In the lobby of his hotel Northcliffe met Colonel House's wife and subjected her to a 'crude embrace'. The shocked House told Steed, 'Northcliffe is gone! He won't live long now.'

On 12 June Northcliffe embarked on a nightmarish train journey to Evian-les-Bains, where Molly was staying. He was accompanied by Steed and a small entourage whom he systematically threatened, harangued and cursed. He informed *The Times*'s foreign correspondent, Sisley Huddleston, that his teeth were bad, his breath stank and that he was no gentleman. He told obscene stories to Miss Rudge, a *Daily Mail* telephonist. He talked indistinctly, disjointedly and incessantly to Steed, at one point insisting that 150 members of *The Times* staff should be dismissed. There were flashes of lucidity but finally Northcliffe choked, screamed and shook his fist in the editor's face. He insulted the railway officials, the hotel staff at Evian and, most brutally of all, Molly herself. He sent such abusive telegrams to London that both Andrew Caird and W. G. Fish issued writs for libel against him. Eventually a Swiss nerve specialist was summoned and, according to Steed, 'certified Northcliffe as insane'. The accuracy of this diagnosis and, indeed, whether it was made at all, has been challenged. Shortly afterwards Northcliffe was escorted back to England and Sir Thomas Horder came to call. Northcliffe brandished his pistol (now unloaded) at the eminent doctor with the words, 'One of [Lloyd] George's bloody knights.' Horder examined Northcliffe and denied that he was mad. Nor, in Sir Thomas's view, was Northcliffe suffering from venereal disease. Though the Wassermann test for syphilis was by no means infallible it was the only examination Northcliffe ever passed. An authority on the subject, Sir Thomas concluded that Northcliffe was the victim of malignant endocarditis, a serious form of blood poisoning in which fever and delirium are prominent symptoms. On balance, this was probably the disease which killed Northcliffe. Some doubt remains. Molly and the family were passionately insistent that Northcliffe should die of a respectable complaint. And doctors notoriously diagnose the infirmities in which they are specialists. Northcliffe himself would have relished the prospect of 'quacktitioners' of one sort or another quarrelling over his corpse.

Northcliffe raged against the dying of the light. His will-power seemed unimpaired even by injections of morphia. He was intermittently violent. He threatened to have *The Times*'s staff ejected from their offices by the police. He railed against Steed: the 'damn nasty bounder... tried to kill me. Tried to knock my eye out. If I had had my gun I would have taken his leg off.' Everything was done to prevent his communicating with the outside world, but he found a telephone in Molly's boudoir. Northcliffe's ghostly voice was heard for the last time in Carmelite House, whispering instructions to the *Mail*'s night editor to release the Chief from his captivity. Dementia recurred. Northcliffe suffered from delusions of poverty: 'My shoes are all I have left in the world. I can't afford to get them soled and heeled.' His mother paid him a poignant last visit, asking the doctor afterwards, 'Is it his head?' On 9 August Horder decided that his patient must have constant fresh air. Northcliffe's own house, 1 Carlton Gardens, was unsuitable so a shelter was built on the roof of the neighbouring house, owned by the Duke of Devonshire. In it Northcliffe spent his final hours in a twilight of consciousness. On 14 August he gently died. His last coherent message was, 'Tell mother she is the only one.' Northcliffe was given a funeral at Westminster Abbey which was said to be 'fit for a king'. He was carried, amid scenes of public mourning which the English are wont to display even for the illustrious dead who were most hated during their lives, to his burial place at St Marylebone Cemetery. Three years later he was joined there by his mother.

Lord Northcliffe's body lay mouldering in the grave but his spirit went marching on. Northcliffe's various wills were contested and his newspaper empire disintegrated. But the emperor himself remained a spectral presence in many lives. J. L. Garvin was just one who found it almost impossible to believe that this 'cataract of human energy' had dried up: 'I feel as one might if Niagara itself were to cease and to vanish.' Surely such mighty generative power could transmit manifestations across the gulf fixed between the mortal and the immortal worlds. Spiritualists such as Conan Doyle, Hannen Swaffer and Northcliffe's sometime secretary and mistress, Louise Owen, focused their occult attention on the departed Chief. Was he there? Had he any news from behind the veil? Sure enough, like the good reporter he was, Northcliffe evaded any celestial censorship, met his deadline and rapped out the haunting staccato sentences:

I am not dead but alive. Can you imagine me inert? Was it my body that lived? It was my mind driven by my will. My mind still lives.

True, not all Northcliffe's utterances were quite consistent with his incorporeal state: 'When on earth I felt my muscles becoming flabby and floppy. Now they are firm and tight. I am not toothless, for my teeth are perfect.' Nor was the Chief as coherent as his earthly audience could have wished: 'Don't chew the end of your pencils when you write. Juicy figs are much better.' Perhaps such inconsequentiality was due to the ethereal interference which so often seems to distort answers from the Other Side. Or perhaps, after all, this was the authentic voice of the great communicator.

Select Bibliography

Lord Beaverbrook	*Men and Power 1916–1918* (1956)
T. Clarke	*My Northcliffe Diary* (1931)
T. Clarke	*Northcliffe in History* (1950)
P. Ferris	*The House of Northcliffe* (1971)
H. Fyfe	*Northcliffe: An Intimate Biography* (1930)
A. M. Gollin	*The Observer and J. L. Garvin* (1960)
H. J. Greenwall	*Northcliffe* (1957)
J. A. Hammerton	*With Northcliffe in Fleet Street* (1952)
The History of 'The Times'	Vols. III and IV (1947 and 1952)
K. Jones	*Fleet Street and Downing Street* (1920)
C. H. King	*Strictly Personal* (1969)
Lord Northcliffe	*At the War* (1916)
Lord Northcliffe	*My Journey Round the World 1921–22* (1923)
M. Pemberton	*Lord Northcliffe* (1922)
R. Pound and G. Harmsworth	*Northcliffe* (1959)
A. P. Ryan	*Lord Northcliffe* (1953)
T. Wilson (Ed.)	*The Political Diaries of C. P. Scott 1911–1928* (1970)
E. Wrench	*Geoffrey Dawson and Our Times* (1955)

Original Sources
British Museum: Northcliffe MSS
New Printing House Square: Northcliffe MSS and documents relating to *The Times*

Arthur Balfour

I

The clearest tribute to the enigmatic character of Arthur James Balfour, statesman and philosopher, is to be found in the number and variety of his nicknames. At Cambridge in the late 1860s his epicene elegance, typified by a fondness for velvet and blue china, earned him the titles of 'Miss Balfour' and 'Pretty Fanny'. By the early 'eighties his foppish airs brought him similar sobriquets in Parliament. Lord Randolph Churchill, regarding him as a member of the high aesthetic band who walked down Piccadilly with a poppy or a lily in their medieval hand, dubbed him 'Mr Postlethwaite'. When, in 1887, Balfour was unexpectedly promoted to the vital front-line post of Chief Secretary for Ireland by his uncle Robert, Lord Salisbury (a stroke of nepotism which inspired the catchphrase 'Bob's your uncle'), Parnell's supporters derided him as the 'scented popinjay', the 'palsied masher', 'Tiger Lily', 'Clara', 'Niminy Piminy'. Soon, however, in bitter acknowledgement of his coercive policies, he was re-christened 'Heliogabalus' after 'the Roman voluptuary who was in the habit of recruiting his debilitated energies in a bath of children's blood'. In Irish demonology he remains 'Bloody'

Balfour. In English high society, on the other hand, he was so charming, so debonair, so chivalrous, that he was hailed as 'Prince Arthur'. Among the 'Souls', that late-Victorian coterie of aristocrats aspiring to be intellectuals, Balfour, their spindle-shanked cynosure, was called 'the adored gazelle'. 'Saki' coined two appellations for him, 'the Ineptitude' and 'Sheer Khan't'. D. H. Lawrence referred to him as an 'old poodle'. The Kaiser denominated him 'a sheep'. Mr Gladstone, who saw through his sleek, androgynous façade earlier than most, prophesying in 1882 that, though the House of Commons laughed at Balfour then, he would one day lead the Conservative Party, knew him as 'artful Arthur'.

The nicknames generally confirm the caricaturists' vision of Balfour as possessing the body of Bertie Wooster and the mind of Jeeves. The patrician refinement and the gentlemanly civilities disguised calculating ruthlessness and striking talents. The fondness for detective stories and the refusal to read newspapers masked a tenacious ambition. The spineless attitudes hid a backbone of steel. Much in Balfour's long career seems to support this simple view — that he was a political poseur. The slug-abed apparently worked undisturbed in his own room during the mornings when he was supposed to be asleep. The 'silk-skinned sybarite whose rest a crumpled rose-leaf would disturb' proved the most resourceful and remorseless Irish Secretary of his age. The dilettante amateur established himself as Salisbury's successor in 1902 with professional adroitness. A year later the golf-loving premier engineered the 'most drastic series of expulsions, resignations and re-shuffles . . . in the twentieth century'. By the subtlest and most sustained campaign of political equivocation in British history the leader who forgot facts, figures and faces managed to keep his party from disintegrating over the issue of tariff reform. During the years immediately before the Great War the socialite who was too delicate to hunt and too sensitive to shoot made himself indispensable to the government in defence matters – even though he was in opposition. Balfour died in 1930 at the age of eighty-two, having spent most of the last fifteen years of his life in the Cabinet. He had become a political habit – a bad one in the view of Lord North-cliffe, who described him as an 'idle septuagenarian'.

Of course, Balfour was a master of the art of self-caricature. He positively invited others to reduce him to an idiosyncratic travesty of his true self. The philosopher of doubt would dither at the top of the great curving double staircase in his London house, 4 Carlton Gardens, appealing to his friends, 'There is absolutely no reason why one should go down one side or the other. What am I to do?' When the politician smuggled himself back into the House of Commons as MP for the City of London in 1906, having just led the Conservative Party to the most disastrous electoral defeat in its history, losing his own Mancunian seat in the process, he raised his pince-nez and surveyed the changed assembly. 'Who is that?' asked Balfour, gesturing towards a new member who was addressing the House, 'He seems on very excellent terms with himself.' 'He may well be,' came a neighbour's reply, 'since he had the honour of beating you at Manchester.' 'Dear me,' was the comment, 'how very interesting.' Studied vagueness was as much a part of the Balfourian burlesque as ironic self-deprecation and serene detachment and aloof disdain. In 1908 Balfour told a 'Soul' that he had won the golf handicap at North Berwick and that the triumph had 'caused far more emotion and surprise in my family than did my becoming Prime Minister. Doubtless also it is more important.' Winston Churchill recalled the occasion when an Irish MP, incensed by Balfour's polished raillery, leapt across the floor and shook his fist at the Leader of the House for fully two minutes. Tories prepared to defend him but Balfour 'regarded the frantic figure with no more and no less than the interest of a biologist examining through a microscope the contortions of a rare and provoked insect'. Of a colleague Balfour once remarked, 'If he had a little more brains he would be a half-wit.' Thus Balfour presented himself to the world as the brilliant, diamond-hard dandy, wise, witty, world-weary and effortlessly superior. The man behind the mannerism was more complex and less attractive.

Not that such a private character can be portrayed with confidence. It was, like Balfour's public career, a locked Chinese box of paradoxes which seemed to defy penetration. In an age which saw the triumph of democracy he was the last hereditary ruler of the Tory party. He was a practical Imperialist who dreamt of a global Anglo-Saxon confederation in which the United States would be Britain's junior partner. He was as blind to the national aspirations of the Irish and the Arabs as he was far-sighted about those of the Jews. The author of the Balfour Declaration knew little about Zionism and was tainted with anti-Semitism. The acme of civilization announced that the happiest fate for the Australian Aborigines would be extermination. The 'most extraordinary *objet d'art* our society has produced', in Maynard Keynes's words, thought that women might be MAs but he drew the line at their becoming MPs. Balfour was the apostle of science as an instrument of social and industrial progress but his own scientific ideas were both crackpot (he asserted that detective stories rested him because they affected 'different lobes of the brain – they draw the blood away') and extravagant (his attempts to improve peat as a fuel lost him a quarter of a million pounds). He was a Leader of the House of Commons who had to ask the Fabian, Beatrice Webb, 'What exactly is a "Trade Union"?', a Prime Minister who confused thousands with millions, a Foreign Secretary who could not distinguish between Somaliland and the Sudan. When he retired from the leadership of the 'Law and Order' party in 1911 Asquith described him as 'the most distinguished member of the greatest deliberative body in the world', yet within two years, by supporting Ulster against a parliamentary majority, Balfour seemed to be fomenting civil war in the United Kingdom. He was a politician who despised politics, a sceptical defender of faith, a logician who flirted with spiritualism, a philosopher who distrusted ideas. He was inscrutable.

H. G. Wells was one of many who 'tormented my brain to get to the bottom of him' only to receive 'a sense of things hidden as it were by depth and mist'. Balfour's character was as evanescent as the personal atmosphere he seemed to breathe inside the vacuum created by his own aloofness. It was impossible to locate the core of his personality. Or perhaps, like an onion, it had no core, just a series of protective layers, grace concealing superciliousness, suavity a cover for sophistry, detachment hiding frigidity, beauty surrounding barrenness. Maybe this was what Margot Asquith meant when she exclaimed, 'Shall I tell you what's the matter with Arthur? He's got no womb . . . no womb!' Perhaps it was to this fundamental sterility that Arthur himself referred when he dismissed the possibility of his marrying with the cryptic words, 'What have I got to offer anyone? Nothing but ashes.' For once he would not elaborate. As Ramsay MacDonald said, Balfour saw 'life from afar'. He dwelt apart, a lonely votary rapt in the mysteries of his own mind, a solitary communicant at the shrine of his own psyche. In his house were many mansions but there was room for only one resident. And, as a 'Soul' remarked, he 'lives with his windows shut and has a few false windows'. Balfour's character was a blank between question marks and his mind was a palimpsest of conflicting opinions. He was 'an island entirely surrounded by urbanity (modified by a few puzzling cross currents) and many determined attempts at invasion have failed'. Or, as another contemporary said, Balfour was 'a living problem, a personality of irreconcilable elements all compact . . . If he were sincere, what a riddle! And if he were not, what a comedy!' Riddle or comedy, comedy or riddle? Balfour was something of both, a beguiling conundrum.

II

Late in life all that Balfour could recollect of his childhood was 'having very tired legs after walking'. It was a revealing memory, for it attested both to his juvenile delicacy and to the fact that his early years were marred, as far as external circumstances went, by no more grave inconvenience than a salutary fatigue. He was fortunate. His mother, born Lady Blanche Mary Harriet Gascoigne Cecil, daughter of the second Marquess of Salisbury, brought up her other, sturdier children with the implacable rigour of one who believed that the tiniest misdemeanour might be their first step on a pilgrimage to Hell. Her Evangelicalism was a passion all the more incandescent for being repressed beneath a glacial patrician hauteur. An aristocratic friend depicted her in 1854, when Arthur was six:

> in Blanche there is such a wonderful power of command and duty that to know her slightly you would think she was a healthy-minded, happy wife, a mother of children, doing all the good she could, and consequently at peace with God and man. But you never could suspect the intense funds of feeling, dashing and flashing and bursting and melting and tearing her at times to pieces. And she looks so quiet, and pure, and almost cold, aye; about as cold as Hecla under its crust of ice.

Arthur later described his mother as clever, amusing and brilliant but, by alternately scorching and freezing her younger children, Lady Blanche blighted their lives. Her third son, Gerald, never concealed his dislike and fear of his mother. Two other sons (one of whom was later banished to Australia after forging a cheque) drank themselves into early graves. Of the daughters, Alice, Arthur's future housekeeper, developed a hatred of men and a neurotic habit of hoarding. And Nora took to winking because it was 'the least tiring expression of emotion'. Thus, even in youth, Arthur's enervated constitution became his great source of strength. It protected him, outwardly at least, from the vitiating effects of his mother's inclemency.

Having sired nine children in eleven years James Balfour, Lady Blanche's husband, broke a blood vessel in a paroxysm of coughing. Tuberculosis developed and by 1856 he was dead. Being the eldest son, Arthur inherited on his coming of age the lion's share of the family fortune, some four million pounds, which made him one of the richest men in Britain. Arthur's grandfather, offspring of a Lowland Scots laird, had made the money in India by purveying supplies to the Navy during the Napoleonic wars. In 1817 he had bought the beautiful, 10,000-acre estate of Whittingehame, just south of Dunbar on the Firth of Forth. Both he and his son James became MPs and played a prominent part in the affairs of East Lothian. Three generations of Balfours professed to live 'on a very simple scale' – in 'drawing-rooms hung with yellow damask and filled with French furniture and Sèvres china'. Arthur evidently imagined that a large shooting lodge, 'a first-class deer forest, as well as grouse moors under sheep and a salmon river' were the natural appurtenances of a civilized existence. Not that he was raised in complete ignorance of working-class distress. As an exercise in piety Arthur and his siblings were even obliged by Lady Blanche to participate in it. During the Lancashire 'cotton famine', caused by the American Civil War, she discharged a few of her servants and gave their wages to the relief fund. In this Lady Blanche evinced, according to one member of the family, 'characteristic ruthlessness for her own personal comfort'. The children were given chores to do and Arthur was surprised to be cast in the role of bootboy to the household. What the dismissed servants thought of this singular act of philanthropy is not recorded.

Nor can it be known how far Arthur's soul had been ravaged by the severities of his mother's salvationism. Physically molly-coddled, he was undoubtedly the victim of a harsh spiritual inquisition and it is significant that he counted his departure for boarding school, at the age of ten, an 'unmixed blessing'. The first of the gilded educational establishments selected for him was Grange School at Hoddesdon, near the Cecils' Hatfield House, in Hertfordshire. Here Arthur was described as attractive and clever but lacking in 'vital energy'; he was allowed to lie down in the afternoons, when 'he liked to have the organ softly played to him in the hall below'. In 1861 he progressed to Eton, just then vindicating itself before the Public School Commission as 'a place *sui generis*', the greatest institution of learning on earth. Actually, Etonian scholarship was increasingly being sacrificed on the altar of Etonian athleticism – the Boating Song was written while Arthur was a pupil. The school seemed less interested in educating the minds and improving the morals of Christian gentlemen than in training the characters and refining the manners of Tory philistines. Arthur's limp physique and poor eyesight (wearing spectacles was regarded as bad form at Eton) denied him success on the playing fields. Nevertheless, like so many of his generation, he became totally imbued with the sporting spirit. He was not only infatuated with golf. As Lord Vansittart wrote, 'his sedate passion for lawn tennis gave him the thrill of a guilty conscience . . . His sliced forc-hand from the base-line evoked in him gleams of pale happiness.' Perhaps life itself, with its elaborate conventions, it empty rewards and its brief span, was but a game. Were not commercial competition, class loyalty and race patriotism simply extensions of team spirit? Certainly Balfour came to regard politics as a game. It was not a game played for real stakes, of course; it would have been a bore to compete for anything as portentous as an increase in the sum of human happiness. It was played among friendly amateurs for fun, for the practice of pleasing forensic strokes and the scoring of elegant debating points, for its own sake. It mattered not who won or lost . . .

Arthur experienced 'unforgettable grace' at Eton. A solitary, effeminate boy, neither 'a hero among my fellows nor a subject of hopeful speculation among my teachers', he might have expected bullying or worse. But he evidently found the Etonian régime mild compared with that of Lady Blanche and he manifested at school 'a beautiful purity of mind' and 'a delightful sort of openness'. Otherwise Eton scarcely contributed to his intellectual development, though it did confirm his prejudice in favour of the general culture of *belles lettres* in an age which more and more stressed the value of utilitarian specialization. Arthur had read Macaulay's *Essays* at home and had been dazzled by the pyrotechnics of that 'showman of supreme genius'. Macaulay, master of the sublime commonplace, was a dangerous model. All too often in later life, when Balfour was not obliged by political exigencies to display the dialectical finesse for which he had such a flair, he slipped into the habit of giving luminous expression to the humdrum ('Care may sit behind the horseman, she never presumes to walk with the caddie') or even making bland pronouncements of the platitudinous. Witness his account of Trinity College, Cambridge, where he went in 1866; not only was the 'kindness' of the dons 'unfailing', but the Master treated him with 'unfailing kindness'. Edwardian writers of *belles lettres* could manufacture such mandarin nothings endlessly, without effort, without thought.

Balfour entered Trinity as a Fellow-Commoner (an archaic rank shortly to be abolished) which gave him the privilege of wearing a blue-and-silver gown and dining at High Table. He thus established an intimate relationship with two senior Fellows, both of whom were in due course to become his brothers-in-law. The first was John Strutt, a distinguished physicist whose achievements were rewarded by a Nobel Prize and a peerage. Edward VII once greeted him with the words, 'Well, Lord Rayleigh, discovering something, I suppose?' – turning to a lady near him – 'He's always at it.' From Strutt Balfour learnt, in an amateurish sort of way, to appreciate the growing importance of science in national life; by augmenting wealth via improved industrial processes science could become a great anti-revolutionary force, easing the lot of the poor and securing the position of the rich. From the other Trinity Fellow, Henry Sidgwick, under whose tutelage he read 'Moral Sciences', Balfour learnt to speculate and to equivocate. A leading light in the 'Apostles', a famous secret society devoted to the discussion of recondite intellectual matters, Sidgwick was unable to decide whether he was an intuitionist or a utilitarian, a believer or an agnostic. Maynard Keynes remarked dismissively that 'He never did anything but wonder whether Christianity was true and prove it wasn't and hope it was.' Lytton Strachey regarded Sidgwick, who was impotent, as a typical representative of 'the Glass Case Age'; he and his like were incapable of penetration, of 'getting either out of themselves or into anything or anybody else'. (Between them Keynes and Strachey were to sabotage the 'Apostles', by electing new members less for their brains than their looks and their willingness to participate in exciting games of Blind Man's Buff.) Sidgwick taught Balfour to see all sides of every issue. From Sidgwick Balfour took his characteristic stance, described by a contemporary as 'shivering in philosophic doubt on the steps of a metaphysical bathing-machine'. The 'Souls'' 'favourite tag of mimicry' was to declare that Balfour's 'reply to any question was "Theoretically: YES . . . Practically: NO"'. As a political rallying cry this clearly left much to be desired. Balfour was always to be a philosopher among politicians, and a politician among philosophers. Yet during the great Edwardian debate, Free Trade v. Protection, his verbal sorcery and casuistical legerdemain for some time concealed his lack of constructive ideas. His very indecisiveness staved off what seemed inevitable — the destruction of the Conservative Party.

What Balfour came to believe in the cold recesses of his heart, what philosophy he finally espoused, who can say? His cogitations often appeared to be just another game, played for the sake of the mental exercise. Or for amusement: 'If there is no future life,' he quipped, 'this world is a bad joke; but whose joke?' Moreover his two main books, *A Defence of Philosophic Doubt* (1879) and *The Foundations of Belief* (1895) were ambiguous at best and at worst contradictory. Like Newman, Balfour used the resources of reason to prove that reason had no resources. The propositions of science, he maintained, were no more susceptible to rational proof than were those of religion. Like Burke, Balfour propounded an ideology to demonstrate the futility of ideas. Certitude was not to be arrived at by reason or argument but by custom and tradition. Authority, not ratiocination, which was a destructive force, provided the only sure foundation for religious faith and for social order. Balfour ranged over sceptical terrain but his conclusions led him down the high road to Conservatism and Christianity. Or did they? The most eloquent passage he ever penned apparently testifies to a profound cosmic pessimism. It was worthy of the radical atheist, Bertrand Russell, who wrote of his conviction 'that all the labours of all the ages, all the devotion, all the inspiration, all the noonday brightness of human genius, are destined to extinction in the vast death of the solar system and that the whole temple of Man's achievement must inevitably be buried beneath the debris of a universe in ruins'. Balfour, having dismissed the past as a history 'of blood and tears, of helpless blundering, of wild revolt, of stupid acquiescence, of empty aspirations', looked into the future and foresaw that

> The energies of our system will decay, the glory of the sun will be dimmed, and the earth, tideless and inert, will no longer tolerate the race which has for a moment disturbed its solitude. Man will go down into the pit and all his thoughts will perish . . . Matter will know itself no longer. Imperishable monuments and immortal deeds, death itself and love stronger than death, will be as though they had never been. Nor will anything that *is* be better or be worse for all that the labour, genius, devotion, and suffering of man have striven through countless generations to effect.

If this was not a testament of nihilistic despair it may at least afford an insight into the spiritual wasteland concealed beneath Balfour's handsome, clever and rich veneer. As a gay undergraduate, as a rising star in the social firmament, as a careless player of a 'scandalous' amount of real tennis, as an amusing performer of the 'Infernals' (his much-loved concertina), as a scholar whose second-class degree was more a reward for ability than work, Balfour attracted human warmth. He did not radiate it. It was as though his emotions had been blasted by his upbringing, as though his interior life had become a petrified wilderness which he saw no purpose in attempting to cultivate. As one of the 'Souls' said, 'He knows that there was once an ice age and that there will be an ice age again.' Neville Chamberlain was one of many who felt that Balfour had 'a heart like a stone'. What, in a heartless world, could have been more appropriate?

III

Balfour's emotional frigidity repelled some members of
the high aristocratic society in which he drifted aimlessly
for nearly a decade after coming down from Cambridge.
Margot Asquith once rebuked him for his coolness:
'You're fond of me and of Ettie [Lady Desborough] and
of Baffy [his niece and biographer, Blanche]; but you
don't really care – you wouldn't mind if we all died.'
Balfour answered, 'I should mind if you all died on the
same day.' H. G. Wells, patronized by the 'Souls',
believed that Balfour might have been 'a very great man
indeed' if his passions had been as hot and his affections
as potent as . . . those of H. G. Wells. Towards the end
of his life Lord Curzon, a very superior 'Soul', summed up
their chief priest thus:

> The truth is that Balfour with his scintillating intellectual
> exterior had no depth of feeling, no profound con-
> victions, and strange to say (in spite of his fascination of
> manner) no real affection. We all knew this, when the
> emergency came he would drop or desert or sacrifice
> any one of us without a pang . . . Were any of us to die
> suddenly he would dine out that night with undisturbed
> complacency, and in the intervals of conversation or
> bridge, would be heard to murmur, 'Poor old George.'

This was somewhat unfair. In 1870 Balfour was touched
by a press report on the Franco-Prussian War and gave
£1,000 to a fund for the relief of its victims. But he immediately regretted the impulse and abjured the newspapers, determining never again 'to lay himself open to
any access of overwhelming pity'. Afterwards, though his
resolution was for a moment melted by Chaim Weizmann's
description of the Jewish pogroms in Russia, Balfour
seldom found himself moved to compassion.

However, he neither lacked nor repressed all sensual

instincts. Shortly after Lady Blanche's death, which occurred in 1872, he fell in love with May Lyttelton, sister of a Cambridge friend. She was tall, amusing and unconventional, with strong reddish colouring and a lively mind. They established an 'understanding'. But before the engagement could be announced she too died, of typhoid, in 1875. Balfour was staggered. He walked the streets of London in a daze. He placed an emerald ring of his mother's in May's coffin. He visited mediums, arranged séances and continued to conduct spiritualist experiments (once achieving good results from 'crystal-gazing') for the rest of his life. He even embarked on a recuperative round-the-world tour with May's brother, who complained that he was 'comatose' most of the time. He never married, later dismissing with 'insolent indifference' the rumour that he was engaged to Margot Tennant, the young termagant who finally became Mrs Asquith: 'No, that is not so. I rather think of having a career of my own.' And though he had romantic friendships, possibly even carnal relations, with two of the leading 'Souls', Mary Elcho and Ettie Desborough, he apparently found it impossible to utter words of vulgar passion: 'they would if said *to* me give such exquisite pain that I could never bring myself to say them to others – even at their desire.' Mary Elcho was not deceived by this fastidiousness: 'of *course* it is because you care less! *feel* less!' She was right. The only ardent declaration Balfour was ever heard to make was addressed to one of Mary Elcho's chows: 'Oh Ching! My fluffy Ching! I *am* so devoted to you! No one knows how greatly I love you!' Where humans were concerned Balfour had the *sang-froid* of an iceberg. It was later suggested that his imagination had been eunuchized, that he was (in Kipling's damning words) 'arid, aloof, incurious, unthinking, unthanking, gelt,' that his affections (if not positively homosexual) had been emasculated. They were simply benumbed. The flesh was willing but the spirit was bleak.

Arthur Balfour, the Prime Minister, in 1903

Arthur Balfour aged nine

The Philosopher-Statesm

When noblesse obliged him to hob-nob with 'the mob', or when necessity forced him into contact with 'those disagreeable accompaniments to a political career', his constituents, Balfour could litterally grow pale with ennui. When receiving public deputations he had constant recourse to the scent spray. He marked the approach of unwanted visitors to Whittingehame with 'complete horror'. He adopted Mark Twain's expression, 'tramps and bounders', to describe them. And sometimes, with other members of his excessively self-absorbed family, he hid among the lime trees near the croquet lawn until the intruders had departed. He was depressed for weeks at the thought of having to attend the annual 'Farm Ball' on his estate. Invitations from neighbours he greeted with 'despairing boredom'. Like his grandmother's intimate friend the 'Iron' Duke of Wellington, after whom he was named, Arthur had a social contempt for his intellectual equals and an intellectual contempt for his social equals. (When a female 'Soul' told him that some of their number were, in a humble spirit, taking classes in ethics he responded drily, 'Humility is good but it is not sufficient for a study of ethics.') Yet he was the spoilt darling of high society and considered no day complete without some sort of evening engagement. In congenial company, that of the very distinguished, the very gifted, the very beautiful or the very rich, no one reflected warmth with such a delightful glow as Balfour.

No one basked in it so radiantly. H. G. Wells said that Balfour 'pleased by being charmed and pleased'. It was 'hopeless to avoid devotion to A.J.B., and I never tried,' wrote Lord Vansittart, 'A great gentleman unaware, his manners were perfect except to foreigners.' A born poodle-faker, Balfour was 'pretty nearly irresistible' to women. His bearing seemed an act of gallantry, his voice was a chaste caress. Consuelo Vanderbilt, who married the Duke of Marlborough, was captivated by Balfour. He was such a delicious change from her husband's usual aristocratic cronies, whose social graces were more or less confined to slapping their legs with a riding crop and who imagined that Americans 'all lived on plantations with Negro slaves and that there were Red Indians ready to scalp us just around the corner' and that the Civil War had been fought between North and South America. She gushed,

> There has, I believe, never been anyone quite like [Balfour] . . . When he spoke in a philosophic vein, it was like listening to Bach. His way of holding his head gave him the appearance of searching the heavens and his blue eyes were absent, and yet intent, as if busy in some abstract world. Both mentally and physically he gave the impression of immense distinction and trans-cendant spirituality.

It was no doubt his visionary air, his remote insouciance, his nimbus of cold light, which constituted Balfour's chief attraction to the opposite sex. He was a challenge. He was a star which, fused by the appropriate idolatry, might flare into a sun.

Even among Balfour's most ecstatic devotees, however, there were those who were 'slightly oppressed by the sense of admiration due' to him. Lady Cynthia Asquith, for example, found it odd that 'in spite of his divine amiability and sweetness and easiness, I still feel shy alone in a room with him.' Others were stifled by the incense-laden atmosphere of Whittingehame, a secular kirk dedicated to the worship of the one true laird, whose lightest words (those, at least, not devoted to 'golfing shop') were treasured up as oracles. (If younger members of the family failed to be sufficiently reverential Balfour grew 'bored' and withered them with 'deadly little blasts of sarcasm'.) Balfour was said to be able to transform the stodgiest pudding of talk into a soufflé. But his efforts were too in-substantial for some tastes. The anti-Imperialist Wilfrid

Scawen Blunt, whom Balfour was to imprison in Ireland in spite of the fact that he was 'a goodish poet and a goodish lawn tennis player and a goodish fellow', dismissed him as 'a pleasant trifler' in conversation. Beatrice Webb thought Balfour mainly mouthed 'froth': 'Says cynical and clever things, which are meant to be cleverer than they turn out to be.' Lord Curzon remarked on his 'cultured ignorance'. Those who were chilled, despite Balfour's enchanting manner, by his lofty self-possession, observed that friendliness for him was a substitute for friendship, that he was fond of everyone and cared for no one.

On the other hand the 'Souls', so nicknamed (to their irritation) because they were always discussing their souls, venerated Balfour wholeheartedly. What was their obeisance worth? Doubtless their social and sexual inter-course – for the 'Souls' were attracted to one another's bodies – took place on a more ethereal level than that of the common-or-garden aristocracy. Their converse, though 'imponderable as gossamer and dew', was surely more animated than that of noblemen whose sole reading was Ruff's *Guide to the Turf.* It was, indeed, fascinating enough on one occasion for its participants, Balfour included, to remain at Harry Cust's table in spite of the fact that his house had caught fire upstairs and, to protect guests against water from the firemen's hoses, footmen passed bath-towels with the port. Whereas Balfour was once abruptly obliged by the unsoulfulness of Lord Essex's after-dinner stories to join the ladies. The evening enter-tainment of the 'Souls', 'Clumps', a guessing game, was possibly more sophisticated than the usual cards. The 'Souls' have even been described as forerunners of the Bloomsbury Group. Yet they created nothing of permanent value in the way of art, literature or ideas. Lord Esher remarked sardonically that Balfour's *Foundations of Belief* 'will give an infinity of trouble to his lady friends and admirers . . . It is really hard when you are the apostle of a

charming sect to trouble their minds with abstract specu-
lations.' The 'Souls' were not much troubled. They found
Burke's *Peerage* more absorbing than Burke's *Reflections*.
Like others of their caste they sought diversion not
edification. They adored their gazelle for his frivolity, for
his command of (what Margot Tennant called) 'the divine
nonsense which makes life liveable'. Beatrice Webb once
achieved the remarkable feat of fracturing Balfour's
composure and quite draining his face of its usual aff-
ability by asking, 'Don't you agree with me, Mr Balfour,
that the only excuse for a dinner-party is that it should end
in a committee?' The 'Souls' wore their culture on their
sleeves like a heraldic badge, a charming and unusual
decoration. It was a chic adjunct to the life of fashion, to
be ranked somewhere between discreet adultery and
immaculate spats. The gentlemen cared more about sole-
cisms than souls; the ladies were not much less interested
in parasols. Perhaps it was not entirely to his credit that in
this elect company Balfour's wan spirit was irradiated with
seraphic brightness.

IV

Few, in his early days, saw Balfour as much more than an
exotic aristocratic butterfly. He adorned London society,
he fluttered from tennis court and concert hall to those
country houses which provided a sufficiently lavish setting
for such a rare specimen. He visited the Duke of Devonshire regularly for Christmas 'theatricals', but despite the
Renaissance-style water-landscaping, cascades rippling
over stone steps six hundred feet long, despite the copper
willow tree which wept tears from every leaf, despite the
carved garlands of fruit and flowers festooning the walls,
Balfour disapproved of Chatsworth: it was 'a very un-
comfortable house'. Balfour seemed too frangible, too

flighty, too epicurean ever to embark on a serious career. He seldom answered letters and the minor inconveniences of life rendered him as 'petulant as a woman'. He was habitually unpunctual and inveterately idle. May Lyttelton recorded in her diary, 'Mr Balfour dangles about and does nothing to an extent that becomes wrong.' And did Lord Salisbury, who had himself been a frail, fastidious, sceptical youth, though he despised the high life of 'Clubland', did uncle Robert perceive in Balfour not a social butterfly but a political chrysalis?

Salisbury was notoriously myopic: as Prime Minister he mistook a photograph of Edward VII for one of General Sir Redvers Buller and he failed to recognize in the flesh not only members of his Cabinet but his own sons. Yet Salisbury had a penetrating mind and he may well have discerned an embryonic ability and a nascent ambition in Balfour. Superficially the smooth, impeccable nephew had little in common with the shambling, bearded uncle, who nearly induced apoplexy in his meticulous sovereign by appearing on one ceremonial occasion in a nice mixture of two uniforms. There were more fundamental differences. Where Balfour was cool and stoical, Salisbury was subject to 'nerve storms'. Balfour was a master of verbal fence, always preferring to say that a man had 'feloniously appropriated other people's property' rather than to call him 'a thief'. Salisbury used a blunderbuss, seldom making a speech which did not contain some 'blazing indiscretion' or vituperative discharge: he once described Disraeli as 'the grain of dirt' clogging the political machine. However, at the most profound level of all the two men were in marked accord. Both were pessimistic and patrician, Christian and Conservative. Both believed that the function of government was to govern; politicians could not and should not do more than administer the law and conduct foreign affairs. Schemes of political improvement were dangerous or ludicrous. Negative formulae were a plausible substitute for positive policies. 'The wise man,' said Balfour, 'is content in a sober and cautious spirit, with a full consciousness of his feeble powers of foresight and the narrow limits of his activity, to deal as they arise with the problems of his own generation.' Uncle and nephew agreed that science might accomplish some painless progress, but even that hope scarcely modified Lord Salisbury's 'firm conviction that we were going to the dogs'. It was not an optimistic sign that, after the installation at Hatfield House of one of the first electric light systems, the bulbs sometimes glowed dull red and the wires sparked so much that the family had to throw cushions at them. But if Balfour and Salisbury were both reactionaries only the latter was a die-hard. Indeed, Balfour claimed that he himself was a Liberal whereas his uncle was a Tory – apparently meaning that he, unlike Salisbury, had never been discovered sleep-walking in front of an open second-floor window, there preparing to repulse 'revolutionary mob leaders'. Balfour was willing to float with the tide of democracy, so long as he floated to the top: the 'classes' must continue to dominate the 'masses'. Salisbury wanted to stem the tide, to perpetuate the traditional system inviolate. No doubt partly with this in mind, he secured his nephew's election in 1874 as Member of Parliament for the family pocket borough of Hertford.

Initially Balfour was a failure. For two years he did not utter a word in the House of Commons. He attracted the disapproval of the Prime Minister, Disraeli, because he 'sat upon his spine'. Mr Gladstone noticed that he 'sprawls all over the house'. The press made jokes about his long 'weak end'. Eventually Balfour broke his silence on a topic carefully selected for its complete lack of interest – Indian currency. It was, he recollected, 'a dull speech, on a dull subject, delivered to an empty House by an anxious beginner'. He did not rise again for another year. After that he spoke infrequently, reluctantly and hesitantly, experiencing on one 'eminently disagreeable' occasion 'the absolute blankness of mind, in which there seemed neither thought nor memory, but only a painful groping for some quite elusive idea'. His initiative was rewarded by Lord Salisbury. The Foreign Secretary appointed the nephew as his private secretary and in 1878 took him to the Congress of Berlin.

Balfour's political advance did not really begin, however, until after the Conservative rout in 1880 and the death of 'the Jew', as Lord Salisbury called Disraeli, a year later. Balfour's progress depended on Salisbury's ascendancy. He therefore resolved that his uncle and not the Tory chief in the Commons, Sir Stafford Northcote, who suffered from weak knees and was 'no more match for Gladstone than a wooden three-decker would be for a Dreadnought', should succeed to the leadership of the Conservative Party. Pleading that he required more room for his long legs, Balfour turned Lord Randolph Churchill's front-bench trio of Tory malcontents into a quartet. It was dubbed 'the Fourth Party' (Parnell's was the third) though it was united in little but a determination to make parliamentary life difficult for the 'Grand Old Man' and impossible for (to employ Lord Randolph's nickname for Northcote) the 'Grand Old Woman'. This, thanks largely to Churchill's outstanding bravura as orator and opportunist, it managed to do. Churchill encouraged Balfour to spread his political wings. From Churchill he learnt to despise friendly auditors and to disparage hostile ones. Balfour slowly metamorphosed himself into that creature unknown to entomology, a butterfly with a sting. The Liberal/Irish 'Kilmainham Treaty' of 1882, 'negotiated in secret with treason', he denounced as 'an infamy'. 'The only way to make Mr Gladstone retract a mis-statement is to send him a lawyer's letter.' Joseph Chamberlain's criticisms of the House of Lords 'consisted in about equal proportions of bad history, bad logic, and bad taste'. Chamberlain riposted effectively by describing Balfour as 'the fourth part of the Fourth Party'. Actually, by 1884 the liaison had served its purpose and Balfour was politely disengaging himself from it, intent on his 'succession to more permanent honours'.

No one needed to teach Balfour the use of social amenity as a method of political advancement. He was the supreme exponent, almost the inventor, of the art. His most damaging criticisms of Sir Stafford Northcote, for example, had been made 'without actually mentioning his name or using any discourteous phrase'. Balfour maintained cordial relations with Lord Randolph Churchill, the next pretender to the Conservative succession, while privately stigmatizing him as a 'half-mad' 'arch-fiend'. Luckily for Balfour, Lord Randolph was a political meteor who shone brightly in the free space of opposition but quickly burnt up in the confined atmosphere of office. In 1886 he resigned from the Chancellorship of the Exchequer in Salisbury's new government over a trivial issue and never regained power. He had incensed too many of his own side by his naked ambition and his caustic pronouncements. He could scarcely expect to assuage the anger of the Tories, now joined by Chamberlainite Liberals intent on preserving the Union with Ireland in the face of Gladstone's Home Rule crusade, for he was unable to resist such flaming provocations as: 'The Irish Question lies in a nutshell; it is that a quick-witted nation are being governed by a stupid party.' Balfour would never insult the Conservatives as Lord Randolph did. He would never even insult the Irish as Lord Salisbury did – his uncle did not conceal his view that they were a race of bog-trotting Hottentots, quite incapable of self-government. True, Balfour had, when provoked, a neat way of saying nasty things. But his invective was delivered with such civility as almost to beguile its victims. His sting seemed to be that of a political lightweight. Nevertheless, early in 1887 Lord Salisbury appointed this framer of soft answers and fair words, who had failed to distinguish himself in two lesser ministerial jobs, to the most onerous and challenging post in his gift, the Chief Secretaryship of Ireland. Balfour's conduct in that office turned on him the undying wrath of the Irish and buttered his political parsnips for life.

Balfour thus became what he said he had no vocation for being, 'a Great Man's Great Man'. Yet such was the difficulty and danger of the Irish situation – Balfour expected to lose either 'life or reputation' there – that few raised the cry of nepotism. His promotion was certainly audacious. But the gasp of consternation and the 'scream of mocking laughter' with which, respectively, Conservatives and Irish greeted it were responses more to the supposed incompetence of the nephew than to the unfair partiality of the uncle. A contemporary newspaper summed up the general opinion:

> It seems like breaking a butterfly to extend Mr Balfour on the rack of Irish politics. He is an elegant, fragile creature, a prey to aristocratic languor, which prevents him from ever assuming any but the limpest attitude. He is also noteworthy for a sublime affectation of intellectual culture, which has proved singularly useless to him in making a mark as a politician ... Mr Balfour's whole life seems to be a protest against being called upon to do anything but sniff a heavily perfumed handkerchief while he sprawls in poses of studied carelessness on the benches of the House of Commons.

How could such an invertebrate parliamentary *flâneur* hope to solve the problem that had come, owing to a combination of acute agrarian distress, the unprecedented strength of the Irish nationalist party under Parnell's iron leadership and Gladstone's espousal of Home Rule, to dominate British politics? To send Balfour to Ireland seemed to Curzon 'like throwing a lame dove among a congregation of angry cats'. The Parnellites relished the prospect of tearing the wings off 'Daddy Long Legs', of drawing the tongue of the 'lisping Hawthorn Bird'. One of them, referring to previous Irish Secretaries, reportedly said, 'We have killed Forster, blinded Beach, smashed up Trevelyan – what shall we do with this weakling?'

They could do nothing with Balfour. Against all expectations, he succeeded. Yet the nature of his triumph, which was purely a rhetorical one, has been much misunderstood. Balfour gained victory after victory, but only in the House of Commons. There, after a hesitant start, he defended his Irish policies with unexampled coolness and resource against some of the most rancorous assaults ever mounted on a minister of the Crown. He infuriated the opposition by the nonchalance with which he dangled his pince-nez, by his dispassionate wit, by his sarcastic repartee, by returning their grenades with that imperturbable forehand volley from the baseline. The points mounted in Balfour's favour, especially after the discrediting of Parnell on account of his adultery with Kitty O'Shea. And the sheer virtuosity of the parliamentary style which Balfour had at last developed served to disguise the emptiness of his actual achievement. For in Ireland he did not succeed; he just avoided overt failure. He could not solve the Irish problem for the simple reason that he never understood what the Irish problem was. Balfour the aristocrat was always insensitive to the needs and aspirations of others, especially the swinish multitude. Balfour the Conservative invariably thought that political disorders were susceptible to administrative remedies. Balfour the bad sailor gave the impression that the Irish problem really resolved itself into the Irish Channel – 'the difference between a calm and a rough passage being merely that between aggravated discomfort and acute agony'. He never realized that the Irish problem was essentially a case of frustrated nationality. If he had studied the condition of John Bull's Other Island thoroughly, if he had not spent fewer than six months there during his four and a half years in office, if he had ventured into the 'beautiful, stagnant desolation' of the interior more than once (in 1890), he might have grasped this fact. Neither the lance of coercion nor the poultice of conciliation could rid the Irish body politic of the poison affecting it as a result of the Union with England.

Balfour's Irish policy was described by his legal officer, Edward 'Coercion' Carson, as one of 'kicks and ha'pence', sticks and carrots. Balfour himself declared, 'I shall be as relentless as Cromwell in enforcing obedience to the law, but, at the same time, I shall be as radical as any reformer in redressing grievances.' The Irish jibe was that Balfour favoured heavy punishments and light railways and that 'mere purposeless human suffering . . . imparted a delicious excitement to his languid life'. The English claim has traditionally been that Balfour ended agrarian crime and that by helping tenants to purchase their land and fostering local industries he initiated the sound policy of 'killing Home Rule by kindness'. All these verdicts are wide of the mark.

Undoubtedly Balfour shared his uncle's disdain for the Irish and thought that a 'licking' would restore them to a proper acceptance of their role in the English scheme of things. He did pass a Crimes Act in 1887 by which the smack of firm government could be duly administered. This did enable him to protect landlords' interests against the 'Plan of Campaign', the systematic refusal to pay rack-rents on selected estates − if this 'grossly illegal', 'socialistic' and 'revolutionary' conspiracy succeeded, Balfour said revealingly, 'Irish land would not be worth three years' purchase? Balfour did support the police who shot down rioters at Mitchelstown and the bailiffs who (using battering-rams paid for out of Secret Service funds) evicted tenants elsewhere. He did resist the improvement of prison conditions for those convicted of political crimes and he was consistently callous about their lot. Referring to the ill-health which dogged the imprisoned MPs, he wondered whether there was 'some mysterious connection between diseased lungs and Irish patriotism'. He congratulated himself that Irish gaols were, at any rate, healthier than Irish slums. (This may have been true, though Balfour drew no moral from it: the death rate in Dublin, even at the beginning of this century, was 27.6 per 1,000, the highest of any city in Europe, higher even than in plague-ridden Calcutta.) Of the death of John Mandeville after a spell behind bars in 1888, Balfour remarked cynically, 'We cannot hope that everybody sent to an Irish prison will prove immortal,' Unlike his disgusted subordinates, Balfour was sardonically amused by William O'Brien's nine-day wonder, a constipation strike. When, on the tenth day, Balfour heard that O'Brien had made a motion he was relieved (not, of course, as relieved as O'Brien) and observed, 'It is curious how few of these fellows seem able to fight like gentlemen.' But none of this constituted what Blunt called 'scientific inhumanity'. By the crude canons of Cromwell, certainly by the more refined standards of the twentieth century, it was not really even repression. The press was free, civil liberties were respected, the rule of law – English law, admittedly – prevailed. And, as a matter of fact, most gaoled priests and politicians did receive special privileges. Poverty was a much more serious evil than coercion and improved harvests and economic revival, not harsh measures, pacified Ireland. Insofar as it achieved anything, coercion weakened the constitutional movement of Parnell, strengthened physical-force nationalism and added a bitter new episode to the tragic saga of Anglo-Irish relations.

As for Balfour's improving schemes . . . kindness is no more a remedy for the afflictions of a conquered nation than sympathy is a cure for cancer. And while the main avenue to Home Rule was blocked, Irishmen, armed with hurleys, would look towards establishing their own right of way. In any case 'constructive Unionism' accomplished little. The hopeful land purchase scheme contained so many complex clauses protecting the owners that it became known as 'Mr Balfour's Puzzle'. It was ineffective. The Catholic university project collapsed. Balfour was not its best advocate, nourishing as he did a dour aversion to Rome and being unable to comprehend how Catholics expected to strengthen their faith by exposing themselves to a liberal education. His Local Government Bill was similarly abortive. Balfour recommended it with the argument, a parody of unidea'd Conservatism, that it was better to do 'a stupid thing which has been done before' than 'a wise thing that has never been done before'. It was promptly 'laughed out of the House and nobody laughed at it more heartily than its author'. The relief works, established in what were euphemistically known as 'congested districts', areas mainly in the West where (as Lord Salisbury explained to Queen Victoria) 'a dense population of half starving multitudes' tried to scratch a living from inadequate land, were misconceived. Balfour set up a Congested Districts Board in 1891 which bought estates, re-settled tenants, improved transport and encouraged fishing, lace-making, weaving and so on. It has recently been claimed (and with unwonted immodesty Balfour himself claimed) that this enterprise was one of his 'crowning achievements' in Ireland. In fact it was a disastrous squandering of precious resources. The work never paid its way and was doomed to disappear once subsidies were withdrawn. The light railways had little effect on local economies. The failure to invest soundly in the East led to large-scale emigration. This Balfour favoured. Indeed, he thought it extraordinary that Irishmen continued to 'squat generation after generation on the bogs and mountains of the inclement West'. He could no more understand what the Irish had to be patriotic about than he could sympathize with the Hibernian partiality for potatoes, which were so prone to disease. It would be much more convenient, he thought, if the Irish lived off lentils.

Balfour was not inhumane: he was unimaginative about those who dwelt on a less exalted plane than his own. He was not brutal, merely unfeeling; he reckoned that 'what made Irish government so difficult was English sentimentality'. He simply did not care about Ireland except as a counter in the English parliamentary game. The triumph of Parnell in proving that *The Times* had used forged letters to implicate him in Irish crime Balfour regarded as 'extremely entertaining'. The ruin of Parnell and his party after the O'Shea divorce scandal he thought 'extraordinarily amusing'. The death of Parnell in 1891 he viewed with 'the detachment of a choir-boy at a funeral service'. Nonetheless, at a subliminal level, Ireland did take its toll on Balfour. He appeared indifferent to his own safety and dangerously absent-minded about the revolver his detectives made him carry. Some even called him 'Balfour the Brave'. But during his years as Chief Secretary his beautiful brown hair turned prematurely grey.

V

Ireland made Balfour, and made it necessary for him to do little more than wait until Lord Salisbury's retirement before succeeding to the premiership. Ireland kept the Tories in power almost continuously for twenty years after 1886 because of the Liberal split over Home Rule. Ireland brought the greatest political figure of the age, Joseph Chamberlain, into the Tory camp and kept him there, in a subordinate role. Ireland distracted the attention and diverted the passion of Englishmen from their own social problems and gave Conservatives the excuse they needed for not tackling them. Ireland seemed to be the cockpit of the struggle for property, aristocracy, Protestantism, empire and civilization, all causes dear to Balfour's heart. Yet Ireland's troubled state, for those who could read the signs of the times, was symptomatic of a widespread desire for radical change at the turn of the century. In particular, the condition-of-England question remained unanswered. Never had there been such hideous poverty amid such ostentatious plenty. Malnutrition was more rife in the Edwardian era than it had been since the great famines of Tudor times. Something had to be done. Balfour became Prime Minister in 1902 because he was the embodiment of the British ruling class's resolve to do nothing – except resist change. And when he was swept from office in the huge landslide of 1906 he recognized 'a faint echo of the same movement which has produced massacres in St Petersburg, riots in Vienna, and Socialist processions in Berlin'. Fortunately, Balfour remarked, his countrymen only caught continental diseases in a mild form. In England discredited politicians do not merely survive, they mutate into respected elder statesmen. Those who live as long as Balfour become sages.

Balfour once said of a parliamentary speech that it was 'unnecessarily' good, meaning that its object could have been achieved with less eloquence and exertion. Salisbury's political heir never made the mistake of drawing too heavily on his limited reserves of energy, especially in the office of Leader of the House of Commons which he occupied, with only a short break, from 1891 to 1902. Indeed, he went to the opposite extreme. He scarcely bothered to acknowledge, let alone lead, rank-and-file Tories. He never thought about politics in bed. Journalists observed him stretching and yawning on the government front bench and wondered 'if he was born tired, like the man who couldn't eat roast beef so exhausted did it make him to reach for the mustard'. Balfour was sparkling, in a sub-Wildean way, when it came to impromptu remarks: 'In that oration there were some things that were true, and some things that were trite; but what was true was trite and what was not trite was not true.' But he never knew what he thought until he heard what he had said, for he was incapable of making the effort to prepare formal speeches. Instead he would flank himself with a knowledgeable minister who would whisper additions and corrections. 'Exactly,' Balfour would respond, and again more sternly, 'Exactly', conveying 'the impression that there was a limit to toleration in these matters and the colleague could be forgiven once but he really must not go on blundering'. Balfour's unruffled passivity had one merit: it instilled confidence into his party. He might be shaken but not stirred. He remained calm even when defending the indefensible, Kitchener's desecration of the Mahdi's corpse after the Sudan campaign in 1898 — among other things the general had toyed both with the large, shapely skull and with the idea of using it as an ink-stand or a drinking-cup. In Blunt's ironical words, Balfour proved 'conclusively that Kitchener was absolutely justified, indeed bound by every principle of right feeling, to blow up the tomb, dig up the body, chuck it into the Nile and what he called "disperse the remains"'. (Kitchener claimed later that he had sent the head back to the Sudan in a kerosene tin; but, as Winston Churchill observed, 'the tin may have contained anything, perhaps ham sandwiches.') Balfour was unmoved by the appeals of sentimentalists. He was unmoved in the darkest days of the Boer War, though he did admit to being somewhat flustered, during what he maladroitly called 'the unhappy entanglement of Ladysmith', at having to give up his Christmas holiday. As well 'try to hustle a glacier', said Saki, as attempt to move 'the Ineptitude'. Balfour's serenity was so perfect that it might almost have been mistaken for complacency.

Of course, Balfour had a lot to be complacent about.

But did he not reveal that he was rather too much at ease with himself by fiddling with words – 'We will neither sacrifice our Empire to the Boers nor our Constitution to the bores' – while men died? Certainly his bland assertions that there had been no reverses during the South African War, simply 'incidents of a protracted campaign' not requiring 'any apology whatever' from the government, caused great popular dissatisfaction. They revealed his inability to come to terms with anything so coarse-grained as the mass mind and his consequent inadequacy as a democratic leader. This was all the more apparent because of the contrast Balfour afforded with the Colonial Secretary and sometime Birmingham screw manufacturer, 'Joe' Chamberlain. They were the passive and the active moods incarnate. As Balfour said, 'The difference between Joe and me is the difference between youth and age: I am age.' And Chamberlain himself remarked, in the same vein, 'Arthur hates difficulties: I love 'em.' With his magnetic personality and his compelling two-pronged programme of imperialism and social reform, Chamberlain might have had a claim to succeed Salisbury. He was disqualified by his radical, middle-class, trading, Nonconformist antecedents. Lord Salisbury's government was so full of his own relations that it was known as the 'Hotel Cecil' and Balfour naturally took over its management. Chamberlain was suspected of planning to convert the Hotel Cecil into a commercial boarding-house. Balfour seemed a guarantee that aristocratic Toryism, with its paternalist, *laissez-faire* ideals, would not be transformed into bourgeois Conservatism, dedicated to the protection of British business. The change could not long be resisted – Balfour's own successors were the iron-merchant Bonar Law and the ironmaster Stanley Baldwin. But Balfour's stubborn, cunning and ultimately disastrous endeavour to preserve old Toryism, patently ossifying as a political creed, was the central fact of his premiership.

97

Balfour's measures were so high Tory that the Liberal victory became inevitable. His Education Act (1902), though it reformed and improved the entire educational system, reflected Balfour's attachment to the old social hierarchy and his detachment from the masses, about whose capacity for learning he was profoundly sceptical. Moreover, it was interpreted by Nonconformists as a method of providing state aid for the impoverished schools of the Established Church. There was evidence for this view. Balfour himself remarked at the time that if the Bill was not passed the Anglican schools were doomed ('I have not cared to dwell upon it too much in public for obvious reasons') and he admitted later that he had never realized 'the Act would mean more expense and more bureaucracy'. His Licensing Act (1904), though it tidied up the muddled laws on alcohol, appeared to the Liberal reformers to be a 'brewers' Bill'. It compensated the licensees of public-houses closed in the interests of sobriety but it did nothing else to encourage temperance. For the Edwardians drink remained 'the shortest way out of Manchester'. To the horror of pacific, internationally-minded Liberals, Balfour began to prepare for the European war which was so generally anticipated. He became 'Godfather of the Dreadnought' and sponsor of the eighteen-pounder gun. He founded the Committee of Imperial Defence. He ended Britain's diplomatic isolation via the Japanese Naval Alliance and the Entente Cordiale with France. The last, incidentally, was widely attributed to the initiative of Edward VII. Balfour rightly denied the responsibility of the monarch, at whose gross tastes and low brow he could hardly repress a shudder of aversion. Balfour's one 'permanent bias' was, as Beatrice Webb noted, 'in favour of personal refinement of thought and feeling', and the King sensed that the Minister condescended to him. The Minister (though he later expended treasures of ingenuity attempting to deny it) provided the estimate on which the royal biographer based his scandalous judgement that the King 'lacked the intellectual resources of a thinker'. Perhaps Edward had shown pique at Balfour's being the first premier to call on his sovereign in a motor car and a homburg hat. Balfour rose above inconvenient conventions: as a Cabinet Minister he had once startled Gladstone by visiting him on a bicycle.

Balfour also united the Liberals in opposition to 'Chinese Slavery', the maltreatment of indentured labourers brought in to work the South African mines. He thought it inconceivably stupid of Milner, the High Commissioner, to have sanctioned the flogging of coolies. The cry of 'Pigtail' echoed throughout the land: Balfour interpreted it not as an expression of genuine moral outrage but as a 'mere electioneering dodge'. He was similarly impervious to criticism over the Aliens Act (1905), which was designed to restrict the influx of foreigners, mainly Jews fleeing from persecution in Eastern Europe. In truth, Balfour was fundamentally lacking in sympathy for those of other, and, as he reckoned, permanently inferior races. Americans, united by blood, language, literature, religion, history and political ideals, he did not regard as foreigners at all. He also pooh-poohed extravagant fears about the 'Yellow Peril'. The 'Black Peril' was the real threat. Indians, for example, though incapable of self-rule, were being egged on towards it by irresponsible intellectuals. Balfour agreed with his Viceroy, Lord Curzon, that 'As long as we rule India we are the greatest power in the world.' But when, during the 1900 famine, twenty million Indians were threatened with death by starvation Balfour refused British aid because it would lead to 'financial irregularity and extravagance' which was 'the most fruitful parent of social troubles'. Other races were a sort of global extension, more or less degenerate, of the British proletariat, to whose needs and aspirations Balfour was equally insensitive. He was intrigued by the behaviour of bacteria but 'slightly bored' by the subject of public health. He was lukewarm about improving the position of Trade Unions (damaged by the House of Lords' decision in 1901 on the Taff Vale case, which made unions liable to be sued for damage done by their members during strikes) or exerting himself to reduce working-class unemployment. Foreign-inspired socialism, he asserted, must not be allowed to 'terrorize us into any such absolutely fatal admission as that it is the duty of the state to find remunerative work for everyone desiring it'. Winston Churchill was not exceptionally prescient in prophesying a huge triumph for the forces of radicalism in 1906.

What made certainty more certain was the fact that, ever since Joseph Chamberlain's famous speech in May 1903 advocating the introduction of protective duties on foreign goods, the Tory party had been tearing itself to pieces. Tariff reform may seem a dry fiscal issue. It obsessed the Edwardians as theology had obsessed the Victorians. England, it was thought, had become the 'workshop of the world' thanks to free trade, and Chamberlain's challenge to this orthodoxy was 'as direct and provocative as the theses which Luther nailed to the church door at Wittenberg'. Chamberlain was an evangelist with an orchid, a seer with an eye-glass. He preached the new gospel with visionary inspiration and men like Leopold Amery literally danced for joy on hearing it. For tariff reform was not merely a way of halting the relative economic decline of Britain, caused by American and German competition. It was not just a method of strengthening imperial ties through a customs union. It was not simply a mode of raising revenue to pay for vital social measures such as old age pensions. Tariff reform represented the glorious hope of regenerating the Right in British politics, of creating a new, vital, democratic form of Conservatism, with a popular programme, led by a spellbinding statesman – if only Balfour would go. Balfour would not go. Despite his apparent indifference to power Balfour was, as a relation said, 'the most ambitious of men'. Perhaps as much for its trappings as for its own sake, he loved office. Devoid of passionate convictions about the fiscal question, he was haunted by the spectre of Sir Robert Peel who split the Conservative Party in 1846. Balfour thus bent his subtle mind to producing a compromise. He delayed, temporized and finally 'nailed his colours to the fence'. He conjured up the policy of 'retaliation', which satisfied all but 'whole-hogging' free-traders and protectionists and metamorphosed the bulk of his party into 'little-piggers'. Quite what 'retaliation' meant nobody knew. In theory it involved the freedom to impose duties on imports from countries which taxed British exports. But it seemed impossible to do this without putting a tariff on foreign corn, and 'stomach taxes' Balfour explicitly rejected. An opponent defied him to clarify the 'little-pigger' philosophy and he obligingly carved, so to speak, a rasher of gammon. On 'a half sheet of note-paper' he fabricated a summary which left everyone more baffled than ever. The Duke of Devonshire's reaction to Balfour's 'hedge within a hedge' was typical: 'I am completely puzzled and distracted by all the arguments *pro* and *con* Free Trade and Protection; but, whichever of them is right, I cannot think that something which is neither, but a little bit of both, can be right.' To one frustrated supporter Balfour wrote, 'You ask me to endorse your interpretation of my original statements [about tariff reform]. This would probably involve my writing you a letter to ask whether I had rightly interpreted your statement of your interpretation, and I do not know that we should be further advanced.' Balfour's dialectical chicanery was such that he even bamboozled himself. He later asked his niece Blanche, 'Was I a Protectionist or a Free Trader in 1903?' She replied, 'That is what all the country wanted to find out.'

Balfour maintained the unity of his party at the expense of its integrity. The sharp practice by which he managed to slice off the protectionist and the free-trading wings of his Cabinet in 1903 involved misleading both sides about his own proposals and concealing the fact that Chamberlain had resigned, while virtually dismissing the three most determined free-traders, among them the Chancellor of the Exchequer. This manoeuvre revealed the Prime Minister at his most unscrupulous. Balfour was likened to a beech tree, 'very beautiful but nothing could live under its shade'. Winston Churchill thought Balfour 'hard', 'cruel' and 'wicked' and remarked that 'Had his life been cast amid the labyrinthine intrigues of the Italian Renaissance, he would not have required to study the works of Machiavelli.' Yet Churchill was unable to repress his admiration for the way in which Balfour managed to hover for so long between the two stools of tariff reform and *laissez-faire* without substantial support. This feat of casuistical levitation was 'the greatest political achievement he had ever known in his long parliamentary life'. Churchill, who deserted to the Liberals over the issue of free trade, was himself the recipient of an ironical rebuke in 1904, which epitomizes Balfour at his most feline.

A hasty reading, for example, of such a phrase as 'Thank God, we have an Opposition' which occurs, I think, in one of your speeches, is apt to lead to misunderstanding. It was rashly interpreted by some as meaning that the policy of the country would be safer in the hands of the Opposition rather than the Government's, a meaning clearly inconsistent with Party loyalty. Obviously, it is equally capable of a quite innocent construction. It might, for example, be a pious recognition of the fact that our heaviest trials are sometimes for our good. Or, again, it might mean that a world in which everybody was agreed would be an exceedingly tedious one;

or, that an effective Opposition made the Party loyalty burn more brightly.

How Balfour relished those exegetical naunces. How he savoured those semantic quibbles. The political struggle became a verbal scrabble, an elaborate game of words in which Balfour permitted himself the occasional luxury of cheating. Chamberlain, after all, not only failed to observe, he failed even to understand, 'the rules of the game'. This justification reconciled few to Balfour's mode of play. The Liberal Augustine Birrell wrote, 'No imagination can be too fertile, no cynicism too extreme, no language too biting, to picture and describe the possible vagaries, gyrations, and somersaults of the ambitious politician in the grip of circumstances.' Balfour's Cecil cousins did not quite approve of him anyway. There was his 'unfortunate love of music'. There was his addiction to speeding along in motors, which exposed him for the 'Middle-Class Monster' he was on his father's side. There was his medicinal use of cocaine, which had evidently rotted his moral fibre. But the Cecils regarded his dissimulation over the fiscal issue as an unpardonable tarnishing of Lord Salisbury's true-blue Toryism. Arthur had 'made mental dishonesty respectable'. Moreover he had done it with such inhuman detachment. The only reverse that evoked a gleam of passion in him was the Duke of Devonshire's resignation in 1903; the Prime Minister was so cross that in order to write the Duke a stiff letter he postponed his bath. Balfour also displayed a flash of anger at the débâcle of 1906. Perhaps, like Harold Wilson after him, he had sat on the fence for so long that the iron had entered into his soul. But no, his placid aplomb was at once restored. He led his party into the wilderness for twenty years and to celebrate his defeat he went out and bought a gramophone.

VI

The keynote of Balfour's life as Leader of His Majesty's Loyal Opposition between 1906 and 1911 was not harmony but discord. This stemmed largely from Balfour's inability to reconcile himself to his own and his party's embarrassing new situation, to the fact that the 'natural rulers' of the country were no longer in power. Of course, defeat involved the making of certain concessions. Balfour found himself compelled to 'go about the country explaining that I am "honest and industrious", like a second footman out of place' and enduring those 'attendant horrors' of public meetings, the 'subsidiary luncheons and dinners, which are fatal to one's temper at the moment, and to one's digestion afterwards'. He was also obliged to compromise with Chamberlain over tariff reform, though the agreed formula remained characteristically ambiguous. But this apart, why should not everyone carry on exactly as before? Balfour returned to the Commons and in his wonted manner delivered himself of some refined and abstruse enquiries about the Liberals' fiscal policy. He was surprised that his appearance was 'the signal for ill-mannered interruptions'. He was more than surprised to receive a devastating rebuke from the new Prime Minister, the much-despised Sir Henry Campbell-Bannerman.

The right hon. gentleman is like the Bourbons. He has learned nothing. He comes back . . . with the same airy graces, the same subtle dialectics, the same light and frivolous way of dealing with great questions. He little knows the temper of the new House of Commons if he thinks these methods will prevail here. The right hon. gentleman has asked certain questions which he seemed to think were posers . . . I have no direct answer to give to them. They are utterly futile, nonsensical and misleading . . . I say, enough of this foolery!

Even Balfour's relations acknowledged this as a magnificent parliamentary triumph for 'C-B'. It was humiliation enough for Balfour to be gored by a man who resembled nothing so much as an enraged sheep, a creature whom he had been accustomed to bait and to guy. But it was a disaster that his habitual forensic technique – the spinning of diaphanous webs in which his adversaries became fatally enmeshed – should be swept aside with such brutal contempt. The journalist H. J. Massingham wrote that the new Members of Parliament thought Balfour's speech 'drivel ... Yet I have heard him make just such a speech – as empty and wandering – and the House has resounded with applause at his cleverness.' Now most MPs, including many of Balfour's own followers, endorsed ' "C-B's" rough but perfectly suitable description of his performance as "foolery"'. Evidently the Liberals were not inclined to favour Balfour's ideal – concord enlivened by mellifluous displays of intellectual counterpoint. They were determined not merely to enjoy power but to exercise it – for the purpose of change.

Or some of them were. Even the execrable Campbell-Bannerman, whose name Lord Salisbury had never been able to remember, was surely enough of a gentleman to desire the preservation of the traditional fabric of society. He framed his bills in such a radical form, Balfour considered, because he needed to satisfy the left wing of his party and because he would thus ensure that they were rejected. As for civilized, intelligent Liberals like Asquith (who succeeded C-B as premier in 1908), Balfour could not believe that they really wanted such subversive measures to pass into law. Was it not clear that 'Liberal policy runs counter to the best thought of the day'? To Liberals intent on implementing old age pensions, land taxes, labour exchanges and national insurance schemes, it was not clear. Balfour had no positive policy of his own (to the discontent of his party he refused to formulate one on the grounds that an opposition must simply oppose) and he could place no faith in the constructive programmes of others. He was unable to attribute to his opponents an idealism which he did not himself share. Indeed, he imagined that the more sophisticated Liberals were, like himself, political Pococurantes. The rest were doubtless dangerous fanatics who had no right to be in the government at all. Luckily the constitution was so organized that the Conservative House of Lords could veto 'revolutionary' legislation. Balfour did not believe that the Lords' powers were best maintained by a refusal to employ them. The Lords existed to protect aristocratic substance from democratic accidents. C-B's suspicion that neither Balfour nor his party had ever 'fully accepted representative institutions' was well founded. With what to a later generation seems breath-taking effrontery, Balfour frankly maintained that the Conservatives 'should still control, whether in power or whether in opposition, the destinies of this great Empire'. It was as much a personal as a party manifesto.

'Mr Balfour's poodle' – this was Lloyd George's famous description of the House of Lords as, obedient to its master's voice, the huge Tory majority therein mangled bill after Liberal bill. The government hounded Balfour unmercifully in the Commons, accusing him of constitutional 'treachery'. He maintained, with playful dramatic licence, that the upper chamber had become a 'theatre of compromise'; British laws should not be 'the hasty and ill-considered offspring of one passionate election' – especially an election won by incontinent Liberals. But whatever the merit of government measures Balfour was inclined to encourage their mutilation. Only thus could he restore Conservative fighting spirit and re-establish his hold over a united party. Admittedly Joseph Chamberlain had suffered a stroke in 1906 and Balfour, having privately obtained a medical opinion of his state, based on photographs, was confident that he would not recover. But the Tory tariff reformers were still on the rampage. Being their leader Balfour was bound to follow them. His policy was to encourage them at all costs to harry the Liberals. So Balfour occasioned the rejection of Lloyd George's Budget in 1909, the two 'Peers v. People' elections of 1910 and the passing of the Parliament Act, which left the Lords shorn of most of their powers, in 1911. It was Balfour's policy, too, which caused unprecedented personal bitterness and political savagery at Westminster. The Duke of Beaufort was so incensed by his opponents that he wanted 'to see Winston Churchill and Lloyd George in the middle of twenty couple of dog-hounds'. Another backwoods nobleman was sufficiently moved to bark during the Budget speeches though, as Lord Lovat explained to Ettie Desborough, he may just have been 'calling to his mate in the gallery'.

At the time the King's private secretary, Lord Knollys, said 'very gravely and emphatically that he thought the Lords mad' to throw out the 'People's Budget'. And recently the historian, Lord Blake, asserted that the Lords were 'insane' to challenge the Commons' traditional power of the purse. Balfour himself gave substance to this verdict by the ease with which he elaborated a foolproof defence of the hereditary peerage on the very grounds of its 'naked absurdity'. But do these years really present one with the spectacle of a demented oligarchy engaged in an act of suicide? Did the gods destroy those whom they had first made mad? To ascribe lunacy to the Lords is to acquit them of responsibility for their actions. They were not mentally deranged but culpably deluded. They perished not for lack of reason but for lack of vision. They were blinded by obscurantist convictions, by caste partisanship and by feudal grandeur. Segregated by the prevailing social *apartheid*, they had no perception of what the great body of their counrtymen thought – Lord Rosebery defended the Dukes as 'a poor but honest class'. The peers mistook social deference for political subservience. They presumed too much on what one contemporary called the Edwardians' 'quasi-religious reverence for rank and titles'. Like Balfour himself, they could see nothing in the Budget except the imposition of a tax on land. Provoked by that 'cad in his soul', Lloyd George, who compared the aristocracy to cheese – 'the older it is the higher it becomes' – they concluded that his measure was a prelude to revolution. The Budget was, Balfour said, 'demagogism in its worst aspect'; it aimed to please 'the "mass" of voters', '"the poor"' at the expense of the rich. That, indeed, was a giddy inversion. The Tories resisted it with wild ululation. Some even attacked Balfour for continuing to fraternize with the enemy on convivial occasions. He retorted that had he known he was to be assailed for attending 'a fancy-dress ball in plain clothes and leaving at 10.30 pm, he would have gone as a harlequin and stayed till four o'clock in the morning'.

This combination of flippancy and hauteur did much to undermine Balfour's leadership of the Conservatives. The very audacity of his arguments during the Budget debates seemed to bespeak an insolent contempt for the intellect of his audience. Churchill reported a 'really delicious' instance of Balfour's attempting to reconcile a previous assertion that the Commons 'settles *uncontrolled* our financial system' with his present view that the Lords had every right to reject the Budget.

If he had said 'the plain is perfectly flat', it would have been understood all the time that the statement was without prejudice to the fact that the world was round. He would never have expected to be reproached for not having mentioned specifically *the normal curvature of the earth's surface*. So when he said the Lords could not touch Money Bills, he never meant that they could not

reject all the Money Bills of the year singly or at a stroke!
That of course went without saying.

Both the Tories and the nation resented such blatant
sophistries. But what finally precipitated Balfour's downfall was not defeat at the hands of 'an unscrupulous and
revolutionary' party in the two elections of 1910. Nor was
it the fact that he had been outmanoeuvred by Asquith,
who secured a royal promise to create enough peers to
ensure the passage of the Parliament Act, 'a gross misuse
of the prerogative' in Balfour's private view. It was not
even the crucial implication of the Lords' loss of power
– the imminent passing of an Irish Home Rule Bill by a
Liberal government now dependent for its majority on
Nationalist MPs. Nor did the Conservative leader de-
part in response to the exellent slogan – BMG, Balfour
Must Go – coined by Leo Maxse, editor of the *National
Review* and trenchant critic of 'mental gymnastics' at
Westminster. No, appropriately enough what discredited
Balfour, and in the end led to his resignation, was a yet
more flagrant display of indecisiveness, equivocation and
detachment.

He vacillated between the 'Hedgers', the peers who
would not oppose their own emasculation for fear of a
worse fate – loss of face, loss of caste, the humiliating
dilution of their ranks – and the 'Ditchers', those who
fought the Parliament Bill to the last ditch and damned the
consequences. Balfour, it was said, blew hot, blew cold
and then ceased to blow at all. For a time he appeared to
espouse the Ditchers' cause. Then he advocated surrender,
dismissing the die-hard stance as 'essentially theatrical',
for 'Music Hall consumption only'. (Lord Northcliffe was
so angered by this shift that he blustered on the telephone
about taking his newspapers into the Radical camp; 'a
worse blackmailing threat' Balfour's secretary had never
heard.) At last, before the Hedgers' victory, Balfour

deserted the field altogether. He went off to take 'the cure' at Bad Gastein. Politics were 'unusually odious'. His own side had not played the game, apart, that is, from Austen Chamberlain who remained loyal to his captain while disagreeing with him — unlike his father, Austen 'always played the game and always lost it'. Balfour brooded over his wrongs, 'a thing which had not happened to me since I was unjustly "complained of" at Eton more than forty years ago'. The party whose unity he had 'strained every nerve' to maintain throughout King Edward's reign was now split over a mere issue of tactics. Yet the schism was deep. Emotions ran high. The peers who had voted for the government were known as 'the Judas group' and ostracized. Balfour's attempts to reconcile conflicting opinions were reviled as hypocrisy. The Ditchers even suspected him 'of having been all through in secret collusion with Asquith'. There was 'universal disquiet' in the party, said a senior Tory, Walter Long, in a letter which Balfour described as 'a bold and brutal invitation for me to retire'. This the Conservative leader did, in November 1911. 'Confident that he would never be equal to taking office again', Balfour was filled with the 'rapture of repose'. On the evening of his resignation he murmured, 'I must ask Leo Maxse to dinner tonight, for we are probably the two happiest men in London.'

VII

Having died as a politician Balfour rose again as a statesman — so, at least, runs the myth about the final part of his career. Certainly the Conservatives were disillusioned with him. He had preserved them neither as the country's natural rulers nor as an élite made in his own image. Amid the sputter of strikers and Suffragettes which preceded the thunder of the guns he seemed only to want a quiet life. Above all, he was too clever by half for 'the stupid party'. He was, as Lloyd George said, 'the only "mind" they have got'. But the Tories sensed that this mind was essentially infertile, a tool of analysis not a matrix of ideas. They recognized, however dimly, that cunning sophisms were no substitute for creative policies. They even rejected Balfour's designated successor, Austen Chamberlain, in favour of the caustic Bonar Law, 'a man of boundless ambition untempered by any nice feeling' in the view of Balfour's secretary. Balfour himself acknowledged that 'it was an advantage to have a leader who was not intellectually much superior to the rest of the party he led.' Lloyd George commented, 'The fools have stumbled on their best man by accident.'

Yet, having been dispensed with by his party, Balfour apparently became indispensable to the nation. Several times he even came close to being resurrected as Prime Minister – in 1913, for example, he proposed himself for that office in an abortive letter of 'advice' to the king. Though he opposed the Liberals vehemently over their policy of granting Home Rule to Ireland – compromise with the Nationalists was 'Eating Dirt' – and virtually incited rebellion in Ulster, Balfour was almost an unofficial member of Asquith's government. The advocate of treason in the name of constitutionalism sat on the important Committee of Imperial Defence. It seemed impossible to exclude him. He was 'a great luxury', said Winston Churchill. Margot Asquith dilated on the 'vast gap that separates Arthur from all his colleagues in everything – prestige, intellect, charm, brilliance'. Moreover there were numberless problems of state that seemed susceptible to purely verbal solutions. That ubiquitous bureaucrat, Maurice Hankey, recalled one defence committee meeting that had reached deadlock.

Suddenly the door opened, and Balfour's tall, loose-limbed figure sauntered into the room and sat down by the Prime Minister. Almost immediately he grasped the points at issue, and there and then, with inimitable skill, he drafted paragraphs which brought the whole sub-committee together. As he strolled back with me after the meeting he made this remark: 'I spent the first part of the afternoon in abusing the Government in the City, and the second part in solving their difficulties at the House of Commons!'

To play on both sides from the middle added a piquant new twist to the political game. Moreover it absolved one of the irksome necessity of playing to win.

The profession and practice of such a philosophy did not disqualify Balfour from membership of the political team selected to beat the Germans. Strolling up Cockspur Street on 29 July 1914 Balfour met Admiral 'Jackie' Fisher, volatile architect of the new navy, who said that Churchill had ordered the fleet up the Channel, so informing Balfour, before the Cabinet itself, that war was inevitable. Within nine months of its outbreak, when Asquith formed his coalition government, Balfour succeeded Churchill as First Lord of the Admiralty. Lloyd George thought that this vital post should be occupied by a younger man but Asquith said Balfour was 'tougher than you think'. The truth was that 'Wait and See' (as Fisher called Asquith) found 'Philosophic Doubter' (as Fisher called Balfour) such a delightfully congenial colleague. Unfortunately, what with his cryptic phrases and his negative attitudes, Balfour proved to be a naval cipher. As Lloyd George wrote, he 'lacked the physical energy, the fertility of resource' to stimulate and organize the senior service during the U-Boat crisis. After hearing the lists of ships sunk, lists made much longer by his failure to implement a convoy system, Balfour could only cry despairingly, 'It is very tiresome. These Germans are intolerable.' Or, holding up his hands, he would give vent to futile ejaculations:

Lord Balfour with Chaim Weizmann at the founding
of the Einstein Institute, Jerusalem, 1925

Lord Balfour with Lloyd George at a garden party, 1922

Shooting party at Blenheim, 1896. Balfour, standing just to the left of the Prince of Wales, preferred bicycling.

(Reproduced by gracious permission of Her Majesty the Queen)

'The Germans must be mad.' His main achievement at the Admiralty was to issue a communiqué immediately after Jutland which conveyed the impression that Britain had suffered a disastrous defeat. It seriously damaged national morale. The fumbling ineptitude of Balfour's régime was exposed by the fact that Churchill himself was requested by the First Lord to draft a more balanced and more reassuring report of the battle. Balfour's frigid unimaginativeness was manifested in his response to the Cabinet's request for an account of the engagement which might have lost Britain the war in an afternoon: 'There is nothing to say to you – only a few anecdotes, and I don't suppose you would care to hear them.' Balfour's lackadaisical ignorance was revealed by the fact that only a month before the destruction of Asquith's government, in December 1916, it came as news to him (provided by C. P. Scott) that Chile was Britain's sole supplier of nitrate, an essential ingredient of high explosives. Fisher understandably inveighed against the 'flabby, effete, apathetic set of philosophic doubters' who were allowing grass to grow in the corridors of the Admiralty. Being their leader and a piano player and a 'Soul', Balfour was chiefly responsible. Fisher exclaimed, 'Souls have no testicles!'

Lord Beaverbrook agreed, though he expressed it somewhat differently: 'Balfour was a hermaphrodite. No one ever saw him naked.' Whatever the truth of all this, it is clear that Balfour's ineffectual spell as First Lord had not stripped him of his political prestige. And, neuter or not, Balfour retained his other feline endowments, especially guile. Though ill at the time, he played a vital part in the shifty manoeuvres by which Lloyd George replaced Asquith as premier. According to Lord Beaverbrook, Balfour was visited in his sick-room by Bonar Law who offered him the Foreign Office if he would serve under Lloyd George. The long, dressing-gowned figure 'jumped up instantly and replied: "Well, you hold a pistol at my head – I must accept."' There was no threat, only the fearful prospect of a wilderness without the red boxes, the private secretaries, the official cars, the pomp and circumstance of power which seemed to keep Balfour younger than his sixty-eight years. Of course, Lloyd George was dangerously lacking in principle – it was both his strength and his weakness, Balfour thought – but the lure of high office overcame any lingering fastidiousness. Asquith never forgave him. He had expected betrayal from a sansculotte Welshman, but for the immaculate Arthur to invest Lloyd George's non-party administration with the pure ethos of Tory respectability – this was treachery indeed. Employing a memorable simile, Winston Churchill wrote that Balfour 'passed from one Cabinet to the other, from the Prime Minister who was his champion to the Prime Minister who had been his most severe critic, like a powerful cat walking delicately and unsoiled across a rather muddy street'.

If Churchill had been seeking a more particular resemblance he might have compared the new Foreign Secretary to the Cheshire Cat. For nothing distinguished Balfour more in his new position than insubstantial charm and desultory vacillation. In print, Lloyd George, vindicating his own judgement, established the orthodox view that Balfour reached his political apotheosis at the Foreign Office. In confidence, when asked what place Balfour would occupy in history, the Prime Minister replied, 'He will be just like the scent on a pocket handkerchief.' Similarly, 'Tiger' Clemenceau hailed Balfour in public as 'the Richelieu of the Congress' at Versailles. Privately, baffled by Balfour's 'now-you-see-it-now-you-don't' mode of discussion and irritated by his purring inconclusiveness, Clemenceau called him 'cette vieille fille'. Churchill, too, expressed heretical reservations about Balfour's achievement: 'if you wanted nothing done, A.J.B. was undoubtedly the best man for the task. There was no one to equal him.' It was fair comment. At Cabinet meetings, where his growing deafness and aptness to doze distanced him from the proceedings, Balfour was more irresolute than ever. He would provide a luminous exposition of both sides of any case, pause, throw up his head, look vaguely out of the window and say hesitantly, 'But if you ask me what course I think we ought to take I must say I feel perplexed.' Committee meetings he treated as academic seminars. He was more interested in refuting Marxism than in formulating a policy towards Bolshevism. Once he was sent an urgent minute by his staff outlining two possible lines of action and asking, 'Which of these two courses do you wish us to adopt?' 'Yes,' replied Balfour. Later he explained, 'When I wrote Yes I only meant that I agreed that there were two courses open.' None of this mattered. Lloyd George required Balfour's ethereal presence at the Foreign Office not for executive vim but for decorative sheen, for the aura of dignity and prestige he lent to the Ministry. Anyway, if war is the continuation of diplomacy by other means, it follows that during wars diplomats are superfluous. Balfour was not a member of the War Cabinet and any important decisions would be taken by the Prime Minister himself. Meanwhile it might be appropriate if his most distinguished lieutenant absented himself entirely – in order to give a personal welcome to Britain's puissant new ally, the United States.

On both sides of the Atlantic voices were raised to condemn it as grotesquely inappropriate. Admiral Fisher expostulated, 'No worse choice than Balfour could have been made to send to America! He is an *"anti-democrat"* to his finger tips.' American newspapers proscribed him as 'an interesting survival', a top-hatted, frock-coated personification of British decadence. Characteristically unperturbed by the abuse, Balfour embraced his mission with uncharacteristic verve. Having inadvertently dissipated his incognito by supplying a Dumfries lift-boy with his autograph, and having rejected the offer of a rubber life-preserving suit – he preferred to drown in his night-shirt – Balfour embarked on the dangerous sea voyage with none of his 'customary groans'. Surprisingly the visit was a success. Balfour admired the American achievement. He had long cherished a fad for bimetallism. He had helped to keep Britain a benevolent neutral in the United States' war with Spain. He had corresponded with President Roosevelt over the desirability of preserving, by means of an Anglo-Saxon confederation, 'the civilization of the white races who have spread their influence over the entire world'. Possibly the war-time alliance might presage the formation of the vast, 'unassailable' racial bloc about which Balfour had dreamt. Without it, he feared, the British Empire 'will probably drop to pieces in the course of the next century'. In public, of course, he confidently asserted, 'British supremacy exists, British supremacy is going to be maintained.' But he recognized that the globe would 'more and more turn on the great Republic as on a pivot'. Balfour accomplished nothing concrete in the United States – American aid remained unhelpfully meagre – but he did strengthen the nebulous transatlantic links. He addressed Congress – the first Briton ever to do so, the first foreigner to do so since Parnell – and his charm apparently transcended the inevitable platitudes. He seemed to have the courage of his clichés – 'same root . . . unique episode . . . common understanding . . . two great branches of the English-speaking race'. He also appealed to the academic snob in President Wilson, seducing him by the frankness with which he admitted the existence of Britain's secret treaties. (Balfour tactfully attributed the President's denial of this knowledge at Versailles to 'a lapse of memory'.) The Foreign Secretary was given an enthusiastic reception at Carnegie Hall and Americans spoke of him in approving terms as a 'real aristocrat'. Of course, he could not please everybody. When touring one of New York's latest skyscrapers he was assured by his hosts that the building was completely fire-proof. Balfour murmured, 'What a pity!'

At Versailles Balfour merged into the long shadow cast by 'the Little Man', as he called Lloyd George. In order to win the peace the Prime Minister evidently did not relish the assistance of a political Hamlet, sure only of the disadvantages of every course of action. On important issues Lloyd George sometimes neglected even to consult his Foreign Secretary – the dynamo had no need of its pylon. This was scarcely surprising if the hostile sketch by Lord Curzon, who succeeded Balfour at the Foreign Office in October 1919 and damned him as a lost 'Soul' and a failed god, is to be believed. Curzon considered Balfour a disaster as Foreign Secretary because of his 'sheer intellectual indolence' and his 'instinctive love of compromise'.

His charm of manner, his extraordinary intellectual distinction, his seeming indifference to petty matters, his power of dialectic, his long and honourable career of public service, blinded all but those who knew from the inside to the lamentable ignorance, indifference and laxity of his régime. He never studied his papers; he never knew the facts; at the Cabinet he had seldom read the morning's Foreign Office telegrams; he never got up a case; he never looked ahead. He trusted to his unique power of improvisation . . . [and] the mental agility which would enable him at the last moment to extricate himself from any complication, however embarrassing.

As an empty diplomatic form, Balfour was reduced to making hollow declarations: the Kaiser was 'the ring-leader in the greatest crime against the human race'; Germany must make reasonable reparations but be rendered 'impotent to renew the war'; Germany's colonies must be confiscated or she would 'deliberately set to work and create a great black army in Central Africa'.

Balfour had to content himself with a rarefied ceremonial role, one he played to perfection. As a later French account had it, 'He assumed the coquetry of old age with so much natural grace that it became him. When one saw him attending a levée of his Sovereign, dressed in his Court uniform and silk knee-breeches and wearing the Order of the Garter, one bowed low before this noble survival of a brilliant past.' Balfour danced Scottish reels. He played lawn tennis — when off form he was suffused by a faint melancholy, but it soon evaporated. He bubbled with ephemeral post-war epigrams — 'everything is now possible, even orthodoxy.' He retailed anecdotes — a favourite concerned Hegel, who, when requested to elucidate a particularly opaque philosophical statement, replied: 'When I wrote that only two people knew what I meant, God Almighty and myself, and now only God Almighty knows.' He indulged in dainty, catty, evanescent gossip. One of Colonel House's staff was acid about Balfour's 'coterie of female cousins, aunts, and nieces' to whom 'he monologues but really says nothing'. Balfour bore his eclipse at Versailles with lunar coolness, wanly conniving at a peace of revenge rather than reconciliation. General Smuts commented bitterly, 'Balfour was a tragedy, a mere dilettante, without force or guidance, when a strong British Foreign Minister might have saved the whole situation.' High on a cloud of unknowing, deep in a spiritual void, Balfour was a disembodied voice crying that for two generations at least there would be no more war.

VIII

But what of the most momentous event in the Foreign Secretary's career? What of the publication of the document with which his name is for ever associated, the Balfour Declaration? That this British aristocrat, with his attenuated human sympathies and his anti-Semitic leanings, should have transformed the Zionist vision into a reality is the central paradox of his life. Of course, in public Balfour condemned anti-Semitism, especially when passing the Aliens Act in 1905. Privately he accepted many of the 'anti-semitic postulates' of Cosima Wagner – at Bayreuth he had been 'a great success' with the composer's widow, whose hatred of the Jews was positively Hitlerian. An unsatisfactory dinner at the Sassoons, where 'the Hebrews were in an actual majority', made Balfour understand the anti-immigrant point of view. His was a conventional prejudice. His friends were accustomed to rail at 'piebald hybrids' and 'rootless cosmopolitans', and at least one 'Soul' endorsed Hilaire Belloc's crude anathemas against the 'vile international slime which has made England its working centre'. But in general the English élite considered aliens preposterous rather than loathsome: the diplomat Sir Mark Sykes took literally the statement of a Japanese officer, 'Our population subsists chiefly on lice', until he was asked, 'What will be the lesult of the Lussian Levolution?' Balfour's race discrimination was essentially a form of class distinction. Like most of his caste, Balfour regarded Jews as exotic proletarians, more or less contemptible figures of fun. He would have appreciated the 'humour' in the King's College Magazine's account of Cambridge May Week in 1913.

Then there was a family of Yids. The Yids came early, because the expense of two extra days at the beginning is really not worth considering, and it is so important for Rachel to see all she can of English social life just at her age. And they were trying so hard to look like anybody else; but though Papa was smoking a cigarette, you knew that he might have been smoking a cigar, and though his coat collar was quite plain you knew that it might have been fur; and as for poor Rachel's nose, it might just as well have been ringed straight away.

This ugly vignette might stand as an epitome of the sinister realities which lurked behind the smiling face of the Edwardian idyll.

Balfour was thus, like many of his contemporaries – Joseph Chamberlain, John Buchan, Mark Sykes, Lord Milner – an anti-Semitic Zionist. He expressed admiration for the cultural, intellectual and religious genius of the Jewish race. He considered that Christian civilization owed the Jews a debt it could not repay. Admittedly, until he met Chaim Weizmann in 1905, he had 'only the most naive and rudimentary notion' of Zionism. But he quickly apprehended that the tragedy of the Jewish diaspora lay less in the resulting persecution and poverty than in 'the malaise of frustrated capacities'. Brought up on the Bible, he immediately recognized the spiritual aspect of Zionism. He appreciated the magic and romantic appeal which Palestine possessed for the Jews – previously he had favoured the scheme to give them a homeland in East Africa. Balfour apparently told Weizmann in 1914 that he was 'deeply moved and interested' by Zionism: 'It is not a dream. It is a great cause and I understand it.' But did Balfour's habitual detachment really desert him over this issue? Was Lord Vansittart right when he claimed that all Balfour ever cared about was Zionism? If so, there were times when he had a perverse way of showing it. At the Admiralty Balfour professed ignorance of the Russian pogroms and at the Foreign Office he refused to intervene on behalf of the Tzar's Jewish subjects. Russia was an ally. What is more, 'the persecutors have a case of their own', one which Balfour was pleased to elaborate on their behalf.

Wherever one went in Eastern Europe one found that by some way or other the Jew got on, and when to this

was added the fact that he belonged to a distinct race
and that he professed a religion which to the people
about him was an object of inherited hatred, and that,
moreover, he was . . . numbered in millions, one could
perhaps understand the desire to keep him down.

The truth was that Balfour was a Zionist because of his
anti-Semitism, not despite it.
Many English Jews perceived the snarl behind the
smile, the fangs behind the grin. Edwin Montagu even
wrote a memorandum entitled 'The Anti-Semitism of the
Present Government.' When Balfour said that Zionism
was 'the Jewish form of patriotism' he seemed to imply
that Jews were unpatriotic Britons. When Balfour wrote
that Zionism was 'a serious endeavour to mitigate the age-
long miseries created for Western civilization by the
presence in its midst of a Body which it too long regarded
as alien and even hostile, but which it was equally unable
to expel or absorb', he appeared to suggest that Jews might
conveniently be repatriated to Palestine. Of course,
Balfour's attitudes towards the Jews, like his attitudes
towards everything else, were complex, tortuous, sibylline,
hedged about with idealistic periphrases, obfuscated by
ambivalent qualifications. But his most profound conviction was that these outlandish figures could never, and
should never, be assimilated into Gentile society. After all
Lenin was a Jew (so, at least, thought Balfour, who would
not have been flattered to learn that his 'brain box' was,
in H. G. Wells's view, 'the very pair of Lenin's') as were
the other leaders of subversive movements throughout
Europe. Zionism would be a stabilizing, conservative
force, a nationalistic counter to 'crazy' international
revolutionaries. It was scarcely an accident that the public
announcement of the Balfour Declaration was made on
the same day, 9 November 1917, as that of the Bolshevik
coup d'état in Petrograd.

Of course, the Balfour Declaration was not the fruit of one man's anti-Semitism; it was a Cabinet document, the product of many motives and many minds. In particular its object was to secure the support of world Jewry, hostile to the Allies as a result of the pogroms, at a time when Germany was apparently winning the war. Moreover a Zionist affirmation might plausibly disguise British imperialism as Jewish self-determination, thus making it acceptable to President Wilson. A British Palestine would prevent France, which was to 'protect' Syria after the war, from threatening the jugular vein of the Empire, Suez. Each of these considerations left its imprint on the Declaration, as did the fact that Arab nationalism was just then being forged into a weapon against the Turks. So many mutually exclusive aims engendered, as the Cabinet Secretary Leopold Amery said, hectic weeks of 'arguments, quarrels, denials, confirmations, secret chats with various interested parties'. Amery (of whom Balfour took 'a very low view', asserting, quite erroneously, that he was 'the son of a Salonika Jew' named Hinri) later claimed that he himself had hatched the final draft of the Declaration moments before the fateful Cabinet meeting which was due to approve it.

Forty-five minutes left. It was truly dramatic. The room was full of tension. You could feel it in the air. You could cut it with a knife. Proposals and counter-proposals chased each other in a bewildering circle. Go-betweens kept on telephoning . . . My desk was full of pieces of paper – discarded formulae. I kept on composing texts and tearing them up. I must have written five, or possibly six. None of them was any good for our purpose . . . No inspiration . . . sheer agony . . . I had to hurry. There were only 12 minutes left . . . Ten minutes . . . Members of the Cabinet began to drift into my room, to see whether I had the text ready . . . I made a last desperate effort on the back of an old memo. I suddenly had a brainwave. Lloyd George came up, glanced at it and exclaimed: 'Yes, that's it'. Balfour had a look and nodded. Milner and Smuts read the brand new text together and dissolved in smiles.

Amery's memory was fallible about the details – he was midwife rather than mother – but his account conveys the breathless excitement which surrounded that portentous birth. When the ministers had concluded, Mark Sykes rushed from the Cabinet room exclaiming triumphantly, 'Dr Weizmann, it's a boy!'

It was a hermaphrodite. Incongruous elements were so combined in the Balfour Declaration as to leave even its authors and begetters mystified.

His Majesty's Government view with favour the establishment in Palestine of a national home for the Jewish people, and will use their best endeavours to facilitate the achievement of this object, it being clearly understood that nothing shall be done which may prejudice the civil and religious rights of existing non-Jewish communities in Palestine, or the rights and political status enjoyed by Jews in any other country.

Did 'national home' mean 'state'? Most Zionists thought not, or at least, not yet. Balfour talked vaguely of 'a focus for national life' which would develop 'in accordance with the ordinary laws of political evolution'. How would the British 'facilitate' matters and how much of Palestine was involved? Nobody knew, least of all Balfour, who piously hoped that the Jews would 'work out their own salvation'. Above all, how was substantial Jewish immigration compatible with the fulfilment of Arab aspirations in Palestine? Balfour asserted that Zionism was 'rooted in age-long traditions, in present need, in future hopes, of far profounder import than the desires and prejudices of the

700,000 Arabs who now inhabit that ancient land'. In short, the Jews might be an unpleasant race, the Arabs were a barbarous one. Anyway, perhaps the problem would never arise. Prince Feisal was in 'deepest sympathy' with the Zionist cause. Balfour predicted that the Arabs, who owed thanks to the British for emancipating them from a brutal oppressor, would not begrudge the Jews 'a small notch, for it is not more geographically, whatever it may be historically', from their territory. Seldom has a prophecy proved so tragically misconceived.

Like the smile on the face of the sphinx, the Balfour Declaration eluded literal interpretation. Like Balfour himself, it was replete with Delphic ambiguities. Few, at the time, were concerned to tease a precise meaning from those oracular phrases. Critics and doubters remained, but all over the world Jews rejoiced at the tidings. In allied, neutral and hostile countries they drank jubilant toasts to the man whose 'declaration read like the first sign of the coming Messiah'. It was, at any rate, clear that the Chosen People were being summoned to a new Exodus, were once more being led towards the Promised Land – the first colony established there was called Balfouria. True, Balfour seemed an unlikely successor to Moses. Was he perhaps an airy-fairy Aaron, a Janus-like Joshua? Jehovah moved in a mysterious way. Certainly the Declaration was 'a trumpet call from Sinai' the echoes of which reached to the uttermost parts of the earth. But amid the euphoria it was forgotten that Balfour's trumpet had never been known to give a certain sound.

IX

No time of life so became Balfour as the white winter of his age. Cool detachment was the fitting mood; desolate beauty was the appropriate style. Balfour seemed to have been born in order to grow old gracefully. And if his hoary self-possession seemed akin to self-absorption, and if his bleached austerity appeared indistinguishable from self-indulgence . . . all was surely forgivable in such an exquisite Nestor. In the public sphere, each year that passed saw Balfour adorned with new honours, the Order of Merit, the Garter, an earldom. As Lord President of the Council he remained in office almost continuously (1919-22 and 1925-29), though without the restless inconveniences of being in power – addressing his peers, he remarked, was 'like talking to a lot of tombstones'. In the private sphere friends and relations continued to beam at him in 'passionate, reverent adoration'. At the great house of Whittingehame they 'revolved like the solar system around the sun, worshipping him with an unveiled idolatry of which he seemed sublimely unconscious'. There were a few iconoclasts. Beatrice Webb found Whittingehame, with its large, formal rooms and its heavy, elaborate luxury, a singularly charmless mansion. As for its owner, she concluded: 'philander, refined and consummate, is Prince Arthur, accustomed always to make others feel what he fails to feel himself.' H. G. Wells, his earlier devotion soured, considered that Balfour had finally become 'a prey to the weak gratifications of vanity and the gentle impulse to pose'. He had not given society an adequate return in mental toil and directive resolution for the wealth and prestige he had so long enjoyed. As his vitality faded Balfour seemed to atrophy into an alabaster attitude. 'He was merely a very eminent person, at last indeed the most eminent person in Britain.'

Balfour's anaemic passions were not quite spent. True, he submitted calmly in 1922 to the Cabinet decision which upset his life-long policy, an 'extremist' one as he acknowledged, towards Ireland. Balfour 'squirmed' at what he regarded as a capitulation to crime but contented himself that both Ulster and Lloyd George's government were preserved intact. However, when disillusioned Tories determined to destroy the latter, Balfour defended both the Coalition and his position in it with rare feeling. At Downing Street he actually pounded the table and vociferated,

> I say, fight them, fight them, fight them. This thing is wrong. Is the lead of Law and Curzon to count for everything and the advice of the rest of us as nothing? This is a revolt and it should be crushed.

The performance apparently drained him, for when he tried to repeat it at the Carlton Club he made one of the feeblest speeches of his career. The Tories disregarded his advice and the government collapsed. Balfour was once more thrown on his own resources and for the first time in his nonchalantly spendthrift life he took to worrying about money. His fortune had mysteriously evaporated. He was no hedonist. Indeed, he might have adopted his motto from Tennyson: 'Hollow, hollow, hollow all delight.' But he had naturally bought the best of everything. As a matter of course he employed one of the finest chefs in London. How could he recoup his losses? At the Hotel Belle Rivage in Geneva, where he went to attend a meeting of the League of Nations, Balfour pulled the handle of a gambling machine so ardently that it broke, spurting its contents all over the floor.

Nor, in his last decade, had Balfour's hand quite lost its political cunning, though his final achievements have about them the familiar look of highly japanned insubstantiality which was Balfour's hallmark. Thus, for example, in 1921/2 Balfour charmed and fascinated everyone at the Washington Conference which, thanks largely to his 'brilliant' guidance, halted the battleship-building race and substituted a four-power pact for the Anglo-Japanese Naval Alliance. Balfour claimed that the Conference was 'an absolutely unmixed benefit to mankind, which carried no seeds of future misfortune'. This was, to employ the word with which Keynes dismissed another of Balfour's formal pronouncements, 'moonshine'. It was the kind of statement Lord Curzon had in mind when he described Balfour's arguments as 'mere soap bubbles, just as iridescent and equally unsubstantial . . . [They] never make the slightest impression on me because, though metaphysically beautiful, they have no connection with the facts.' For the Washington Conference limited no armaments except capital ships (already outdated), it ignored the nagging problem of war debts and, by giving the Japanese local superiority in the Pacific, it prepared the ground for Allied disasters in the Far East during the Second World War. In 1926, at the Imperial Conference, Balfour performed his last feat of verbal hocus-pocus. This was the celebrated Balfour Definition, a contradiction in terms if ever there was one. In it Balfour conjured up an acceptable formula to express the anomalous relationship between Great Britain and the Dominions:

> equal in status, in no way subordinate one to another in any aspect of their domestic or internal affairs, though united by a common allegiance to the Crown, and freely associated as members of the British Commonwealth of Nations.

Lesser breeds, Indians, Africans, Arabs, were without the definition. But this scarcely mattered for it was little more than foam on the ebb-tide of empire.

Slowly, with characteristic dignity and coolness, Balfour himself slipped away. Like snow in the desert he was visibly tending not to be. A fatalist, a sceptic about the worth of human endeavour, he had always regarded terrestrial existence as a game, important perhaps in terms of winning salvation, profoundly insignificant in its own right and in its end. Not for nothing had Kipling written,

The Foundations of Philosophic Doubt
Are based on this single premiss
'Shall I be able to get out
To Wimbledon in time for tennis?'

But even games, Balfour said, should not be taken too
seriously. Life was nothing but ashes. It was a mere ante-
chamber to eternity, and death was no more alarming than
the passage from one room to another. Of course, suffering
was unpleasant ('I am a coward in regard to pain') and
Balfour bemoaned the loss of his teeth. He also complained
of poor hearing and referred to Whittingehame, where all
the guests in the last year of his life were 'blind, deaf, halt
or maim', as a 'Cripples' Home'. But, though he seemed
moved by the farewell visit of Chaim Weizmann, and
though money worries recurred (he wondered whether the
family would be able to eat after his departure), nothing
could really shake his composure of mind or disturb his
tranquillity of spirit. He slept naturally, peacefully, soul-
fully to the last. For some time he shilly-shallied on the
brink of eternity. And then, imperceptibly but unequivoc-
ally, the rigidity of death replaced the frigidity of life. On
19 March 1930, surrounded by his family, he passed from
fleeting doubt into perpetual certainty. All over the world
the Jewish Prayer of Remembrance, the A'skara, was in-
toned. Candles flickered in synagogues to mourn the passing of Arthur. By his own wish he was buried not in
Westminster Abbey but in the family cemetery at
Whittingehame. Balfour's final act of detachment was
complete.

ARTHUR BALFOUR

Select Bibliography

Lady C. Asquith	*Diaries 1915–1918* (1968)
A. J. Balfour	*Chapters of Autobiography* (1930)
A. J. Balfour	*Speeches on Zionism* (1928)
Lady Frances Balfour	*Ne Obliviscaris* (1930)
N. Blewett	*The Peers, the Parties and the People* (1972)
W. S. Churchill	*Lord Randolph Churchill* (1951 edn.)
B. E. C. Dugdale	*Arthur James Balfour* (1937)
L. P. Curtis	*Coercion and Conciliation in Ireland 1880–1892* (1963)
J. L. Garvin and J. Amery	*The Life of Joseph Chamberlain* (1932–68)
A. M. Gollin	*Balfour's Burden* (1955)
R. Jenkins	*Mr Balfour's Poodle* (1954)
D. Judd	*Balfour and the British Empire* (1968)
I. Malcolm	*Lord Balfour: A Memory* (1930)
Lord Rayleigh	*Lord Balfour and His Relation to Science* (1930)
E. T. Raymond	*Mr Balfour* (1920)
K. Rose	*Superior Person* (1969)
L. Stein	*The Balfour Declaration* (1961)
K. Young	*Arthur James Balfour* (1963)
S. H. Zebel	*Balfour* (1973)

Original Sources
British Museum: Balfour MSS

Mrs Pankhurst

I

Mrs Emmeline Pankhurst became the most famous and
the most notorious woman of her day by means of violence.
Violence, after all, was a male prerogative. Its employment
by this new Joan of Arc and her Suffragette minions was at
once a castrating threat to the lords of humankind and a
vile outrage against all notions of feminine propriety. But
Mrs Pankhurst's own violence was less striking as a form
of political agitation than as a mode of personal dominance. With clenched fists and a fierce tilt of her chin she
confessed to a group of intimates, 'I *love* fighting!' The
moral force and the evangelistic power of her oratory
stemmed from a harnessed Niagara of passion. Her leadership of the militant movement was won by a combination of overwhelming charisma and histrionic dare-devilry.
It was maintained by a sectarian ruthlessness and a dis-
position to 'smash' those who challenged her autocracy.
It was sealed by a turbulent determination to secure her
place in the temple of fame not just by crusading for the
women's vote but by embracing martyrdom. As she said, 'If
men will not do us justice, they shall do us violence.' Nowhere was Mrs Pankhurst's maenadic fury so unconstrained

133

as in prison. A fellow-gaolbird described her confrontation with two visiting officials,

> the men apparently embarrassed and explanatory, the slight form, clad in a long cloak, her head enwrapped in chiffon, rigid with anger. From time to time the arm is raised in a short sharp gesture of incredible violence, to fall again quickly; the whole figure silhouetted against the prison wall reminds one...of a strange archaic relief from the fallen Selinonte temple, – Dian urging on her hounds to devour Actaeon. The voice rises like an angry sea – a terrible cadence in it never heard from a platform – then dies down to a still stranger sonority, the very essence of contempt and defiance. And yet her back shows dolphin-like above her anger, and from such a contest she will emerge as a giant refreshed with wine.

Mrs Pankhurst's friend, the composer Ethel Smyth, sought in many ways to account for the absolute sovereignty of the Suffragette queen. Was it her unscrupulous single-mindedness, her sacred indignation, her magical personality, her 'crystal purity of spirit', her bewitching voice? The composer of *The Wreckers* concluded that one element in Mrs Pankhurst dominated all the rest, 'the sublime and terrific violence of her soul'.

Yet what most intrigued Edwardians about Mrs Pankhurst was the extraordinary contrast between her 'she-male' aggressiveness and her lady-like looks. For it was notorious that feminists were vinegary harridans like those great women's leaders of the previous generation, the mannish Susan B. Anthony and the forbidding Lydia Becker. The stereotype was perpetuated in hackneyed epigrams, trite slogans and cheap jibes: 'Women who wanted women's rights also wanted women's charms'; 'Women's Rights are Men's Lefts'; 'There are three sexes, masculine, feminine and Miss Becker.' The desire for equal rights was obviously a symptom of deep-seated female neurosis. Lord Northcliffe was typical in imagining that he had probed to the root of the matter by describing Suffragettes, in Max Beerbohm's phrase, as 'the unenjoyed'. But Mrs Pankhurst was beautiful. She had the face, it was often said, of a weary saint. A mother and widow, she resembled a virgin rather than a virago. With her svelte pre-Raphaelite figure borne majestically erect, with her clear, olive complexion and full, rosy cheeks, with her raven-black hair, with her delicately pencilled eyebrows and deep violet-blue eyes, above all with her entrancingly melodious voice, she was the very antithesis of the frustrated spinster and the soured old maid of popular mythology. Americans especially were transfixed by her. They expected a bloomered revolutionary with a cropped head, blue spectacles and a billycock hat. They received a slender, cultivated, soft-toned, fashionably garbed gentlewoman whose visage 'recalled the pansy by its shape and a kind of velvety bloom on the expression'. One newspaper exclaimed, 'Can this pale, frail woman have terrified Mr Asquith and created an uproar in the Commons? Why she looks more like a quiet housewife going shopping.' Paradoxically enough, the outward appearance expressed much of the inner reality. It was not just that Mrs Pankhurst actually did adore shopping, the drama of a sale and the excitement of employing sharp wits and sharper elbows to secure a bargain – 'With your perpetual *Come* on! *Come* on!' she once scolded Ethel Smyth in Regent Street, 'You are as bad as a husband.' Nor was it simply that Mrs Pankhurst revelled in the pretty clothes she bought and in adorning herself with a coquettish grace which was all the more artful for seeming to be artless. No, the truth was that Mrs Pankhurst not only looked like a perfect Edwardian lady, in essentials she was a perfect Edwardian lady.

Her manner was so modest, so dignified, so proper, that one Suffragette described her as 'the best bred human being I ever met'. Mrs Pankhurst had worshipped her husband with all the ardour of a romantic and all the abasement of a domestic. Glorying in the matrimonial bond, she had seemed to acknowledge that her place was in the home, and she had expended energy and ingenuity on (what Ruskin had defined as the wife's cardinal task) its 'sweet ordering'. She had brought up her children in the familiar bourgeois way, imposing strict discipline, insisting that they finish their lumpy porridge, forbidding her astigmatic son to wear spectacles, chastising recalcitrance, and once instructing the servants to tie her second daughter Sylvia to a bed all day long for refusing to take her cod liver oil. Never a scholar herself, Mrs Pankhurst had set less store by education than by 'accomplishments' – her eldest daughter Christabel was 'too highly strung' to benefit from school, though she was permitted to take classes in logic as well as French and dressmaking. A domestic ornament which any man would have been proud to possess, Mrs Pankhurst disapproved of ugly feminist breaches of decorum, Helen Taylor's trousers, for example, or the short skirts and shorter hair affected by Annie Besant. She was intensely fastidious, once insisting that her family should leave a Socialist meeting because she had found a bug on her glove. Her main worry in prison seems to have been the vermin and the stained underclothes which she was obliged to wear. Being so 'meticulously dainty' in her personal habits Mrs Pankhurst could never have realized, so Ethel Smyth reckoned, that during and after hunger-and-thirst strikes, her body, feeding off its own tissue, emitted a 'strange, pervasive, sweetish odour of corruption'. Mrs Pankhurst was as much of a Puritan as was consistent with being a Francophile – she found it 'odd how what is quite ordinary in French immediately becomes coarse and improper in English'. She was disturbed by the subject of sex and never instructed her children in its mysteries. When she sent the young Suffragette, Annie Kenney, to 'rouse' London for the cause in 1906, Mrs Pankhurst warned her to speak publicly to no one of the opposite sex except policemen. (Christabel mimicked her mother's prudery, even going so far as to ban the use of 'coarse screen blocks' for printing *The Suffragette* – 'A woman's paper ought to be a finished and almost dainty production however robust the point of view expressed in it.') In short, then, Mrs Pankhurst was very much an orthodox woman of her age and class. She created the Suffragette Movement in her own image.

This may seem a contentious claim, for the traditional view of the militant Edwardian feminist is that she was a stark reaction against the docile Victorian female. The Suffragette Movement is generally seen as an expression of the pent-up rage of middle-class matrons who had for too long been inhibited by feminine gentility and patronized by masculine chivalry. Their campaign is usually presented as a violent protest against being treated as children and idiots politically, as angels and slaves domestically, against the whole gamut of ideas embodied in the patriarchal maxim, 'My wife and I are one and I am he.' It is explained as an explosive revolt against nineteenth century stereotypes which represented women as nymphs of superior intuition and rarefied emotion who should nevertheless honour and obey, suffer and be still. These depicted women as weaker vessels, their creative power drained by the menstrual flow and their intellects porous from an early evolutionary arrest 'necessitated', in Herbert Spencer's opinion, 'by the reservation of vital power to meet the cost of reproduction', who should nevertheless be paragons of high-minded purity. The Suffragettes themselves asserted that their rebellion signalled, in the words of Mrs Pethick-Lawrence, 'the discovery of woman by herself, the realization of her own powers, the overthrow by herself of traditions and conventions that were the real bondage... The world and the press cried "unladylike" and forthwith women themselves turned down the word "lady".' Christabel, it has been said, 'lit a fire which consumed the past'. The historian George Dangerfield maintained that Pankhurstian militancy, combined, at the end of the Edwardian era, with assaults on the body politic by subversive strikers, pugnacious peers and belligerent Irish Unionists, contributed to 'the strange death of Liberal England'. In fact the Suffragette Movement was more notable as a manifestation of the strange survival of Conservative England. It was not the first blast of the trumpet of Women's Liberation so much as the last trump of Victorian religious revivalism. It did not so much herald the birth of the New Woman as proclaim the vitality of the Old Lady.

Charles Dickens defined a lady as one who was doubtful about the propriety of attending a christening, considering the implications of human birth. But the Victorian lady was less of a helpless, insipid prig than she has been painted. Many women were prepared, in the tradition of Florence Nightingale and Josephine Butler, to renounce a degree of respectability in order to uphold a higher ideal of morality. Suffragette self-mortification, what Mrs Pankhurst called the 'heroic sacrifice by which alone the soul of civilization is saved', was an intensified form of the Victorian lady's spirit of self-denying service. Suffragette militancy was more extreme in England than elsewhere precisely because Mrs Pankhurst and her fellows were so confident of their superior social status and their elevated moral role.

On the other hand, there were limits. 'Rise up, women!' cried Mrs Pankhurst — but so far and no further. In order to vindicate their policy and to preserve their caste the Suffragettes needed to conform slavishly, when out of the fray, to the dictates of convention. Even when engaged in hostilities the rebels liked to pretend that they were victims.

Christabel went to great lengths to explain that spitting at a policeman was the only form of assault she could commit with her arms pinioned and that in any case it had been nothing more than a lady-like ' "pout", a perfectly dry purse of the mouth'. Nothing distressed Mrs Pankhurst more than the stiff collars, trilby hats and other masculine trappings sported by a few of her adherents. And she would have been horrified by American feminists who had questioned accepted sexual ethics, by Elizabeth Cady Stanton, for example, who denounced 'hypocritical prating about purity' as 'one of man's most effective engines for our division and subjugation'. Shocked beyond words at her daughter Sylvia's unmarried motherhood (itself a deliberate, socialistic flouting of gentlewomanly standards) Mrs Pankhurst would have been outraged still further had she known that a revolution in feminine sensibility of more profound significance than the suffrage insurrection was being engendered almost on her doorstep.

It was conceived in a Bloomsbury drawing-room on 11 August 1908 at about five o'clock in the afternoon. Vanessa Bell and her sister Virginia, shortly to be Mrs Woolf, were having tea.

> Suddenly the door opened and the long and sinister figure of Mr Lytton Strachey stood on the threshold. He pointed his finger at a stain on Vanessa's white dress. 'Semen?' he said. Can one really say it? I thought and we burst out laughing. With that one word all barriers of reticence and reserve went down. A flood of the sacred fluid seemed to overwhelm us. Sex permeated our conversation. The word bugger was never far from our lips. We discussed copulation with the same excitement and openness that we had discussed the nature of good.

Too much can be made of a symbolic moment; too much has been made of a narcissistic group. Nevertheless, in

Bloomsbury, to quote the well-worn witticism, all the couples were triangles and lived in squares, whereas even to speak of sexual freedom for women (though not, of course, for men) had been taboo under the Victorian dispensation. Mrs Pankhurst proposed to sustain and refine that dispensation. Enfranchised women could enforce virtue by law. With her obsessive concern for purity Mrs Pankhurst stiffened the sinews of Mrs Grundy and summoned up blood-curdling images of her own about the incipient degeneration of the race. Her message was that chastity belts must be tightened up all round. Moreover she connived at the customary subjection of her sex in other spheres, education, employment and, especially, in the home. For she aimed exclusively to win 'Votes for Women', or as radical opponents more accurately described it, referring to her willingness to see only a higher class of females enfranchised, 'Votes for Ladies'. (It was no accident that the Women's Liberation Movement of the 1960s began in America where female emancipation had never been understood solely in narrow terms of the vote and where women were traditionally more independent – it would have been difficult, if not impossible, to find an English feminist rebuking her sisters, as Emma Goldmann did, for keeping their mouths shut and their wombs open.) By exercising despotic control over the movement Mrs Pankhurst even denied Suffragettes the experience of democratic participation, the achievement of which was its object. By fostering a quasi-religious hero-worship of herself and of Christabel Mrs Pankhurst imposed on her disciples, in the disillusioned words of one of their number, 'a thousand servitudes in order to win one small symbol of liberty...A slave woman with a vote will still be essentially a slave.' However vigorous their evangelism, Suffragette ladies in the missionary position were still essentially supine.

All the same, it must be acknowledged that Mrs Pank-

hurst was a missionary of consummate brilliance. She was
the messianic leader of a 'moral crusade'. She was the
inspired prophetess of a 'spiritual awakening'. She was the
courageous general of a secular salvation army engaged in
a 'Holy War for the emancipation of our sex'. She was a
hot-gospeller conducting 'the greatest mission the world
has ever known . . . to free half the human race, and through
that freedom to save the rest'. She was a preacher against
vice, and its consequential 'loathsome disease', whose
sermons were inspired by the vision of a new apocalypse.

The fire of suffering whose flame is upon our sisters in
prison is burning us also. For we suffer with them, we
partake of their affliction, and we shall share their
victory by-and-by. This fire will breathe into the ear of,
many a sleeper the one word 'Awake', and she will arise
to slumber no more. It will descend with the gift of
tongues upon many who have hitherto been dumb, and
they will go forth to preach the news of deliverance. Its
light will be seen afar off by many who suffer and are
sorrowful and oppressed, and will irradiate their lives
with a new hope. . . For the spirit which is in women
to-day cannot be quenched; it is stronger than all
earthly potentates and powers; it is stronger than all
tyranny, cruelty and oppression; it is stronger even than
death itself.

The more violent their movement became, the more Mrs
Pankhurst and Christabel stressed its sacred and moral
character, its 'supernatural quality which, as it were, raises
the hair and freezes the blood of those grosser beings',
men. *The Suffragette*'s comment on the campaign of arson
reflected its belief that no mortal incendiary was at work:
'The people that walk in darkness shall see a great light.'
Mrs Pankhurst was hailed as the 'Illuminator of women'.
On platform, podium, or plinth, her eyes now smouldering
with pathos, now flashing with excitement, she seemed

transfigured. On the demonstration or in the mêlée she was possessed by a divine fury, a fury which she compared to Christ's when he cast the money-changers out of the temple and destroyed the Gadarene swine. She was never more vibrant than when enjoying the limelight (what compensated those poor Suffragettes who languished in obscurity? she wondered pityingly). She was never more thrilled than when taking part in some act of militancy. On the first skirmish in the House of Commons, in 1906, a Suffragette, observing her leader prostrate on the marble floor under two large policemen, rushed to her aid. She was greeted by a fearless and amused glance from a pair of sparkling amethyst eyes. Mrs Pankhurst was having the time of her life. She had seized the time. The hour was surely at hand which would vindicate her faith in the feminist millennium and realize her hope of personal glory.

II

With a theatrical flair which was never to desert her Mrs Pankhurst, *née* Emmeline Goulden, entered the world on the anniversary of the storming of the Bastille, 14 July 1858. At the time, the happy event was regarded as a sad anti-climax. Victorian parents were wont to describe the birth of a girl as 'our fiasco', and Robert Goulden, though otherwise enlightened and progressive, was no exception. Emmeline later overheard her father lamenting the fact that she 'wasn't born a lad'. Her mother, a pretty farmer's daughter from the Isle of Man, shared her husband's belief in women's rights. But despite the availability of contraceptives she allowed herself to become a breeding-machine. And she considered that her girls should devote themselves to dusting, arranging flowers and fetching their brothers' slippers. Emmeline inherited her father's thespian talents – as well as having worked himself up from errand boy to owner of a cotton printing business, Goulden was Manchester's foremost amateur actor — and she created emotional scenes over the inconsistency between her mother's principles and practice. Emmeline was conscious of being stronger, brighter, bolder than her brothers. They knew her as 'the dictionary' because she read so much, her favourite books being *Uncle Tom's Cabin*, Carlyle's *French Revolution* and Bunyan's *Holy War*. She was early inclined towards rebellion by stories of her paternal grandfather who had narrowly escaped with his life at the 'Peterloo' Massacre of 1819 and had been press-ganged, returning after years in the navy to find no trace of his family or friends. Imbued with the romance of action and adventure, Emmeline demonstrated her juvenile support for radicalism by staging a daring tableau. At a meeting of rough Mancunian factory workers, during the election of 1868, she and a younger sister paraded the Liberal colours by hoisting their green dresses to reveal red petticoats. An outraged nursery maid whisked them home and the disgraced exhibitionists were confined to bed. There, perhaps, Emmeline consoled herself by sating her imagination once again in the drama of the true 'hero of her heart', King Charles the Martyr.

Emmeline engaged in few other youthful pranks for, being the eldest girl in a large family, she was forced to mature quickly. At the age of fourteen she attended her first suffrage meeting, addressed by Lydia Becker. Miss Becker was subsequently to utter in Emmeline's presence the bitter cry of outcast spinsterdom: 'Married women have all the plums of life!' But in 1872 she merely confirmed the young novice's faith in the gospel of votes for women. Later that year Emmeline was sent from Manchester dame school to the Ecole Normale in Paris where her 'bosom friendship' with a dashing fellow pupil, Noémie de Rochefort, daughter of an exiled Communard nobleman, strengthened her liberal ideas and her taste for excitement. The much-vaunted moral discipline and intellectual training of the Ecole Normale affected her hardly at all. She enjoyed the course on embroidery and learnt to sew with skill and enthusiasm. As for chemistry and book-keeping...a knowledge of such dismal subjects could only cramp a smart young lady's style. But Paris – gay, republican, sophisticated, fashionable Paris – captivated her. She wanted to stay for ever. But for this plum, and for all the other plums of life, to fall into her lap, she needed a husband. Noémie produced a suitor who was complaisant in everything but the question of a dowry. This Emmeline's father indignantly refused to pay. Hard-headed Englishmen tended to regard marriage as a matter of purchase just as prostitution was a matter of hire, and Robert Goulden was determined not to make a rich present of his daughter to an improvident and licentious Frenchman. Emmeline, in a state of rage and humiliation, was recalled to grimy, provincial Manchester. Its only compensation was that there she attracted everyone's attention. From the top of her head, crowned with a fetching little bonnet or a scarlet ribbon knotted with elaborate carelessness, to the tips of her minute, elegantly-shod feet, she was every inch the 'finished' young lady. Inwardly still a diffident girl, Emmeline, aged twenty, had all the outward self-possession of a woman.

If a husband was the 'Open Sesame' to ecstasy in Paris how much more was this so in Manchester, where Emmeline had no function and no duty but to adorn her parents' home. Such service was perfect serfdom. Her spirit yearned to harness itself to the yoke of some liberating idealism...or idealist. She was determined 'only to give herself to an important man'. Of course, she would not flirt; that was 'degrading'. A lady revealed her want of a mate with refined circumspection; as one contemporary journal wrote, 'Half the art of the woman of the world consists in doing disgusting things delicately.' However,

Mrs Pankhurst, the Suffragette Queen

Mrs Pankhurst travels
First Class

Mrs Pankhurst and
Christabel in prison
uniform

when she found her prospective spouse she kindled his ardour so directly that Mrs Goulden accused Emmeline of 'throwing herself' at him. Richard Marsden Pankhurst, Ll.D., with his carroty beard and a piping treble voice which often caused him to be mistaken for a woman, seemed an improbable key to bliss. He was twice Emmeline's age. He had always lived with his Baptist parents and never left the house for an hour without telling them where he was going. A scholarly barrister, he was small, unprepossessing and so physically incompetent that his wife always had to do the carving. Still, he had beautiful hands. And in other respects the 'Red Doctor' was a distinctly glamorous figure. He was the most prominent and the most flaming radical in 'Cottonopolis'. He was a pioneer of every advanced faith and a 'standard-bearer of every forlorn hope'. He was a democrat, a republican, a communist, a Home Ruler, a pacifist, an internationalist, an agnostic. He was an opponent of imperialism and the House of Lords – it was 'a public abattoir' in which human rights were butchered. He was a proponent of free secular education and women's rights – clawing the air with his long, curved finger-nails, he once exclaimed, 'Why are women so patient? Why don't you force us to give you the vote? Why don't you scratch our eyes out?' In short, Dr Pankhurst was an extremist and he courted Emmeline with an impetuosity that matched her own. On 8 September 1879 he wrote to 'Dear Miss Goulden' trying to interest her, 'one of the party of progress', in the movement for female higher education. On 23 September he addressed her as 'Dearest Treasure', assured her that 'Every struggling cause shall be ours' and rejoiced at the prospect 'of two lives made one by that love which seeks more the other than self'. Emmeline was so transported by the eloquence and devotion of this glorious revolutionary that she proposed they should enter into a 'free union'. The Doctor quickly explained that to violate sexual orthodoxy was to invite social damnation and thus to miss their chance of reforming the world. Emmeline learnt the lesson well and reconciled herself to defying convention in a brown velvet wedding-dress. Discovering too late that a superfluous row of brass buttons down the front made her look 'like a little page boy', she burst into tears.

On the eve of the marriage Mrs Goulden embarked on an explanation of what were euphemistically known as the duties of a bride: 'I want to talk to you.' Emmeline replied, 'I do not want to listen.' Maybe she knew already. Or perhaps she preferred to be instructed by the mild-mannered fire-eater whose helpmate she was to be. If so she proved a quick pupil. In the space of five years she gave birth to four children, Christabel (1880), Sylvia (1882), Henry Francis (1884) and Adela (1885). Christabel alone she nursed and the bond established between the feline daughter and the passionate mother was preternaturally strong. Other Pankhurstian ties were to dissolve like cobwebs; Adela was to be exiled to Australia for denying Christabel's infallibility and for the same sin Sylvia was to be excommunicated amidst her mother's public regrets that she was entitled to bear the family name. Whereas, talking to a friend in Holloway Prison, Mrs Pankhurst 'dwelt upon the name of her daughter "Christabel the Anointed One", the young deliverer who was to emancipate the new generation of women'. Despite a professed atheism Mrs Pankhurst had a profound, if misty, religious sense. And whatever the psychological explanation for her adoration of Christabel, who bore a marked physical resemblance to her earthly father, Mrs Pankhurst was to deem her firstborn the Saviour of womankind – though at this early stage she was ambitious for Christabel to become a dancer. Unlike many of her contemporaries, Mrs Pankhurst never pretended to believe that babies were made by a species of remote control. But Christabel she conceived to be immaculate.

Meanwhile the domestic scene absorbed Mrs Pankhurst's attention. She was an indifferent manager. She
spent too little on mutton and too much on bon-bons. She
complained of sick headaches and languished in bed for
days with hot water bottles, a prey to boredom and
irritation. Though unable to finish the stiff course of
reading which the Doctor, at her insistence, had pre-
scribed, she was a compulsive skimmer of light novels.
Luckily the 'devoted service' of their Welsh nurse freed her
from mundane chores, including the care of the children.
Mrs Pankhurst's role was to beautify the home. Though
most of the Doctor's legal work was in Manchester, she
persuaded him in 1886 to move to London, 'where everybody wants to be'. She decorated their Bloomsbury house
in her favourite colour, yellow. And, loving 'comfort and
the pretty things of life', she furnished it with more than
oriental splendour, with Japanese blinds, embroidery and
coloured beads, with Chinese teapots, Persian plates,
Indian brasses, Turkish rugs. The expense was to be met
by starting a fancy goods shop – in all she embarked on
three such artistic missions to the housewife, each one
called Emersons, each one opening with radiant expectations, each one closing in dismal failure. The children
learnt to live plainly. Their mother would tolerate 'no
likes and dislikes'. They ate milk puddings and wore blue
serge knickers. The régime may have taken its toll on the
delicate son, who died of diphtheria in 1888. Mrs
Pankhurst was prostrated with grief. The following year
she bore, with great difficulty and some danger, a substitute, another son, also delicate. Though known as
Harry, he was given his deceased brother's names, Henry
Francis. He was also to die prematurely, the victim,
Sylvia thought, of his mother's neglect. By contrast the
Pankhurst women were all blessed with a vigorous longevity – the female of the species was more vital than
the male.

Mrs Pankhurst did not trick out her Bloomsbury house to provide an elegant domestic setting so much as a spectacular political set, an ornate backcloth to the radical salon over which she dreamt of presiding. The Pankhurst 'At Home' was to be a splendid stage, draped with arabesques of white gauze and garlands of purple heliotrope, on which she could play the leading lady while the vanguard of the march of mind acted as supporting cast. She did perform as hostess to many progressive writers and politicians. And at her house in 1889 Mrs Pankhurst, Josephine Butler, Elizabeth Cady Stanton and others founded the Women's Franchise League. It was a protest against the timid constitutional methods of what they called the 'Spinster Suffrage Party' led by Lydia Becker and Millicent Fawcett. The Franchise League soon dissolved for lack of funds, the very circumstance which was to mar and then to close Mrs Pankhurst's salon and to send the family back to Manchester in 1893. But straitened means never checked Mrs Pankhurst's quicksilver ways. She broke with her father forever when her husband abandoned the Liberal party for socialism in the first of his three unsuccessful attempts to enter Parliament. And when the Doctor became involved in a libel case, a result of describing the Holy Ghost as 'the foggy member of the Trinity' whose credentials he would like to examine in the witness-box, Mrs Pankhurst attacked the judge. She accused him of being part of

> a conspiracy to crush the public life of an honourable public man. It is to be regretted that there should be found on the English Bench a judge who will lend his aid to a disreputable section of the Tory Party in doing their dirty work; but for what other reason were you ever placed where you are?

Recognizing a member of the 'shrieking sisterhood' when he heard one, his lordship wisely disregarded this act of provocation. Nothing exasperated Mrs Pankhurst more than indifference. It was death in life, doom of her hopes for immortal renown. She exclaimed fiercely, 'I want to go to prison for contempt of court!'

Whatever the cost, Mrs Pankhurst would not be ignored. Back in Manchester she gained in confidence and competence as a speaker on behalf of suffragism and socialism. In 1894 she was elected to the Chorlton Board of Poor Law Guardians, controllers of the workhouse. There she discovered destitute waifs shivering for want of undergarments because the matron had been too modest to discuss their provision with the authorities. Scorning the false delicacy of the socially insecure, Mrs Pankhurst, called 'My Lady' by the paupers, saw that the need was supplied. Employing her 'passionate and persuasive' oratory, she helped to ease the lot of the unemployed and to effect other workhouse reforms. Unfortunately her stormy rhetoric was apt to cloud her philanthropic perspicacity. She insisted that the bread of the poor should be 'buttered with margarine'. And by 1897, considering the Chorlton workhouse so improved that children were worse off in the average working-class home, she proposed to increase the authority of the Guardians in order 'to cancel parental power' and assume direct wardship of children whose welfare was jeopardized by their parents' 'inability' or 'evil conduct'. Understandably, one of her opponents on the board inscribed on his blotting paper this injunction to himself: 'Keep your temper!' The Manchester magistrates must have written themselves a similar rubric, for they refused in 1896 to bestow on Mrs Pankhurst the public martyrdom she craved over the affair of Boggart Hole Clough. This was a natural amphitheatre in one of the city's parks where the Independent Labour Party (ILP) held open-air meetings, illegally in the view of the Council. Mrs Pankhurst and other socialist leaders defied the ban. At rally after rally Mrs

Pankhurst, in her pink straw bonnet, 'her mellow, effortless tones carrying far beyond the shouts of excited men', challenged the magistrates to convict her. She promised to pay no fine and 'put upon the bench the full responsibility' of committing her to Strangeways Gaol. They sensibly denied her that seductive accolade. After a complex legal wrangle the City Council was defeated and what was, in effect, the dress rehearsal for the Suffragette drama ended in triumph. It was quickly followed by disaster. In 1898, exhausted by tempestuous political involvements and drained by his efforts to support the family, Dr Pankhurst paid his last debt to nature. Summoned home from the Continent, where she had been taking Christabel to visit Noémie, Mrs Pankhurst read the news of his death in a passenger's evening paper on the train from London. She shrieked aloud in her anguish. So stricken by misery and loneliness was she that Sylvia had to sleep with her in the matrimonial bed. On her husband's headstone Mrs Pankhurst had carved Walt Whitman's words, 'Faithful and true — my loving comrade.' The Pankhurst Memorial Hall was so named in the Red Doctor's honour. To his widow's incredulous fury the branch of the ILP, whose headquarters it was, barred the entry of women.

III

Mrs Pankhurst was thus obliged, at the age of forty, to become an employed lady (a state fast ceasing to be a contradiction in terms) and from this novel experience she was to draw powder and shot enough to fill the militant woman's magazine. The Doctor's possessions were sold to pay his debts. The family moved from a select Crescent to a prosaic Street (though the smaller house was carefully chosen for its 'air of distinction'). And Mrs Pankhurst resigned as an unpaid Poor Law Guardian and became a

salaried Registrar of Births and Deaths. Her duties
brought her into close contact with the squalid wretched-
ness of working-class life and she was quick to diagnose
the worst ills as moral ones. Sweated labour, rape, incest,
illegitimacy, prostitution, the white slave traffic – such
wicked forms of social and sexual exploitation could only
be eradicated by enfranchised womanhood. Until the vote
was won these evils were to afford a justification for
Suffragette violence, which had the merit of being directed
against property, not persons. Everywhere Mrs Pankhurst
looked it was apparent that the chief victims of injustice
were females. Behind every poor man, she observed,
stood a still poorer woman. Elected in 1900 as an ILP
candidate to the Manchester School Board, she discovered
that there was little or no technical training provided for
girls, even in the baking and confectionery trades. Females
were a fettered sub-proletariat, 'a servant class'. Christabel
agreed, but she lacked her mother's faith in, and pre-
occupation with, Labour. Now assisting the radical
suffragist Eva Gore-Booth, whose blonde neuralgic head
she would massage for hours, much to the jealous annoy-
ance of Mrs Pankhurst, Christabel accused socialists and
trade unionists of wanting 'beef-steaks and butter for
working men; tea and bread for working women'. By
1903 mother and daughter were together belabouring
friends in the ILP on behalf of the women's cause. The
response of Bruce Glasier, who regarded female suffrage
as a bourgeois diversion from the socialist highway, was
typical.

At last get roused and speak with something like scorn
of their miserable individualist sexism, and virtually
tell them that the ILP will not stir a finger more than it
has done for all the women suffragists in creation.
Really the pair are not seeking democratic freedom but
self-importance... Christabel paints her eyebrows

grossly and looks selfish, lazy and wilful. They want to be ladies and lack the humility of real heroinism.

Certainly Mrs Pankhurst was arrogant. Courage alone would scarcely have sustained her had she not felt herself to be pregnant with a world-important message. Its delivery would be marked by signs, wonders and vociferations for she was, as Lloyd George said, 'a big woman, but narrow'. There was, indeed, to be a frenetic quality about her actions, a hysterical note to her rhetoric. Christabel claimed that her mother's voices were of God. Prejudiced persons found it all too easy to disparage Mrs Pankhurst's procedures as. . . essentially feminine.

It was obvious to Mrs Pankhurst that all males, whatever their political persuasion, were locked in a vicious conspiracy against those whom they were wont to call, in that revealing metonymy, 'the Sex'. Was it not clear that women were kept down so that men could more conveniently get up to no good? Women were a recumbent indication of men's rampant inclinations. Lust, said Bernard Shaw, was the greatest single obstacle to female emancipation, just as 'the cry for the vote is often really the cry for the key to one's bedroom'. Of course, men disguised their desire to maintain political power, for it was really the power to consort with prostitutes, the power to assault children, the power to infect their wives with syphilis. They concealed their desires behind arguments of impeccable respectability. For example, it was obvious that females could not become aldermen because there was no such word as 'alderwomen', let alone 'alderpersons'. Women should be excluded from Parliament for it would not do to have Lord Chancellors eloping or Prime Ministers in an interesting condition – why, there might be knitting on the Woolsack and *accouchements* on the front bench. Then again, canvassing was surely a form of licensed soliciting. Domestic happiness could hardly be sustained,

said Labouchere, Parliamentary leader of the Anti-Suf-
fragists, 'if a man is perpetually leaving his own wife and
visiting another man's wife on the plea that he wanted to
be a town councillor'.

The 'Antis' had axioms to meet every occasion.
Proper women, emotional and illogical, did not want the
vote; militant, masculine-minded suffragists demonstrated
their unworthiness to exercise it. Females would not use
the vote; female voters would neglect their families.
Women would vote with their husbands or priests; women
would cause domestic or religious dissension by voting
against their husbands or priests. Women did not understand politics; women would outnumber men, vote *en bloc*,
change the laws and impose 'a crushing tax on bachelors'.
Women did not defend the state or earn its wealth and
therefore had no title to vote; women fighters and workers
were so unladylike as to be disqualified from the franchise.
Women were essentially domestic creatures; women were
better off working as volunteers for one of the big political
parties. The vote would mean nothing to women; the vote
accorded with the dignity of man. In short, men were men
and women were women and never the twain should meet
inside a polling-booth – where who knew what indescri-
bable indecencies might take place.

Mrs Pankhurst was not deceived. It did not require a
Freud to see the ballot box, with its suggestive orifice, as a
symbol of man's sovereign promiscuity. As Ethel Smyth
later wrote to Mrs Pankhurst, all men, from bishops
down, were 'tainted by the brothel ideas of the sanctity of
women's bodies and hence fail to be horrified at venereal
disease'. Only a moral crusade could free women from
captivity and men from iniquity. 'Women,' proclaimed
Mrs Pankhurst to her friends, 'We must have an independent woman's movement. Come to my house tomorrow
and we will arrange it.' So, imperiously, on 10 October
1903, the Women's Social and Political Union (WSPU)

was formed. Its ends were 'Votes for Women and Chastity for Men.' Its means, in a motto endlessly reiterated, were 'Deeds not Words.'

At first the WSPU seemed little more than an ambitious 'family party'. Mrs Pankhurst maintained a rigid matriarchal discipline. Christabel, now training as a barrister though excluded by her sex from the bar, exercised her celebrated skill as an organizer. Sylvia, Adela and even Harry also served. However, the Pankhursts were joined by the purposeful Mrs Flora Drummond whose life had been blighted by the fact that she was under regulation height to become a post-mistress. She was nicknamed 'Bluebell', 'the Precocious Piglet', and finally, because she so loved to command Suffragette parades, 'the General'. Another early ally was the intellectual Teresa Billington – unfortunately her sexual habits were somewhat natural and she was soon to break with the movement because it was 'socially exclusive, punctiliously correct, gracefully fashionable, ultra-respectable and narrowly religious'. Hannah Mitchell, renegade from a Labour Church where they sang hymns like 'The Red Flag', was a useful recruit until she succumbed to a nervous breakdown – none of the Pankhurst family showed the slightest sympathy. Most valuable of all was the tractable, attractive Lancashire mill-hand (she had lost the finger of one hand in a mill), Annie Kenney. Called by her 'still small voice', she became the most winning of 'Mrs Pankhurst's suffrage missionaries,' as they were termed, preaching of her conviction that the vote would end poverty, bring Paradise and do the washing. It was Annie Kenney who advised the WSPU to conduct its propaganda at the Lancashire Wakes, or travelling fairs. Soon its members were competing for the attention of the public with merry-go-rounds and Aunt Sallies, and emptying the booths of tooth drawers, vendors of quack medicines, fortune tellers and religious revivalists of other persuasions.

Her crusade lifted Mrs Pankhurst to a condition of almost permanent effervescence. She was determined that 'Votes for Women' would be achieved now. The millennium was imminent – or would be if exhortation could make it so. She lived 'in a frenzy of suspense; all the woes of the world, all the sorrows of women hung, one would say, in the balance'. By 1905 Sylvia was quite worried about her mother's state.

Far into the night she railed against the treachery of men and bemoaned the impotence of women! 'Poor women!' The overburdened mothers, the sweated workers, the outcasts of the streets, the orphan children of the workhouse mingled in the imagery of her discourse. She appeared so greatly to distress herself that I feared for her health and her reason. On some later occasion, when, after a night of these agonies. . . she began again to declaim, I gazed at her in sorrowful concern. . . Suddenly turning on me with a smile, she struck me lightly on the arm: 'Don't look at me like that! Bless you, your old mother likes it. This is what I call life!'

It was in this spirit that Mrs Pankhurst embarked on her first act of militancy. When, in May 1905, a Private Member's Bill for woman's suffrage was talked out by Labouchere and his friends with porcine jokes about 'the Sex', she organized a demonstration of protest. The police jostled and then expelled her from the precincts of Parliament. So, outside Westminster Abbey, she addressed the crowd. At last she was in her element, a petticoated Parnell, a Savonarola in silk stockings. Her body taut, her eyes alight, her tones tremulous with anger, she was no longer just a woman speaker. She was the voice of womanhood, 'maternity pleading for the race'. Mrs Pankhurst would accomplish the downfall of Labouchere morally, by harsh words, and not physically, as she had planned, by a fine trip-wire.

After this convulsion there was an anticlimactic pause in the progress of the movement. As his government drifted towards dissolution Balfour rightly assured the WSPU that women's suffrage was not 'in the swim'. Street-corner meetings in Lancashire, even those summoned by Christabel's muffin bell, caused only insignificant ripples. The movement needed to make a mighty national splash. All Mrs Pankhurst's instincts cried out for martyrdom. The women's cause must become an issue of blood. But at the moment, for the sake of her registrarship, Mrs Pankhurst could not afford to spill her own. She would send her beloved daughter. Christabel should make the sacrifice and win the glory. On 13 October 1905 Sir Edward Grey was to address supporters at Manchester's Free Trade Hall. Christabel announced, 'I shall sleep in prison tonight.' When Grey refused to pledge a future Liberal government to 'Votes for Women', she and Annie Kenney created a disturbance. They were expelled from the meeting, a steward covering Annie's pretty face with his hat, and arrested amidst further struggles outside, when Christabel spat at her policeman. On refusing to pay the fines, they were sentenced to short terms of imprisonment. At this stage Mrs Pankhurst succumbed to a moment of panic. Perhaps she was intimidated by the police; later she had such a dread of the inspector who regularly arrested her that she would turn pale at the mention of his name – the Suffragettes tried to kidnap him but unhappily they attacked the wrong man. Anyway the mother offered to dash the cup of suffering from her daughter's lips. Christabel knew it must be drained to the lees if womankind were to be saved: 'Mother, if you pay my fine I will never go home.' She went to gaol, where, Annie Kenney reported, she looked 'very coy and pretty in her prison cap. She took my hand and held it tenderly as though I were a lost child being guided home.'

Christabel's act was hailed as a piece of arrant, impertinent, unmaidenly folly which should have been punished by 'the discipline of the nursery': the bad publicity was the best publicity that the WSPU had ever enjoyed. The *Daily Mail* coined for its members the insulting diminutive 'Suffragette', a nickname they eagerly embraced. According to the press Mrs Pankhurst and her daughters were 'crazy hooligans, their followers were shrieking hysterics, their policy was wild delirium'. But all over the country female hearts responded to the call to sacrifice. The Suffragette creed, though written as a *jeu d'esprit* (in 1908), expressed genuine feelings of reverence for Mrs Pankhurst and a real sense that the movement owed its soul to the intercession of Christabel.

I believe in Emmeline Pankhurst – founder of the Women's Social and Political Union. And in Christabel Pankhurst, her eldest daughter, our Lady, who was inspired by the passion for Liberty, born to be a leader of women. She descended into prison; the seventh day she returned again to the world. She was entertained to breakfast, and sat on the right hand of her mother, our glorious Leader. From thence she went forth to judge both the Government and the Antis. I believe in Votes for Women on the same terms as men, the policy of the Women's Social and Political Union, the equality of the sexes, Representation for Taxation, the necessity for militant tactics, and Freedom Everlasting.

Mrs Pankhurst was not amused – her sense of humour was, indeed, about as rudimentary as that of the great Queen. But the Suffragette sovereign did not spurn less blasphemous forms of idolatry. Her own newspaper was to proclaim her 'a creative genius whose deeds and words are her masterpieces'. Personal adulation helped to swell the ranks of the militants and to establish their *esprit de corps*. It was understandable that a Lancashire Suffragette, homeward bound after a London rally, should ask directions for a railway station called St Pankhurst.

Mrs Pankhurst demanded crescendo. During the general election of 1906 the campaign was still being conducted on a relatively small scale. Ministers were heckled by 'vixens in velvet'. Churchill was 'hen-pecked' in Manchester. Balfour's sister, close to tears, begged the Suffragettes not to interrupt Arthur's meetings: 'He could not stand it.' The priorities of the victorious Liberals were clearly not those of Mrs Pankhurst and it became essential to concert all Suffragette efforts in London. A 'Women's Parliament' met on 16 February 1906 at Caxton Hall, near what Mrs Pankhurst contemptuously called the 'Men's Parliament'. Wearing regal black and 'the dignity of a mother who has known great sorrow', Mrs Pankhurst played on the feelings of her hearers, exercising what H. N. Brailsford called 'her almost intolerable power to move'. She spoke quietly, in an accent still marked by the Lancastrian twang ('Join uzz!') which she had wanted her children to lose. Her phrases were plain. Her theme was almost a cliché. She made hardly a gesture with her lorgnette. But her bearing was an exclamation mark. Her eyes blazed as though she nursed some secret fire. Her personality was charged with magnetic force, all the more palpable for seeming to be suppressed. Her voice thrilled with emotion, poignant, mournful, edged with terrible menace. That voice was, said Ethel Smyth, 'a stringed instrument in the hands of a great artist' – though the composer noted with surprise that in church, where Mrs Pankhurst joined 'loudly, fervently and even gloatingly in the hymns', she 'sang flatter than I should have thought it possible to sing'. Anyway, such was her performance that many women 'silently pledged their faith to her for life'. And the Caxton Hall audience rose in a body to follow Mrs Pankhurst as she marched on the Parliament of men. Soaked by torrential rain, they were at first denied entry and then admitted in small batches. Nothing was achieved. Only one MP, Keir Hardie, veteran leader of the ILP, showed any real sympathy for the Suffragettes. And his compassion for women in general was a symptom of his passion for the Pankhurst women in particular. Rumour-mongers scented hanky-panky, hinted that Hardie knew Emmeline better than he should have done – 'Verily,' said Bruce Glasier, 'Mrs Pankhurst has been the Delilah that has cut our Samson's locks.' And he undoubtedly did have carnal knowledge of Sylvia. Despite a gallant struggle Hardie was virtually impotent in Parliament – as Christabel complained, 'the Private Member is a very rudimentary organ.' Mrs Pankhurst wept, raged and implored him to do more for the women's cause. Instead, in April 1906, he combined with Sylvia to stop her, for sound tactical reasons, making a disturbance in the Ladies' Gallery of the House of Commons. 'You have baulked me – both of you!' cried Mrs Pankhurst, in one of those *prima donna* paroxysms that punctuated her life, 'I thought there would have been one little niche in the temple of fame for me!'

IV

Later that month Mrs Pankhurst achieved her purpose, if entry to the temple of fame may indeed be secured via expulsion from the senate of Albion. Crying, 'Divide, divide!' over a suffragist resolution being moved by Keir Hardie, she and her acolytes were bundled from the Ladies' Gallery amid uproar. What a ravishing adventure! The glare of publicity quite made Mrs Pankhurst's skin glow. More than ever she had faith in the cause she served. Such drama, such *éclat*, such idealism – here was fulfilment of which she had scarcely dared dream. The movement was the fount of her seething emotions, the focus of her 'desperate heart-hunger'. Mrs Pankhurst instinctively knew, as Mrs Pethick-Lawrence wrote, that she had been 'cast for a great role...She could have been a queen on the stage or in the salon. Circumstances had baulked her.' Now Mrs Pankhurst's 'daemon' drove her on to realize her destiny. She was uniquely well qualified to be proselytizer-in-chief, an aloof high priestess with 'a witch's charm' (Suffragettes often told her that had she 'lived in earlier days she would have been burnt as a witch'). Nothing should thwart Mrs Pankhurst now. With ever-increasing urgency she heckled, agitated, led processions and deputations, campaigned in by-elections, addressed meetings, was ejected from meetings and created disgraceful scenes. But other Suffragettes were being arrested and imprisoned. Mrs Pankhurst would not be outdone in self-abnegation. In March 1907 she gave up her registrarship, packed all her belongings and embarked on the glory trail for good, travelling the country with a repertoire of speeches which kept her bathed in limelight. She did not scruple to sacrifice even her frail adolescent son Harry. With disastrous consequences to his health, she apprenticed him to a Buddhist builder of slums in Glasgow who shortly went bankrupt.

Mrs Pankhurst herself was better off as a full-time evangelist. Her expensive clothes and extravagant ways could be justified as professional necessities and the access of so many silked and satinned ladies to the cause, though it occasioned some internal dissent, filled the war chest. The support of the affluent Pethick-Lawrences was especially valuable. Believing themselves to be, as Mrs Pethick-Lawrence later said, 'agents of unseen forces that are guiding the evolution of the world', husband and wife worked so busily that they had to make appointments even to see each other. Fred Pethick-Lawrence was a clever, altruistic lawyer who helped Christabel to manage the efficient WSPU organization and edited the newspaper,

Votes for Women. Elegant and well-born ('All our family go to Heaven'), Emmeline Pethick-Lawrence became treasurer of the WSPU. Like other Suffragettes she had previously been engaged in a bizarre form of Edwardian philanthropy, the endeavour to restore to the brutalized urban masses their lost sense of the pulsating joy of Merrie England by means of folk songs and Morris dances. Now she invested her eurhythmic exuberance in 'the greatest spiritual and moral awakening that has taken place for centuries'. With the rapt expression of a visionary or a somnambulist, she roused well-bred young ladies to yield up their money or their lives to the movement: 'Come with us! Come! Come! You will come!' But like Mrs Pankhurst, who rejoiced that her daughter was a political genius limited by none of her mother's human weaknesses, Mrs Pethick-Lawrence always deferred to Christabel. As for Mr Pethick-Lawrence, he found the eldest Miss Pankhurst 'quite irresistible'. Indeed, the Pethick-Lawrences and Christabel all lived at Clement's Inn, above the expanding offices of the WSPU. There they formed an intimate group from which Mrs Pankhurst was, as she complained to Sylvia with scalding tears of jealousy, virtually excluded.

However, Mrs Pankhurst was invariably on hand during crises and she was always summoned from the 'preaching platform' to conduct 'executions'. There was, for example, the sad case of Mrs Montefiore who sucked cocaine lozenges, had been involved in some 'scandal' and lacked that humble 'delicacy of heart' so vital to ladies 'who work in this cause'. A Suffragette reported, 'Mrs Pankhurst was heated and spoke plainly – as she can! – in the interview with her which was practically a dismissal; she seems to have been overheard speaking to her daughter even more plainly, a most unfortunate thing.' Another woman was formally censured by a packed committee of paid Suffragette organizers under Mrs Pankhurst's direction, without a hearing or even a notification that she was being tried. In 1907 disaffected Suffragettes, led by Teresa Billington ('a wrecker' in Mrs Pankhurst's view) and that gallant old sandal-wearing, fruit-juice-drinking, theosophizing suffragist Mrs Despard, protested about the WSPU's severing its links with the Independent Labour Party. They criticized the gradual exclusion of working-class women from the Suffragette ranks and the policy of 'Votes for Ladies'.

What might have been a revolution in the female condition seemed to have become a charade of rebellion mounted for the self-aggrandizement of its star mummers. According to Teresa Billington-Greig*, the Suffragettes' poverty of spirit was summed up in such remarks as, ' "I do interrupt meetings but I am a perfect lady,' " and ' "I knocked off a policeman's helmet, but I only want a little thing, a quite respectable thing – a vote." ' The dissidents tried to use constitutional means to destroy the power of the ruling clique. With a dramatic gesture Mrs Pankhurst declared, 'I shall tear up the constitution!' So she did, causing the first great schism in the Suffragette body – the secessionists formed a new sect, the Women's Freedom League. Mrs Pankhurst never seemed to grasp the incongruity of her new position, autocrat of a movement dedicated to the extension of democracy. But then an uncultivated mind was as much the attribute of an Edwardian lady as was a 'cultured' mien. Christabel said proudly that her mother was feminine to a degree 'in her ability to "jump", as it is called, to a conclusion'. A woman thinking was like a dog standing on its hind legs... Mrs Pankhurst had no pretensions to mannish intellectual subtlety: as she told Ethel Smyth, 'I am simply an agitator.'

Agitation brought its due recompense. Early in 1908 Mrs Pankhurst was assaulted by a gang of roughs during

* As she became on her marriage.

a Devon by-election. In a fainting state, convinced that they intended to roll her around Newton Abbot in a barrel, she was rescued by the police. Still white, weak and shaken, she determined now to graduate into the noble company of Suffragette martyrs, to attain her 'Holloway degree'. Taking as her cue the adoring cries from Caxton Hall – 'Mrs Pankhurst must not go! We cannot spare her!' – she limped, with a band of twelve disciples, towards the men's Parliament. On the way she was arrested as 'a common brawler', a charge she indignantly rebutted. Found guilty, she would neither pay a fine nor be bound over to keep the peace. So, in her fiftieth year (Mrs Pankhurst would never give her age in court), she was sentenced to her first term of imprisonment – six weeks in the Second (unprivileged) Division. It was, she recollected later, like being buried alive. The Black Maria was 'a hearse of many coffins', each one enclosing a blasted female soul. Holloway was an underworld of the debased, the despairing and the depraved – one of the subterranean cells in which Mrs Pankhurst was entombed was made intolerable to her not so much by the plank bed, the damp, the cockroaches, the disgusting sanitary conditions, as by obscene graffiti carved on the door. The public disrobing ('Unfasten your chests', instructed the wardress), the ritual search, the filthy bath, all these were dehumanizing indignities. But nothing affronted and demoralized Mrs Pankhurst more than the prison uniform. The clumsy, mis-mated shoes, the coarse brown woollen stockings with red stripes, (lack of garters made her feel naked) the 'hideous prison dress stamped all over with the broad arrow of disgrace', the 'small Dutch cap' which, as Lady Constance Lytton noted, had to be treated with 'the utmost reverence' because it was 'white and starched' – these were grave clothes indeed. Most sinister of all were the nether garments, old, patched and discoloured in 'a revolting and suggestive manner'; the Suffragette actress

Kitty Marion described these 'undies' as 'ugly reflections' of the authorities' minds. Christabel said that prison itself was emblematic of women's political bondage. But to Mrs Pankhurst confinement was purgatory. The lack of reading matter (the Bible was only good for summoning up fits of feminist rage) troubled a mind not given to repose. The loneliness tormented a spirit incapable of serenity. Mrs Pankhurst's migraines recurred and she was transferred to the prison hospital. There the enforced inactivity so galled her that she pleaded for something to sew.

Unprompted, the government released Mrs Pankhurst before the end of her sentence. She was thus able to achieve a sensational apotheosis on the stage of the Albert Hall, where Suffragettes had gathered to celebrate the culmination of a 'self-denial week' which raised over £7,000 for the cause. Her skin was almost transparent. Her face shone with an unearthly pallor. Her eyes were deep-sunken, yet irradiated with a zealot's light. Her voice rose again to its wonted pitch. 'The old cry was "you will never rouse women." We have done what they thought, and what they hoped was impossible; we women are roused!' Wave upon wave of emotion broke over Mrs Pankhurst. The huge audience hurrahed; women sprang from their seats, stretching their hands towards her. One Suffragette later wrote that Mrs Pankhurst held out a light to the world, led the crusade with supreme inspiration.

She was... a mighty spirit in a fragile frame, endowed with superb courage, mental and physical, an indomitable will, great natural dignity at all times and the keenest sense of duty. Her wonderful eloquence and beautiful voice appealed to all, and stirred all hearts with a desire to help her carry on the fight. She had an indescribably gracious personality, and her courteous manner carried with it such straightness of purpose...

Mrs Pankhurst was unique, because to know her was to love her and to love her was to follow her.

To be sure, her 'feelings on sex problems' were 'rigid and wanting in elasticity', but she was so 'plucky', such 'a perfect brick', that no act of self-surrender was too extravagant to perform in her name. Suffragettes 'raided' the House of Commons in furniture vans. They harangued MPs from the river. They distributed leaflets by balloon. They chained themselves to railings. They insinuated themselves into meetings by forging tickets, by hiding in organ lofts, by squirming under platforms. They permeated Society: one Suffragette reportedly entered a reception 'disguised as a lady'. They even made so bold as to invade the sanctuary of the golf course and on one lamentable occasion they caused Mr Asquith to foozle his drive. Above all they processed, with marshals, bands, pageantry, insignia and colours – green for hope, purple for dignity, white for purity. They consciously modelled themselves on the Salvation Army, which had counted it all honour to be a 'jail-bird for Jesus'. But even though the Suffragettes mounted the largest political demonstration ever seen in Britain – perhaps half a million people, many drawn by curiosity, rallied at Hyde Park in June 1908 – the vote seemed as distant as ever. Mrs Pankhurst had marched under a huge banner inscribed with the word RECTITUDE. But it was apparent to her that Asquith's morally flaccid government could neither aspire to rectitude itself nor respond to that quality in others. Feverishly Mrs Pankhurst searched round for some new expedient, perhaps an Irish rather than a Salvationist one. 'I want to be tried for sedition,' she cried.

In the summer of 1908 Mrs Pankhurst condoned, though she did not initiate, the first deliberate Suffragette attack on property, the dispatch of two 'flinty messages', as she called them, through the windows of 10 Downing

Street. In October, having issued a handbill urging the populace to help Suffragettes '*RUSH the House of Commons*', Mrs Pankhurst, Christabel and 'General' Drummond were arrested. Lady Constance Lytton, a strict vegetarian won over to the cause by perceiving in the maltreatment of a sheep on its way to the slaughterhouse a revelation of 'the position of women throughout the world', visited the Bow Street cells and was struck by the 'splendour of defiance and indignation' which pervaded Mrs Pankhurst's countenance. The prisoner complained of the cold – the blankets were 'almost certainly verminous'. A friendly MP hastened to the Savoy hotel which quickly provided comfortable beds and a table set with damask cloths, 'silver, flowers, tall wax candles, gaily coloured fruit'. Three waiters served an elaborate meal while the gaolers looked on with respectful awe. At the trial Mrs Pankhurst was keen that Christabel should demonstrate her legal expertise. And Christabel did, indeed, achieve the great coup of summoning two members of the government, Lloyd George and Herbert Gladstone, as witnesses of the incitement to breach the peace. The Suffragettes and the press made much of Christabel's clever cross-examination and more of her fresh white muslin dress with the broad band of purple, white and green stripes around her lissome waist, of the silky curls with just a hint of gold in them clustering demurely about her neck, of her alabaster skin and rose-petal cheeks, more exquisitely flushed than usual. But though she was 'bright and dainty as a newly opened flower' and though she up-staged both magistrate and ministers, Christabel could not steal the scene from so experienced a tragedienne as her mother. With 'mournful melody' Mrs Pankhurst expatiated on the 'difficulty which women have in throwing off their natural diffidence', on their patience, self-restraint and lack of hysteria. She concluded with a flourish, 'We are here, not because we are law-breakers; we are here in our efforts to become lawmakers.' Even the police were moved to tears. The magistrate, who had been accused of presiding over 'the Star Chamber of the twentieth century', sentenced her to three months in Holloway. This time she would not submit to being stripped and searched. And after a week she broke the soul-searing silence. As they tramped, in single file, round the prison yard she cried out, 'Christabel, stand still till I come to you!' Trembling, she linked arms with her daughter and began talking to her in low, vibrant tones. A wardress rushed up: 'I shall listen to everything you say!' 'You are welcome to do that, but I shall insist on my right to speak to my daughter!' Pandemonium broke loose, whistles were blown, more wardresses arrived and the Suffragette leader was marched off to solitary confinement amid the excited shouts of her supporters, 'Three cheers for Mrs Pankhurst!'

V

How could that applause be prolonged? How could Mrs Pankhurst sustain the Suffragettes' spirit and the movement's momentum? Her own early 'cerebral excitement', noticed by the Holloway authorities, was soon deadened by protracted incarceration. And no new tactic, certainly not the systematic defiance of prison rules which Mrs Pankhurst pronouned official policy at her release breakfast, seemed capable of moving the government. Admittedly Suffragette morale was still buoyed up by the rapture of self-denial and, what Lady Constance Lytton experienced at Cannon Row Police Station after her first arrest, 'the delights of that full, unfettered companionship' with those who worked for the cause. Many of Lady Con's fellows lived on that high emotional level (though none of them followed her example in prison – in an ecstasy of self-laceration she attempted to inscribe the motto 'Votes for Women' on her chest with a needle) and their hero-worship was not confined to Mrs Pankhurst. One Suffragette appealed to Helen Ogston, who had flogged the male curs attacking her at a political meeting, 'Let me touch the hand that used the dog-whip!' Other Suffragettes were ravished by the actor Forbes-Robertson's speech which ended with this invocation:

Mary Wollstonecraft! John Stuart Mill! May your spirits, your beautiful, noble and generous spirits, look down upon us, and assist and encourage us to soften the hearts of those opposed to us! And when the hour of our victory comes – as most certainly it will – may the Master of all convey to you the joyous news, that you may rejoice greatly with us.

For some reason Mr Asquith remained unaffected by the intercession of the feminist saints. Perhaps Mrs Pankhurst and Christabel sensed what really stirred him – the fear that Suffragettes might tear off all his clothes. At any rate, by the autumn of 1909 the WSPU leaders adopted more forceful measures. These, spontaneously developed by the rank and file, were the hustling of Cabinet Ministers wherever possible, the hunger strike and the destruction of private property. The last particularly offended public feeling. Mrs Pankhurst proclaimed that to stop it would be 'folly, weakness and wickedness' and a betrayal of her 'sacred trust'.

The appeal for greater self-sacrifice was ever Mrs Pankhurst's recipe for success. 'Just as it is in the hottest furnace that steel is most finely tempered, so it is in this hour of fiercest trial that the great spirit of women is being called forth...every successive act of repression brings new recruits to the corps for active service.' As the Suffragettes mortified their flesh they sanctified the soul of the movement. Neither stone walls nor iron bars could contain such spiritual force, and Christabel claimed that only now, as emaciated women burst their bonds, was it possible to understand 'the true manner and meaning of the miracles of old times'. The suffering of the hunger strikers was made that much more sublime when the authorities resorted to forcible feeding. The politicians called it 'hospital treatment'. The Suffragettes knew it as a 'violation' of their starved bodies, a kind of oral, nasal or rectal rape symbolizing the base treatment to which women had been subjected by men throughout the ages. Mrs Pankhurst denounced this 'torture' unsparingly, but she found it difficult to disguise the elements of artifice and illogic in her impeachment. Wearing the aspect of violent rebels her Suffragettes provoked the government, but when it duly retaliated they took on the air of blameless victims. Mrs Pankhurst was both a militant who courted martyrdom as a means of inspiring women to cast off their shackles and a lady who condemned persecution as an outrage against the privileges of her sex. She brazened out the incongruity, nowhere with greater panache than on her first visit to the United States in October 1909. An Amazon of 'genteel feminine appearance', Boadicea attired in a violet chiffon velvet gown lined with dull green silk, she won 'wild hurrahs' from a Carnegie Hall audience with her first words, 'I am what you call a hooligan!' Her triumphal tour not only raised money for the Suffragettes, it gave 'a distinct fillip' to the suffragist movement in the United States, though Mrs Pankhurst found the 'definite opposition' of the English male more manageable than the 'half-amused indifference which I see in the men of America'. This transatlantic trip involved Mrs Pankhurst in a supreme sacrifice of her own. She had gone in the knowledge that her son Harry, having been sent (against doctor's advice) to work on the land after the failure of the Buddhist builder, was seriously ill with infantile paralysis. Others could nurse him, she thought; only she could fulfil her mission. On her return she was greeted with a giant banner announcing 'No Surrender. Welcome Mrs Pankhurst, Liberator of Women', and the news that Harry would never walk again. In despair she exclaimed, 'He would be better dead!' He soon was, his mother's anguish being aggravated by the presence of a rival, Harry's sweetheart, at his deathbed. After the funeral, Sylvia recalled, Mrs Pankhurst 'was broken as I had never seen her; huddled together without a care for her appearance, she seemed an old, plain, cheerless woman. Her utter dejection moved me more than her vanished charm.'

Despite this bereavement Mrs Pankhurst remained an old woman in a hurry. She was 'unscrupulous', as Teresa Billington-Greig wrote, in never counting the cost of her acts but 'human and appealing' in paying the price with a pang and sorrowing over it. Still, after campaigning against Asquith in forty constituencies during the first election of 1910, Mrs Pankhurst unwillingly agreed to a suspension of what Christabel called 'mild militancy'. The hope was that the new Parliament would pass an all-party 'Conciliation Bill' giving votes to about a million female property-owners, ladies to the last woman. Asquith opposed it on principle. Of course, he held the traditional view that women's 'natural sphere is not the turmoil and dust of politics, but the circle of social and domestic life'. And he enjoyed the caressing company of frivolous women of his own circle too much to risk their being metamorphosed into prickly seekers after notoriety, certainly dangerous and probably demented, like Mrs Pankhurst. She would scarcely have permitted the Prime Minister to take her hand, as he took that of Viscount Esher's daughter when she sat beside him on a sofa at Garsington, and cause it (in Lytton Strachey's words) to 'feel his erected instrument under his trousers'. However, Asquith had sound, political reasons for regarding the Suffragettes as

'Toryettes' and for resisting the enfranchisement of women who would be predominantly Conservative. Seeing the proposed voters in terms of their class as much as their sex, he resisted the Conciliation Bill as undemocratic. Thus on 18 November 1910, 'Black Friday', Mrs Pankhurst resumed hostilities.

She led a huge phalanx of Suffragettes on Parliament. When the police (unfortunately a rough contingent from the East End unaccustomed to the ways of ladies) barred their progress, a violent and prolonged struggle ensued. Its sexual overtones were shockingly pronounced. The women described many cases of brutal and indecent assault, the most frequent complaint being that their breasts were twisted, pinched, screwed, nipped and wrung. One policeman clutched a Suffragette by the thigh: 'Unhand it, sir!' 'My old dear, I can grip you where I like today.' Another policeman accompanied his 'consciously sensual' actions by a remark which exposed their psychological root: 'You have been wanting this for a long time, haven't you?' Mrs Pankhurst was horrified. 'Is there not a man in the House of Commons who will stand up for us?' she expostulated. The new Home Secretary, Winston Churchill, obliged by releasing about a hundred arrested women, those who had not broken windows. Their detention and trial, with another election pending, was not to the 'public advantage'. The following day Mrs Pankhurst announced to the Women's Parliament, 'I am going to Downing Street: come along all of you!' The police were taken by surprise. Asquith and Augustine Birrell incautiously showed their faces and they were mobbed in what came to be known as the Battle of Downing Street. The Prime Minister, looking white and frightened, like a fascinated rabbit, had some broken glass stuffed down his neck before effecting his escape in a taxi. The Chief Secretary for Ireland became the victim of what he indignantly termed 'a brutal, outrageous and unprovoked assault... it may have lamed me for life.' The

> hags... pulled me about and hustled me, 'stroked' my face, knocked off my hat and kicked it about, and one whose unpleasant features yet dwell in my memory harangued me with 'Oh! you wicked man; you must be a wicked man not to help us.'

Mrs Pankhurst and her myrmidons were arrested, but again the charges were dropped. With the prospect of reviving the Conciliation Bill and in an access of loyalty summoned up by the approaching coronation of George V, the widow of the Red Republican Doctor resumed the truce.

She did so reluctantly. Mrs Pankhurst came not to bring peace but the sword. By now danger was her element. Excitement was her salamander's fire. Drama was her drug. Unresting, unceasing, she continued the campaign by other means. She organized resistance to the national census – women did not count so they should not be numbered. (*Punch* inevitably remarked that the ladies had taken leave of their census.) She inveighed more frequently against the white slave traffic and sexual assaults upon children, flaying her male auditors unmercifully. 'Men!...men!...I know what shame is in your hearts!' she cried at one meeting. Masculine heads bowed. Such contrition! 'What DEARS men are!' she enthused to Ethel Smyth afterwards, her 'wonderful light-holding eyes shining like stars'. In her fast motor, the present of an American admirer, Mrs Pankhurst toured the country impressing audiences by her 'absolute sincerity, her freedom from all cant, pose and artificiality'. She rode like an empress, not even getting out of the car when it was stopped by punctures, leaving everything to her young chauffeuse – whose parents considered that in serving such a 'dreadful woman' their daughter was being embraced by 'the dark arms of Hell'. On one occasion, though, Mrs Pankhurst did alight. Driving to a rally at the

Albert Hall the car struck a member of the booing, jeering crowd. Hatred and menace were in the air as Mrs Pankhurst leapt out to succour 'the blowzy victim of Suffragette brutality'. Like one born to command Mrs Pankhurst ordered a policeman to fetch an ambulance. Her obvious distress, her sincere regret that because of the meeting she could not take the injured woman to hospital, transformed the bystanders' mood. Soon they were solacing her, taking a collection for her, urging her not to be late. Her face, 'soft with pity, radiant with love, was the face of an angel'. Safely back in the motor Mrs Pankhurst could be heard fulminating in a furious undertone, 'Drunken old beast. I wish we'd run her over.'

While the armistice lasted at home Mrs Pankhurst felt constrained to make two more sorties to the United States, in 1910 and 1911. The challenge of new audiences made the blood sing in her veins. Americans welcomed her as 'the fourteen-inch gun of the militant suffrage party'. Americans were amused by her accounts of how Mr Asquith had been forced to slide through a mail chute to evade the Suffragettes. Americans did not scoff at her claim that Californian women owed their enfranchisement, won in 1911, 'very largely to the impetus given to the movement by the agitation in England'. Above all Americans were susceptible to her brand of genteel revivalism. When she addressed a suffrage convention in Louisville the *Lexington Herald* reported,

The moment she appeared on the platform one realized by what power of personality she has become the best loved and best hated woman in England. We have seen William Jennings Bryan capture a convention. We have seen those we account greater than Bryan dominate men. We have never seen any personality that instantly impressed itself more than does Mrs Pankhurst. A gentlewoman she is, evidently, in all that sweet word implies; but a leader with a courage to stake all on the cast of a die.

Better than Britain, the United States, later home of Elmer Gantry and Aimée Semple Macpherson, recognized Mrs Pankhurst for what she was, an old-fashioned Holiness preacher. Americans realized that she was primarily 'out for purity'. After an address at Milwaukee the audience crowded eagerly round her at the rostrum ejaculating, 'You are a God-send!' 'God give you health!' 'You've converted me!' Shortly afterwards Mrs Pankhurst heard that the government had finally 'torpedoed' (the word was Lloyd George's) the Conciliation Bill. 'Protest imperative,' she cabled. By January 1912 she had returned to England. Her new watchwords were 'Sedition' and 'The Women's Revolution'.

VI

The Suffragette agitation reached its climax just at a time when Mrs Pankhurst was experiencing what Sylvia called 'the flood-tide of the last great energies of her personality'. In this period, immediately before the First World War, the most full-blooded Suffragette violence coincided with the most consummate Suffragette puritanism. The harshness of male retaliation and the extremism of Mrs Pankhurst and her eldest daughter drove their forces underground, replaced open demonstration by secret arson. 'Militancy,' wrote Christabel, 'is doing the work of purification.' By winning women the power to outlaw vice, Suffragette violence aimed to end all violence, especially that done to white slaves, assaulted children and the like. But as the subversives dwelt upon the evils of the opposite sex, as they embraced the 'scientific' doctrine that 'life is feminine' and that the male element is 'primarily an excrescence, a superfluity, a waste product of nature', as they consorted furtively together, so their feminist impulses quickened. Homosexuality is the ultimate expression of male or female chauvinism, just as incest is the ultimate expression of social snobbery. And some of Mrs Pankhurst's followers prosecuted the sex war with such vehemence that it is impossible to discount some kind of sapphic incentive – one Suffragette advocated the segregation of married women on the grounds that they were 'contaminated'. Other evidence confirms the supposition. Mrs Pethick-Lawrence and Annie Kenney paraded their attraction for one another so openly that Teresa Billington-Greig 'saw it as something unbalanced and primitive and possibly dangerous to the movement'. Christabel sent hothouse missives to the WSPU secretary, Mrs Tuke: 'My dear and darling Pansy...with very very much love'. And Ethel Smyth, with her mannish hats, her tweed jackets and her green, purple and white ties, fell passionately in love with Mrs Pankhurst (who forgave her sartorial eccentricity). Dame Ethel was later to develop a similar infatuation for Virginia Woolf, who described her wooing as 'hideous and horrid and melancholy sad. It is like being caught by a giant crab.'

Mrs Pankhurst did not spurn this novel attachment. True, her deepest feelings were always bound up with Christabel ('my fellow – a born bachelor', said Ethel Smyth). And, wholly engaged in her mission, Mrs Pankhurst had held aloof from other emotional entanglements. But, as Ethel Smyth wrote to her 'darling Em',

I am the glorious exception for you – and I think it is the crowning achievement of my life to have made you love me. And proof of your cleverness to have found me – and found a new gift in yourself – the friendship you give me. Yes, I also am getting more and more 'off' men.

Ethel Smyth was a powerful woman and her advances were difficult to resist. Mrs Pankhurst did not try. At this fraught stage of her career, the fabric of her slight body wasted by repeated hunger strikes, the wings of her swift spirit clipped by constant imprisonments, this intimacy seemed to satisfy her most profound psychological needs. Mrs Pankhurst had always accepted the traditional view that woman's moral nature was infinitely superior to man's. Ladies were the better half, though, of course, the sexes should be absolutely equal in terms of civil rights. She had invariably exalted chastity as the female virtue to which males should aspire. But by 1913 she endorsed Christabel's assertion that most of women's ailments and disabilities stemmed from diseases contracted from those seventy-five per cent of males suffering from gonorrhoea and syphilis. Men seemed incapable of following the Pankhursts' admonition to conserve 'the complex seminal fluid, with its wonderfully invigorating influence', despite Christabel's warning that 'the secretion of the testicles. . . if wrongfully used. . . is so potent that it may figuratively be classed with the secretions of the poison fangs of venomous reptiles.' Thus women should avoid their embraces altogether. Mrs Pankhurst positively advised against marriage 'unless you care so much that you cannot help it'. Not, of course, that she favoured Lesbianism. But she found much-needed comfort in the bosom of Ethel Smyth, who wrote to 'my treasure and my pride',

> I lie awake at night sometimes and see you like Atlas, bearing up the world of women on your head. I can't tell you what I think of you. . . If you were to come in now all I could do would be to hold you in my arms. . . and be silent.

Mrs Pankhurst responded as warmly to Ethel Smyth's endearments as she did to her music. She also found the composer an able tutor in the *recherché* art of breaking

Mrs Pankhurst in
about 1904

Mrs Pankhurst being
arrested near Buckingham
Palace in 1914

Mrs Pankhurst, Nurse Pine
and detectives

Mrs Pankhurst in New York after her release from Ellis Island, 1913

windows. Together they went to practise on Hook Heath.
Mrs Pankhurst's first stone shot backwards, narrowly
missing Ethel Smyth's dog. Wearing a scowl of ferocious
concentration, Mrs Pankhurst tried and tried again.
Finally she hit the target and 'a smile of such beatitude –
the smile of a baby that has blown a watch open – stole
across her countenance'.

In fact 'the argument of the stone', as deployed by Mrs
Pankhurst, proved singularly ineffective; for, leading an
assault by some of 'our bad, bold ones' on 10 Downing
Street in March 1912, both her missiles flew wide of the
mark. And although the Prime Minister's windows were
smashed, and although the main shopping streets of
London resounded to the tinkle of glass as cohorts of
fashionably dressed women produced hammers from
handbags and flints from muffs, the effect was to enrage
the public not to coerce the politicians. Mrs Pankhurst's
indisputably great achievement had been to make women's
suffrage a major national issue, something forty years of
constitutional agitation had failed to do. Now her sight
was dimmed by floods of dazzling limelight, her vision
was obscured by cataracts of sectarian enthusiasm. She
talked grandiosely of destroying governments but she
failed to perceive that her violence was back-firing, that it
was chiefly, like her stone-throwing, a danger to her own
followers. The 'madness of the militants' was universally
condemned. They were fanatics, hysterics, unfit to vote.
No less a person than Sir Almroth Wright said so, in a
letter to *The Times*. More, the eminent bacteriologist
indicted women in general as tending to become morally
warped and mentally sick in response to 'the reverber-
ations of their physiological emergencies' – sexual frustration, menstrual tension, menopausal disorder and
Lesbian perversion. This was somewhat strong for contemporary taste and the letter was denounced as porno-
graphy. But militant behaviour certainly seemed to

confirm Leo Maxse's view that 'female suffrage would be worse than a German invasion in the way of a national calamity.' Lloyd George was not alone in thinking that Christabel had lost all sense of reality: 'It's just like going to a lunatic asylum and talking to a man who thinks he's God Almighty.' Even the Anti-Suffragist movement was temporarily able to mask the fundamental absurdity of its position – for the more successfully its female members conducted their campaign the more decisively they demonstrated women's fitness to participate in politics. Mrs Pankhurst ignored 'the priceless Antis'. Back in 'that horrible Holloway' she kept up her spirits by joining in the Suffragette sing-song, her 'queer cracked voice' rising tunelessly to the strains of the 'March of the Women' as its composer, Ethel Smyth, conducted from a cell window 'in almost Bacchic frenzy with a toothbrush'.

Suffering from bronchitis, she was soon released to face a much more serious charge than stone-throwing. With the Pethick-Lawrences (Christabel escaped to concert future operations from the safety and comfort of Paris) Mrs Pankhurst was accused of conspiracy to damage property. The trial was notable both for its revelation that the Suffragettes kept a code-book in which Cabinet Ministers were identified by the names of 'the commonest weeds' and for Mrs Pankhurst's spirited defence. 'Swifter and more impassioned than a tigress', she was 'by turns petulant, imperious and appealing'. Her hottest denial was reserved for the allegation that the WSPU was a collection of 'unimportant wild women'. It contained ladies like herself (indeed, she owed her leadership to her superior social standing) ladies who would not dream of biting, kicking or wielding hatpins. 'We have always put up an honourable fight.' The jury were impressed by the purity of her motives, but they found her guilty and she was sentenced to nine months' imprisonment. With her fellows she went on hunger strike. Holloway became a Gehenna, as all around her Suffragettes endured the agony of being stuffed like Christmas turkeys. Eventually a deputation of doctors and nurses proposed to subject Mrs Pankhurst to the same revolting treatment. 'If any of you dare take a step inside this cell, I shall defend myself!' she threatened, seizing a heavy earthenware chamber-pot. They withdrew in disarray. The government apparently feared the lengths to which Mrs Pankhurst would go if they fed her by force. So, a wraith, she was freed. She journeyed to Paris to recuperate amid an orgy of shopping.

Now Mrs Pankhurst and her daughter began to talk in terms of guerilla tactics, civil war. The Pethick-Lawrences demurred and in one of 'her summer-storms of anger' Mrs Pankhurst blazed, 'If you do not support Christabel's policy we shall smash you!' The Pethick-Lawrences departed for Canada unperturbed. On their return, in October 1912, they discovered what an 'extreme and violent person' Mrs Pankhurst was, how 'ruthless', how 'insensitive to ordinary human considerations', 'like some irresistible force of nature – a tidal wave, or a river in full flood'. The Pethick-Lawrences were treated like pariahs, no one would talk to them, their offices had vanished. Finally Mrs Pankhurst (gladdened by regaining spiritual possession of Christabel) announced their expulsion from the WSPU. Having supported her dictatorship in 1907, they could only challenge it now at the expense of the cause 'to which we have contributed our life-blood'. So they accepted the *coup*, continued to edit *Votes for Women* (Christabel began a rival paper, *The Suffragette*) and allowed Mrs Pankhurst to veil the rift, to plead for union and to foment bolder militancy. Like some accomplished high-wire artist, she gave a dizzying performance (Fred Pethick-Lawrence admired it as a means of winning sympathy and condemned it as an exercise in 'play-acting') which inspired the Albert Hall audience with the vertigo of her own self-sacrifice. She lamented the sorrows of women who had 'exposed themselves to the indecent violence' of the mob. She mourned the fate of outraged and diseased young girls. She concluded, 'Be militant each in your own way. . . I incite this meeting to rebellion. I say to the Government: You have not dared to take the leaders of Ulster for their incitement to rebellion. Take me if you dare.' The 'Panks' thus triumphed over the 'Peths', but the loss of its less extreme wing left the movement sadly unbalanced. Having excommunicated the Pethick-Lawrences, Mrs Pankhurst never communicated with them again.

The Suffragettes burned to vote. Public buildings and private houses went up in flames. Letter-boxes were assaulted, railway stations were attacked, telephone wires were cut, orchids were destroyed, putting greens were damaged with acid, works of art were defaced, churches were gutted, bombs were planted. One exploded, destroying Lloyd George's new house at Walton, the 'Bombazines' or 'Outragettes' leaving as sinister evidence of their guilt 'two broken hat-pins, a hairpin, and a golosh indisputably feminine'. Old ladies bought gun licences to terrify the authorities. Envelopes containing red pepper and snuff were sent to all Cabinet Ministers. Mrs Pankhurst took full responsibility for everything. But in April 1913 she pleaded innocent to the charge of inciting to commit a felony on the grounds that she had not done so 'wickedly and maliciously'. From the bench the 'red-robed mumbler, cruel, hard' (as a Suffragette called him) dismissed Mrs Pankhurst's plea and her justification – it included a tale about a judge being found dead in a brothel which his lordship found both irrelevant and improper. The rest of her defence consisted of a searing condemnation of London's 'regulated traffic. . . in little children. . . [who are] being trained to minister to the vicious pleasures of persons who ought to know better in their positions in life'. From the dock Mrs Pankhurst breathed fiery defiance:

I feel I have done my duty. I look upon myself as a prisoner of war. I am under no moral obligation to conform to, or in any way accept, the sentence imposed upon me. . . I shall fight, I shall fight, I shall fight, from the moment I enter prison.

She was condemned to three years' penal servitude. The 'Cat and Mouse' Act, recently passed, ensured that released hunger-strikers could be re-arrested at will to continue their sentences. Nevertheless starvation was the limbo through which she must pass to attain even temporary freedom. For ten days Mrs Pankhurst endured its pains, depressed, miserable, spurning the delicacies thoughtfully placed in her cell. Only once was she roused, when the prison governor, smelling strongly of drink, offered to fetch her a minister. Her conscience was clear!

Finally Mrs Pankhurst was liberated 'on licence', a document which, with a mummer's flourish, she tore up in front of the governor as her valedictory act: 'I have no intention of obeying this infamous law.' The 'Queen' then dragged her macerated carcase through the prison gates, to be greeted rapturously by her 'subjects', who had been keeping long vigil outside. Soon she was recovering, revelling in the 'sportingness' of the struggle, eating fish and drinking champagne, complaining that to have her movements spied on by the police was an 'intolerable insult'. 'All the old Adam (or, Eve, which is better) is coming back, and I begin to realize the glorious fight ahead of me.' The fight consisted of rhythmic rounds of detentions and releases (ten of each in the fifteen months before the armistice of August 1914) interspersed by moments of high excitement as she addressed meetings or evaded capture. At this she became adept, with the help of veiled decoys dressed in her clothes. She had only to cry, 'Women, they are arresting me!' for her specially trained bodyguard of athletic young women to leap to the rescue, wielding Indian clubs. After one escape she exulted, 'The girl who had her head cut open would not have it stitched as she wanted to keep the scar as big as possible! The real warrior spirit!' Mrs Pankhurst paid for the drama with pounds of flesh. By refusing to rest or to drink, she made her fasts quick indeed, but deathly. That her periods of liberty were purchased at a fearful price can be seen in her description of the effects of hunger, thirst and sleep strikes.

> The body cannot endure the loss of moisture. It cries out in protest with every nerve. The muscles waste, the skin becomes shrunken and flabby, the facial appearance alters horribly...Every natural function is, of course, suspended...The body becomes cold and shivery, there is constant headache and nausea, and sometimes there is fever. The mouth and tongue become coated and swollen, the throat thickens and the voice sinks to a thready whisper.

Having refused to let the prison doctor examine her ('I gave him one of my storms..."You are a Government torturer." ') Mrs Pankhurst would emerge, desiccated, skeletal, the yellow parchment skin so tightly drawn over her face that it seemed the bones must break through, to be kept in 'cotton wool' until she was sufficiently recovered to endure the hell once more. This cycle of suffering touched the wardresses themselves, over whom she had established a social ascendancy – 'All the women officers are now devoted to me...perfect angels.' The Suffragettes interrupted church services, chanting their own litany:

> Save Emmeline Pankhurst
> Spare her! Spare her!
> Give her light and set her free
> Save her! Save her!
> Hear us while we pray to thee.

Among the fascinated observers of Mrs Pankhurst's terrible waxing and waning only Christabel seemed to endure her mother's progressive mummification with unmoved fortitude. Ethel Smyth commented that in allowing her aged parent to act as scapegoat for womankind Christabel 'goes one better than God who sacrified his son – a young person!!' It was a remark which Mrs Pankhurst neither forgot nor forgave.

No one actually liked Mrs Pankhurst and Christabel: the Suffragette leaders were either abominated or worshipped. Mrs Pankhurst's evident fanaticism offended the many. Her nobly borne torments inspired the few to emulate, even to outdo her in eccentric feats of chivalry. Some, though prohibited from taking life, attempted personal violence – Philip Snowden found it necessary to protect one of his political meetings by employing as stewards wardresses from a lunatic asylum. Others made vain and embarrassing appeals to the Archbishop of Canterbury and to the yet more sacred person of the sovereign. Emily Wilding Davison, writhing with desire to make the ultimate surrender, to achieve what she called 'the supreme consummation of sacrifice', committed suicide by throwing herself in front of the monarch's horse as it raced in the Derby. (For the Suffragettes it was a sensation; for the British public it was 'such bad manners to the King'.) A specific protest against the 'slow murder' of Mrs Pankhurst by 'Iscariot politicians' was the slashing of Velasquez's 'Rokeby' Venus by Mary Richardson, a radical Suffragette who later attempted to start a communist nunnery. With the tortured logic that is the first refuge of fanatics everywhere, she argued that justice was an element of beauty as much as colour and form. 'I have tried to destroy the picture of the most beautiful woman in mythological history as a protest against the government for destroying Mrs Pankhurst, who is the most beautiful character in modern history.' At a safe distance Mrs

Pankhurst attracted more than she repelled. Admittedly the United States Immigration authorities attempted to bar her entry in October 1913, detaining her on Ellis Island as a person suspected, ironically enough, of 'moral turpitude'. But the chorus of scorn and execration which greeted this affront to 'the best known of living women', claimed by some Americans to be a 'spiritual giantess' and a 'revolutionary hero' in the same class as Washington, Jefferson and Lincoln (not to mention Mrs Pankhurst's threat to go on hunger strike) secured her quick release. The headlines blazed, 'Mrs Pankhurst beats Uncle Sam.' For Mrs Pankhurst it was another 'thrilling adventure' which swelled her audiences and her takings in the United States – as Suffragette numbers dwindled she became obsessed with increasing 'monied' support. For Alice Paul and those who were to form the American Women's Party, it was a further call to employ the methods of their transatlantic sisters. Alice Paul, schooled in the Suffragette struggle, possessed an indomitable will and seems in certain respects to have modelled herself on Mrs Pankhurst, most notably in a commitment to militancy which no ridicule, no failure and no argument could shake. Ethel Smyth's judgement of Mrs Pankhurst might equally have applied to her American counterpart: as well try to hold up an avalanche with a child's spade as persuade her out of an idea that had once taken root in her mind.

Could nothing check Mrs Pankhurst's inexorable course? Among others, Sylvia attempted to divert her mother into more democratic and pacific ways, but she was ignominiously swept aside. Now Mrs Pankhurst carried on the fight for its own sake, sought martyrdom as an end in itself. For it was clear that militant tactics were actually postponing victory and that Suffragettes could never compete with, say, Irish Unionists (who were anyway monopolizing the government's attention) when it came to coercion. The inconsistency between Mrs Pankhurst's avowed aims and the means she employed to realize them was not due simply to a lady-like lack of logic. As Dr Mary Gordon, the psychiatrist at Holloway who had taken a professional interest in the Suffragette leader, explained, the WSPU had 'fire not form'. It

> leapt into being like a flame.... It released vast stores of unconscious energy... It cohered fiercely, ignoring thinking... and good order... It swept where it listed, and when its work was done died down and out... Such spiritual upheavals are always irrational, and irrational human types are swept into them as high priests.

By 1914 Mrs Pankhurst was the focus of a small, intense, chiliastic cult. Its satisfactions lay in immediate emotional climaxes, 'the exaltation, the rapture of battle,' rather than in final fulfilment, when, as Christabel prophesied, joy would mingle with 'regret that the most glorious chapter in women's history is closed'. Countrywide conversion would deprive the chief evangelist of her *raison d'être*. Only an earth-shaking event could stop Mrs Pankhurst's agitation, could afford a more sublime afflatus, could demand a more heroic sacrifice. It was provided by the outbreak of the Great War. At first Mrs Pankhurst and Christabel saw this as God's vengeance upon men for subjecting women through the ages to their lusts. After a few days, however, they were vouchsafed a new revelation: this was another holy war and the enemy was not man but German. Sexual chauvinism submitted to the paramount claims of racial jingoism.

VII

Armageddon provided a fitting new part for an experienced old trooper. It involved Mrs Pankhurst in nothing less than acting as the chief preserver of English civilization. Naturally the war must be won, at whatever cost in blood and money. Mrs Pankhurst became the flail of slackers, shirkers and strikers. She exhorted men to join the colours. She encouraged ladies to distribute white feathers. She rampaged for conscription. She led a huge procession of women demanding 'The Right to Serve'. They would strike or riot, she warned, if they were not permitted to fill male jobs and so free men for the trenches. But perhaps even more important than military success was spiritual victory. Mrs Pankhurst expressed delight that Lord Kitchener had impressed on his soldiers 'the duty to keep themselves clean and pure'. However, there were more insidious perils than germs – Germans! They were everywhere; not just in obvious places, such as Belgian nunneries and British pacifist organizations. They infested the Stock Exchange, the Churches, Westminster, the War Office, even the WSPU itself. Mrs Pankhurst called for their elimination from the government with such vehemence that her remarks verged on treason, and in 1915 she was arrested (though at once released) during a rally in Trafalgar Square. For the same reason *Britannia*, as *The Suffragette* had been re-christened, was often raided by the police. The *Daily Mail* was fairly outdone and Lord Northcliffe revised his hostile opinion of Mrs Pankhurst. They vied with one another in patriotic proscription. Ethel Smyth recorded that, on the day Asquith resigned, Mrs Pankhurst found Lord Northcliffe bouncing up and down in his chair crying:

'*I* did it... *I* did it'; and timing the 'I' on the down bounce. Mrs Pankhurst, much astonished, said something about the worst of the lot, the Foreign Office, being still in the saddle. Whereupon he leapt up, patted her on the back, and said: 'Don't you worry, my dear girl, we'll get 'em all out.'

Lord Northcliffe might have been less cordial, and less familiar, had he known that Mrs Pankhurst reckoned the root of all Germany's evil lay in its being 'a male nation', which had violated Belgium and was attempting to repeat the outrage on the 'feminine' state of France. He might also have nursed doubts about the explanation, which Mrs Pankhurst's bellicose new role had afforded her, of a puzzling pre-war phenomenon: the stewards who had ejected Suffragettes from political meetings most brutally all spoke with thick, guttural accents. They were, of course, Huns.

Mrs Pankhurst attempted to foster British civilization in other ways. When her scheme to start a home for illegitimate war babies foundered, owing to a 'lamentable lack of public spirit', she adopted four little girls herself, setting up house in London with the formidable Sister Pine, who had nursed her so diligently after hunger strikes. Perhaps Mrs Pankhurst sought recompense for the loss of Harry (whom she still mourned in moods of dejection) or even of Sylvia and Adela (whom she publicly disowned for their pacifism). Unfortunately, though, her maternal instincts remained erratic. She taught the girls to curtsy but she neglected their education. She promised, 'If you're very good you'll get the name of Pankhurst', but it was not to be – after a decade or so the children proved too expensive and three of them were handed over to rich guardians, while Christabel adopted the fourth. Meanwhile the girls had, and were, attractive properties; Mrs Pankhurst carefully rehearsed them in the business of hugging and kissing her for the benefit of photographers. Her flair for publicity never failed. Even the King had advised Lloyd George 'to make use of Mrs Pankhurst'. In 1916 she went on another tour of North America, interspersing propagandist speeches on the war with lectures on 'social hygiene' – the prevention of venereal disease. In 1917 she travelled to Russia, under official auspices, in a vain attempt to instil fighting spirit into Kerensky's armies by appeals to the soldiers' wives. She was thrilled by the female 'Battalions of Death' who paraded before her, but they proved to be aptly named, at first derided by the Russian troops they were supposed to inspire and then well-nigh exterminated by the Germans they were supposed to kill. The mind of the Russian masses had clearly been poisoned by Hun agents and Kerensky himself was obviously sick in body and weak in will. As Mrs Pankhurst departed, the Provisional Government was teetering towards its downfall and she received a sinister warning that the new World Enemy was to be Bolshevism. It had actually been suggested that her safety could not be assured in the streets of Petrograd unless she wore hideous 'proletarian' clothes.

The purifying fire of Mrs Pankhurst's present convictions seemed to devour her past. She never paused, never hesitated, never looked back. She despised 'potterers', waverers, compromisers, reminiscers. Perhaps the crowning irony of Mrs Pankhurst's career was her vitriolic attack on Asquith when, in 1916, he announced his conversion to female suffrage. It was more important, she asserted, for all servicemen to be enfranchised. Votes for women could take second place. Asquith was guilty of using women as 'catspaws' to 'dish' the defenders of the realm 'while any and every crank, coward or traitor, is to be free to vote as usual'. However, her sex had patently earned the ballot. In 1918 Lloyd George, anxious to avoid a renewal of Suffragette militancy, at last did justice to women – to those, at least, over thirty. The triumph of enfranchisement was marred for Mrs Pankhurst by the fact that Christabel, standing as a candidate at Smethwick on the ticket of a man she had so often denounced as 'Oily' George, was defeated by a Socialist. Bernard Shaw's acid comments on the general election were understandable. Instead of elevating politics to a nobler plane

MRS PANKHURST

Women voted for hanging the Kaiser; rallied hysterically round the worst male candidates; threw out all the women candidates of tried ability, integrity and devotion; and elected just one titled lady of great wealth and singular demagogic fascination.

Of course this proved nothing, except perhaps the soundness of Mrs Poyser's celebrated judgement that women were fools, God having made them to match men. Mrs Pankhurst, at any rate, had no time to consider the effects of women's suffrage. To do so might have involved her in that untimeliest of fates – anticlimax. In 1918, and once more in 1919, she toured North America at Lloyd George's behest. Again she was the inspired preacher, uttering fiery comminations, speaking with tongue of flame, bearing the torch for her new mission. Its practical aim was the abolition of the proletariat by assimilating its members into the bourgeoisie. Its spiritual purpose was to cleanse the world of the pestilence of Bolshevism. Spawned by a German Jew, the germ of Bolshevism had spread a mental infection akin to venereal disease. The sores on the body politic should be cauterized. The public mind should be purged. 'It would be an excellent thing,' wrote Mrs Pankhurst in the *New York Tribune*, 'if all the books written before the war, and many that have been written since 1914, could be burned in one great conflagration.'

In her declining years Mrs Pankhurst was obliged to orate less from fullness of soul than from emptiness of purse. Ever optimistic, capable of earning $500 a speech, she believed that 'financial Nirvana was imminent', but she was tormented in practice by abysmal penury. The flood of Suffragette cash had evaporated, her testimonial fund had produced only a disappointing trickle and she remained habitually improvident. 'I cannot reduce my standard to one of constant pinch and save.' Was it not economy to buy the best? How could she take the stage without a suitable costume? Anyway, she could not resist dashing feathered hats, elegant velvet gowns, finely wrought lace, soft leather gloves, delicate kid shoes. But when Ethel Smyth offered her money Mrs Pankhurst's pride was wounded and they were permanently estranged. So between 1920 and '24, sponsored by the National Council for Combating Venereal Disease, Mrs Pankhurst spent most of her time lecturing in Canada on 'social hygiene'. With her accustomed panache she insisted that her meetings should be advertised as 'public health demonstrations' and she filled theatres, halls and churches all over the country. Branding sexual misconduct as 'moral Bolshevism', advocating the exclusion of all but eugenically sound Anglo-Saxon immigrants, she lifted the whole question of VD, as the *Toronto Globe* said, 'from the purely medical to the realm of the spiritual'. She had a sharply temporal riposte, though, for the Mayor of Bathurst, New Brunswick, who showed her his new Home for Fallen Women: 'And where, pray, is your Home for Fallen Men?' Mrs Pankhurst liked Toronto, a 'city of churches, trees and kind hearts', and she so favoured the dominion as a bastion of the British Empire that she became a Canadian citizen. But by 1925 the winters had become intolerable. After a long recuperative spell in Bermuda, where frequent 'At Homes' failed to alleviate her boredom, she travelled to Juan-les-Pins on the French Riviera. There, with Christabel and 'Pansy' Tuke, she embarked on an enterprise which, had it succeeded, would have brought her career to a truly bizarre conclusion. Among the expatriate community, cosy and secluded, she opened 'The English Teashop of Good Hope'.

It was a hopeless venture, doomed from the start and quickly abandoned. Yet some found it less astonishing than Mrs Pankhurst's final apotheosis as a Conservative *grande dame*, which was considered 'a denial of her whole life's work'. She returned to London. She expressed horror at the socialistic distemper which was the General Strike. She impressed Mr Baldwin by disdaining the proffered microphone and transmitting the faintest vibrations of that extraordinary voice from the past to the farthest corners of the Albert Hall. She was adopted as Tory candidate for the forlorn seat of Whitechapel. She descended into the abyss of the East End to live among her constituents, some of whom had been infected with the communist virus spread by her daughter Sylvia. Frail and withered, Mrs Pankhurst still managed on the platform to transfigure herself into the radiant prophetess of former times. True, the purport of her message had altered: now the extension of the suffrage to irresponsible 'flappers' did not find favour in her sight. But she still campaigned for righteousness: now she was agonized by the fear that growing sexual equality involved men's dragging women down to their own base level. What with short skirts, lipstick, jazz, cigarettes, contraceptives, a new age of immorality seemed to be dawning – unless Mr Baldwin intervened. To cap it all, Sylvia was 'carrying on' with an Italian socialist! The news of her illegitimate baby brought down Mrs Pankhurst's exquisitely coiffured silver hairs with sorrow to the grave. For hours she wept. She would be stigmatized with her daughter's shame, would never be able to speak in public again. From Stygian despair she rallied gamely for a while. Then she relapsed and Christabel removed her to the polite privacy of a Hampstead nursing home. There, at the end of her seventieth year and at the height of the London season, on 14 June 1928, Mrs Pankhurst's tempestuous spirit at last forsook her ravaged body. Her dramatic instinct was impeccable. After lying in state, surrounded by bouquets of flowers and a Suffragette guard of honour, all arrayed in purple, green and white, after scenes of great public emotion – women sobbed, kissed the funeral pall, knelt on the pavements as the cortège passed – her mortal remains were laid to rest at Brompton Cemetery. In the same hour the House of Lords passed the measure giving all adult women the vote.

Two years later a statue of Mrs Pankhurst was erected near the Houses of Parliament. There she poses still, a refined, feminine figure clad in a long coat with a fur collar, her outstretched hand clasping a lorgnette. In bronze, as in flesh, she is every inch the lady on her pedestal.

At the unveiling ceremony traffic was diverted around Parliament Square, Mr Baldwin delivered a speech of unparalleled banality and the music, conducted by Ethel Smyth, was provided by the band of the Metropolitan Police. A heretic, duly qualified for sainthood by apostasy and death, had been canonized – so, at least, went the popular myth. In fact, Mrs Pankhurst had been a bigot for orthodoxy, a martyr for morality. Her nonconformity consisted of nothing but uncompromising dedication to strait-laced dogmas and obdurate scorn for the constitutional suffragists' maxim that the last infirmity of noble minds was to do ill that good might come. Mrs Pankhurst conveyed her invincible sense of rectitude to her daughters, as their remarkable careers demonstrate. Adela, having been a militant Suffragette, an extreme radical and an active trade unionist, became a fervent imperialist just in time to effect a last reconciliation with her mother. Following the rightward path, Adela condemned criticism of Hitler and Mussolini during the 1930s, deplored the outbreak of war and was interned in Australia in 1943 for expressing pro-Japanese sentiments. Mrs Pankhurst was implacable towards her second daughter. Sylvia crusaded for everything from Esperanto to vegetarianism and was by turns a socialist, a pacifist, a Bolshevist (she was imprisoned in 1920 for inciting the British fleet to mutiny), a free-lance revolutionary, an anti-Fascist. She became so obsessed by Italy's rape of Ethiopia that she spent her last twenty-five years championing the feudal theocracy of the Emperor Haile Selassie, Elect of God, Lion of Judah, King of Zion. Having for so long prophesied the feminist millennium, Dame Christabel (as she became in 1936) devoted the rest of her life to predicting the Millennium *tout court*. She became a travelling evangelist of the Second Advent. This would be ushered in by a 'season of tribulation and world-purification' and might be foretold by any number of auguries, from the return of the Jews to Jerusalem to an earth tremor in New York. As Mrs Pethick-Lawrence once ruefully observed, 'The Pankhursts did nothing by halves.' At the infernal centre of the daughters' causes chafed the mother's violent spirit. That spirit has never been laid. It is the spirit of zealotry, it haunts the modern world and its manifestations are legion.

Select Bibliography

T. Billington-Greig	*The Militant Suffrage Movement* (1912)
R. Fulford	*Votes for Women* (1976 edn.)
B. Harrison	*Separate Spheres* (1978)
A. Kenney	*Memories of a Militant* (1924)
D. Mitchell	*The Fighting Pankhursts* (1967)
D. Mitchell	*Queen Christabel* (1977)
D. Morgan	*Suffragists and Liberals* (1975)
C. Pankhurst	*Unshackled* (1959)
E. Pankhurst	*My Own Story* (1914)
S. Pankhurst	*The Suffragette* (1911)
S. Pankhurst	*The Suffragette Movement* (1931)
S. Pankhurst	*The Life of Emmeline Pankhurst* (1935)
E. Pethick-Lawrence	*My Part in a Changing World* (1938)
A. Raeburn	*The Militant Suffragettes* (1973)
A. Rosen	*Rise Up, Women!* (1974)
C. Rover	*Women's Suffrage and Party Politics in Britain 1866–1914* (1967)
E. Smyth	*Female Pipings in Eden* (1933)
R. Strachey	*The Cause* (1928)

Original Sources
Fawcett Library: Suffragette MSS
Girton College, Cambridge: a few letters from Christabel Pankhurst, other Suffragette MSS and copies of *Votes for Women* and *The Suffragette*
London Museum: Ethel Smyth's letters to Mrs. Pankhurst and other Suffragette MSS

General Baden-Powell

I

Few men have been so idolized as Robert Stephenson Smyth Baden-Powell, defender of Mafeking and founder of the Boy Scout Movement. The famous siege made it clear to the world, even to the unfriendly New York *World*, that Baden-Powell had written 'a new page in the annals of human heroism'. Those modest-jaunty messages ('All well. Four hours bombardment. One dog killed.') perfectly conjured up that fabled English soldier, so often subsequently burlesqued, whose wounds hurt only when he laughed. When Mafeking was relieved, amid an unprecedented orgy of rejoicing, patriotic biographers competed to represent Baden-Powell as a demigod. It was stated 'on good authority that not once did he cry in the whole of babyhood'. 'B-P' was 'the ideal English schoolboy, and the ideal British officer. . . a hero in the best sense of the word, living cleanly, despising viciousness equally with effeminacy'. It was surely no accident that those famous initials also stood for British Pluck. Even asleep B-P was a paragon, a figure of romance and adventure who might have walked straight out of the pages of the *Boy's Own Paper*.

Once, after two months of wandering, he got into a hotel and, after dinner, into a bed. But it would not do, he says; in a twinkling he had whipped the blankets off the bed and was lying outside on mother earth, with the rain beating upon his face, and deep in refreshing slumber...However soundly he sleeps, if any one comes within ten yards of him, tread he never so softly, Baden-Powell wakes up without fail, and with a brain cleared for action.

Not that B-P was much given to repose. Had not the war-like Matabele dubbed him 'Impeesa', 'the wolf-that-never-sleeps'? And was not sleeping, especially sleeping under too many covers, calculated to lead to dreams, bad dreams, the kind that weaken a fellow? B-P always took measures to ensure that his own bed was properly ventilated. He placed it under the canopy of heaven and made it the same at each end 'so that both head and feet feel the benefit of the fresh air'. He slept, as it were, with a stiff upper lip. Such trifling eccentricities actually enhanced the Chief Scout's heroic glamour. Generations of his followers needed no exhortation to worship the Founder in the days of their youth.

The adulation has naturally inspired a hostile reaction. Nowadays B-P is no longer saluted as 'one of the greatest generals of modern times'. Instead he is hailed as 'a somewhat ridiculous and vain little Colonel'. 'Seldom,' asserts a recent historian, 'has one man ever built such a successful career out of incompetence.' B-P has been denounced as the victim of 'an almost frenzied ambition'. He has been exposed as a liar who, over the years, systematically inflated his estimate of the number of Boers held at bay around Mafeking. He has been vilified as a racialist who fed the white population of the besieged township on oyster patties and turkey while subjecting the blacks to slow starvation on a diet of horse soup and a porridge which tasted like bill-sticker's paste. He has been decried as a hypocrite, the champion hog-hunter and pig-sticker who advocated kindness to animals. He has been condemned as a philistine – he scorned contemporary painting and poetry as well as the wasteful modern habit of teaching French and music, and he experienced 'particular pleasure' when a shell destroyed one of the pianos at the convent in Mafeking. He has been branded as a reactionary – in Matabeleland he discovered gold mines surrounded by forts and hankered thus to 'simplify' the English 'labour question', 'keeping the workers in and the agitators out'. He has been stigmatized as an aggressive imperialist who purposed to turn lads into rifle-shooting flag-waggers. He has been declared everything from faddist to fascist, here obsessed by the vicious properties of 'suppressed perspiration' and the need to douse the 'racial organ' regularly in cold water, there willing to permit Mussolini ('a very charming, humorous and human man') to apply Scouting methods to his own youth movement, the Balilla. Even P. G. Wodehouse has not spared B-P, for surely that splendid empire-building, Matabele-bashing creation, Major Brabazon Plank (the initials tell the tale), is less a satire on Colonel Blimp in general than on General Baden-Powell in particular. Against this heavy-calibre bore Bertie Wooster inveighed with unwonted venom:

> On his own showing, he had for years been horning in uninvited on the aborigines of Brazil, the Congo and elsewhere, and not one of them apparently had had the enterprise to get after him with a spear or to say it with poisoned darts from the family blowpipe.

The Boy Scouts Association itself, long held in check by the longevity of Lady Baden-Powell, who guarded her husband's reputation fiercely and believed that Scouting must never be changed because it 'is flawless and complete

and perfect as HE LAID IT OUT', now seems to
acknowledge that its founder was human and fallible,
quite as liable as other men to get his woggle in a tangle.
According to a reappraisal lately published under the
Association's auspices, B-P's mind lacked any 'depth of
intelligence' and his character was marred by a tendency
towards egotistical self-advertisement. He even trans-
gressed against his own decalogue, the Scout Law.

Of course the Baden-Powell myth merited its debunk-
ing. But who shall debunk the debunkers themselves? In
their eagerness to dash the Edwardian soldier-saint from
his pedestal B-P's adversaries have been unwarrantably
iconoclastic. It is absurd to pretend, for example, that the
saviour of Mafeking was strikingly inept as a military
commander, especially when one considers his British
rivals during the Boer War. They were a bizarre collection:
the bloated Buller, with his baggage-train full of kitchen
equipment; the monocled Warren, owlishly concerned
about the safety of his oxen; the insomniac Hart, who was
roused to fury by the sight of a sleeping man; the dapper
Roberts, with his aversion to cats; the ruthless Kitchener,
described by a subaltern as 'the most talented murderer
[of his own men] the war has produced'. One can understand why it was rumoured among the Boers that to fire
at a British general was a capital offence; and why Queen
Victoria's private secretary wrote to Arthur Balfour in
January 1900, 'I see you think everything has now been
supplied to the generals but brains! For these I imagine the
Primate is arranging a special day of intercession.' What is
more, Baden-Powell's detractors cannot scout the success
of Scouting itself. B-P created the largest and most
flourishing youth movement the world has ever seen. In
the seventy years since its foundation, in 1908, about
eighty million boys have become Scouts and nearly fifty
million girls Guides, and the organization is established
in more than a hundred countries. B-P's friend and assistant,

Sir Percy Everett, made the point graphically in his obituary tribute in 1941.

> No Chief, no Prince, no King, no Saint was ever mourned by so great a company of boys and girls, of men and women in every land. No other leader in the history of men gathered under one banner, in his own life-time, so great a multitude of followers of all ages, of all races, of all colours, of all creeds.

If B-P required a monument he had only to look around the globe – at myriads of bare-kneed young replicas making their elders' lives a perfect hell by whistling and singing under all difficulties and doing good turns every day.

B-P himself whistled and sang under all difficulties – at Mafeking he 'warbled music hall ditties from morning till night'. It was a curious trait, of a piece with his jolly juvenile penchant for exploding cigars and practical jokes of all sorts, for comic disguises, for amateur theatricals, for acting the goat and for playing the piano with his toes. Still, it affords a valuable clue, a *clou* even, to Baden-Powell's true nature and to his place in Edwardian England.

B-P's critics have suggested that at Mafeking he was a charlatan presiding over a charade. They have argued that Scouting was militarism in masquerade. They have claimed that it was Baden-Powell's sinister, social-Darwinist aim not merely to avert British decadence but to establish British racial superiority by means of woodcraft – in the spirit of Mussolini, who later contemplated reafforesting the Apennines in order to create a harsher climate and thus transform the soft Italians into hardy 'Nordic Aryans'. The charges are not without foundation. But they impute to B-P a seasoned sophistication of which he was entirely innocent. For the whole of his 'extraordinarily happy life' he was, indeed, a perennial singing school-boy, a permanent whistling adolescent, a case of arrested development *con brio*. He was unabashedly a 'boy-man' and he recommended the condition as one to which his Scoutmasters should aspire. Only thus would they be filled with 'that bright, cheery spirit of adventure' which was 'the life-blood' of their work. Or rather play, for B-P always insisted that Scouting was essentially a matter of 'fun and jollity', a game. Life itself, he said, should be looked on 'as a game, and the world as a playground', and happiness as the goal. In general B-P himself was blissfully blithe-spirited, testifying to the mood by an unusual mannerism – rubbing his hands together. But perpetual immaturity was not always a joyously carefree condition. There were, for example, those fretting anxieties about 'self-abuse'; working up, 'with your hand or otherwise,' 'a pleasant feeling in your private parts' led to public headaches, palpitations of the heart and eventual idiocy, not to mention 'several awful diseases. . . one especially that rots away the inside of the men's mouths, their noses, and eyes, etc.' And despite the bluff manner with which B-P pronounced on the sombre problems of his day (mostly jeremiads against slouching slackers, 'solitary soakers' and 'soft, sloppy cigarette-suckers') he must have been uneasily aware that his political solutions were callow, his social nostrums were naive and his philosophical panaceas were puerile. A breezy air could by no means disperse the yellow fog of difficulties which rubbed its back against Edwardian window-panes. At times B-P sang to keep his spirits up. At times he whistled in the dark.

By and large, though, B-P managed to escape from the perplexing realm of adulthood into a merry Never-Never Land peopled by the figments of G. A. Henty, Fenimore Cooper, Conan Doyle, Robert Louis Stevenson, Alexandre Dumas, Rudyard Kipling. He transformed the most mundane settings, via fantasy, into exotic scenes of high adventure.

Have you never seen the buffaloes roaming in Kensington Gardens past the very spot where Gil Blas met the robbers behind the trees? Can't you see the smoke from the Sioux lodges under the shadow of the Albert Memorial? I have seen them there these sixty years.

If, during tea-party chatter, 'the word saddle, or rifle, or billy, or some other attribute of camp life' was casually mentioned, 'visions of the veldt' would suddenly rise before B-P's inner eye and 'off goes my mind at a tangent to play with its toys'. He reverted unashamedly to childhood, particularly in the performance of japes, pranks and larks. In fancy he even retreated into infancy. Once, when walking along a sea-side esplanade with a friend, he suddenly sat down on the kerb, placed his billycock hat on his knees and began to sob into a large red handkerchief. To an inquiring policeman he solemnly explained that he had 'just that moment tumbled out of his nurse's arms and the silly woman had gone on without noticing it'. But B-P was not content with imagined romance or artificial entertainment. He travelled to remote countries in search of the authentic article. He spied in Montenegro. He chased brigands in Afghanistan. He fished in Tasmania. He ventured into the interior of Brazil – 'my wig, there are some pretty funny wonders to be met with in the jungles there, not forgetting snakes seventy feet long and frogs two feet across.' All his life B-P suffered from 'camp sickness...hunger to be out in the wilds'. He was never happier than when spooring, stalking and hunting – boars or Boers, it did not seem to matter which, though his most ecstatic moments were spent attempting to bag the biggest game of all, those 'laughing black fiends' the Matabele.

Finally, however, B-P created for himself a boy's own kingdom, replete with secret signs, initiation rites, ceremonial beads, arcane litanies, queer hats, totem poles and knives with attachments for removing stones from horses' hooves. It was a kingdom in which there were no complexities, no uncertainties: spies were 'foreign-looking'; men with waxed moustaches were untrustworthy; 'heels worn down on the inside signify weakness and indecision of character.' Moreover it was a kingdom united by simple tribal loyalties and governed by a straightforward code of honour. One 'played the game' and there were no doubts about what was, and what was not, cricket. Growing lads aspired to be 'white men', to be 'manly' – which actually implied the evasion of manhood. 'Manliness' denoted a postponement of pubescence in favour of the healthy, ingenuous virtues of flannel-shirted, khaki-shorted youth. Edwardians, worried about the corrupting effects of a degenerate culture, a culture spawned in mean city streets and manufactured in dark satanic mills, found it natural to seek social rejuvenation by juvenile means. No doubt all men are but children of a larger growth. Nevertheless, B-P's contemporaries, faced with the threat of imperial decline, whether through foreign competition, domestic conflict or racial deteriora-tion, were especially prone to bury their heads in the golden sand-pit of childhood. Edwardians cherished a nostalgia for the nursery. With Kenneth Grahame they yearned to re-live those pre-pubertal dream days in Arcady. They wallowed in the escapist whimsy of *Peter Pan* and longed 'always to be a little boy and have fun'. Hardened cynics might opine, in the manner of P. G. Wodehouse contemplating his fictional Boy Scouts as they spoored the family cat across the drawing-room carpet, or imitated the cry of the turnip in order to deceive rabbits, or perpetrated mayhem with their sticks, that 'what this country needs is somebody like King Herod'. But it was not surprising that a civilization which revelled in its own retardation, should have embraced Scouting. It was appropriate that a society which was not prepared to grow up should have worshipped a hero whose motto was 'Be Prepared' (based on the famous initials), a motto at once so stirring as an adolescent challenge and so twaddling as an adult exhortation.

II

One of B-P's own heroes was the famous Elizabethan adventurer rescued from death at the hands of the blood-thirsty Chickahominies by Princess Pocahontas, Captain John Smith, from whom his mother's family claimed descent. Like much else in B-P's career this was a piece of colourful embroidery. But his true origins, though by no means the stuff of which camp-fire yarns could be spun, were not entirely bereft of romance. His mother, Henrietta Grace Smyth, was the daughter of an admiral and the grand-niece of Nelson. When she was twenty-one, in 1845, Admiral Smyth received a visit from his old friend the Rev. Baden Powell, F.R.S., Savilian Professor of Geometry at Oxford. Powell, aged forty-nine and twice widowed, was an imposing figure. He was a distinguished scientist, the forthright ally of Darwin. He was an eminent theologian, the stern enemy of 'Puseyite perversion' and Judaic heresy — he went through the family Prayer Books systematically crossing out the word 'Sabbath' and sub-stituting 'Lord's Day' and was said to have Sunday 'on the brain'. He was a staunch moralist, permitting his children to look at the illustrations in Dickens's novels but putting them on their honour not to read the text. In the presence of this learned divine young Henrietta Smyth was filled with a frozen awe, which thawed only when they found themselves alone together in front of the dining-room hearth.

I was warming one of my feet at the fire when my blushes were suddenly called forth by observing this philosopher Mr Powell dart a glance at it, give a deep sigh and exclaim aloud, though evidently unconscious that it was heard – 'Yes, perfect.'

The Professor suggested a 'short walk' and Henrietta was agitated and elated to discover that they held the same advanced views on the important subject of religious education. On a second walk he proposed to her and, the match being 'quite desirable', no difficulties were put in the couple's way. During their delectable fifteen years of marriage Henrietta gave birth to ten children, six of whom survived into adulthood. Her most famous son entered what he was to term 'the 'Varsity of Life' in 1857. He was christened Robert Stephenson after one of his godfathers, who had built the first successful steam locomotive, 'The Rocket'. It was thus to be expected that, unlike most small boys, Stephe (as he was called) would fulfil his early ambition to become an engine driver. Such was his youthful ardour that he later piloted a train carrying his regiment across India spankingly enough to rouse the Colonel; it was an audacious feat, for Sir Baker Russell, a fire-eater whose bristling moustache and choleric behaviour gave him an unnerving resemblance to a boar, was accustomed to punish miscreants by jamming his helmet down on his head and charging into them at full tilt on his horse.

In 1860 the Rev. Baden Powell died, his main bequest to his wife and children being a brilliant reputation. Even that was tarnished by his courageous contribution to a once-famous, now-forgotten book entitled *Essays and Reviews* (1860). It attempted to reconcile old theology with new science and was consequently regarded by pious Victorians as having been vomited out of the jaws of Hell. Henrietta asserted her unchanging devotion to the Professor's memory by changing the family surname to Baden-Powell and insisting on the new form with such vehemence that other relations nicknamed her 'Old Mrs

Hyphen'. Unmoved, she bent herself ruthlessly to preserve the Baden-Powells' proper place in caste-ridden
nineteenth-century London society on the modest income
she now enjoyed. She tapped all the resources of the
intellectual Establishment to which her husband had
belonged. Influential friends secured her boys, Stephe
included, closed scholarships at public schools. Ruskin
was consulted about Stephe's vexatious habit of painting
with both hands (on occasion with both feet) and encouraged him in his ambidexterity. Thackeray came to
dinner and once, when young Stephe attempted to join
the party, paid him a shilling to go away – the earliest
recorded instance of bob-a-jobbery. Above all the Baden-
Powells practised thrift, a virtue which Stephe never
grew tired of preaching: 'A Scout is thrifty', and even the
Second Class variety must have at least sixpence in a
savings bank. B-P believed that thrift would somehow
'bring money to all'. Frugality would enrich the destitute,
presumably, just as fasting would feed the hungry. But
this is not to suggest that Stephe lacked the high degree of
juvenile idealism usually attributed to him, and illustrated
by the following manifesto, issued when he was eight.

LAWS FOR ME WHEN I AM OLD. I will have the
poor people to be as rich as we are, and they ought by
rights to be as happy as we are, and all who go across the
crossings shall give the poor crossing sweepers some
money and you ought to thank God for what he has
given us and He has made the poor people to be poor
and the rich people to be rich, and I can tell you how
to be good, now I will tell you. You must pray to God
whenever you can but you cannot be good with only
praying but you must also try very hard to be good.

This document is remarkable not because B-P wrote it as a
boy but because he might have written it as a man. In tone
and content (almost, indeed, in style) it foreshadows the

woolly earnestness and the obtuse benevolence of those perky adult pi-jaws which became familiar to millions of Boy Scouts. Stephe had inherited much of his father's high-mindedness but little of his mind.

It was understandable, therefore, that B-P should have developed in acute form the blunt soldier's customary distrust for 'eggheads'. Three of the major 'snags in life' were, he considered, 'wine, women and highbrows'. He worried that the advent of motor-cars, bicycles and elevators would cause boys to 'grow brains instead of brawn'. He even condemned the emphasis on 'book-instruction' in public schools, which should have been concentrating on '*character education*'. This was odd. For training the character was precisely what the public schools prided themselves on doing *par excellence*. By means of competitive games, muscular Christianity, sexual segregation, strict discipline, elaborate ritual and physical hardship, they aimed to produce a sound, gentlemanly élite which would govern and defend the Empire. And the main criticism directed against the public schools was that they succeeded in fostering a class distinguished not just by emotional immaturity but by intellectual callowness, its typical representative being the distinguished politician Sir Thomas Inskip, of whom it was said that 'he could look with frank and fearless gaze on any prospect, however appalling – and fail to see it'. B-P's reservations about the public schools were actually those of Kipling, whose *Stalky & Co* was a protest against pedagogic restraints (such as compulsory games – productive of 'muddied oafs' and 'flannelled fools') on the joyful barbarian freedoms of boyhood. B-P thought the civilized English should imitate the savage Matabele, who licked their adolescents into shape by covering them with white daub and sending them alone for a month into the bush. As a matter of fact Charterhouse, where Stephe went on leaving his Tunbridge Wells preparatory school in 1870, offered few

Lord Baden-Powell, Chief Scout of the world, aged eighty

Stephe at Charterhouse

Captain Baden-Powell aged twenty-six

B-P on stage

impediments to Stalkyish independence, to the practice of Spartan chivalry and Machiavellian chicanery. As for intellectual impedimenta of the kind provided by modern culture and ideas, the school was disinclined to clutter fledgling minds with such stuff. It suited B-P to a tee. His general blast against the public schools was really a particular puff for Charterhouse. All his life he remained the most loyal of Old Boys and one of his sharpest disappointments during the siege of Mafeking was that he could find no other Carthusian with whom to celebrate Founder's Day. By way of delightful compensation B-P learnt that the chaps at Charterhouse had elected him patron of their newly formed 'League of Health and Manliness'.

Stephe's Headmaster, the Rev. Dr William Haig Brown (known to his pupils as Old Bill), was, appropriately enough, 'a man of "infinite jest" '. He encouraged, and once even assisted, Stephe and his fellows in battles against the town 'cads'. He was unable or unwilling to prevent Stephe visiting a forbidden copse near the school: 'It was here that I imagined myself a backwoodsman, a trapper, and an Indian scout.' He crept about warily 'looking for "sign"'. He snared, skinned and cooked rabbits. He read pirate stories, played hide-and-seek, built dams, constructed tree-houses, shot and stuffed birds. He learned the woodland lore which 'helped me as a youngster to find my soul'. Not, of course, that Stephe was unhealthily soulful; he once fought a decadent youth for maintaining that Sir Henry Irving's fingers tapered at the tips. Old Bill did not mind that Stephe was rather a 'duffer' at 'footer'. 'Bathing-Towel', as he was nicknamed, played in goal where he disconcerted the opposition by uttering Redskin war-cries and his own team by donning a second pair of boots at half-time, no doubt to alleviate the evil effects of suppressed perspiration. Old Bill even seemed to condone Stephe's total lack of interest in his studies – as a cub, Impeesa slept through many of his lessons, presumably breathing through his nose, a habit he was to recommend to Scouts as a preventive against both thirst and giving one's self away to an enemy by snoring. It was enough for the Head that this slight, freckled, gingery youth was 'always cheerful, perfectly straight and clean in every way'. Not all the masters were quite so tolerant. The mathematics 'beak', especially, lamented Stephe's refusal to confine his comic antics to the stage and deplored his 'tendency to buffoonery'.

Lewis Carroll would have concurred. For when Stephe came before the don behind the pseudonym, the Rev. Charles Dodgson refused to admit him to Christ Church, Oxford, because Mathematics was evidently Greek to him. The Regius Professor of Greek, Benjamin Jowett, despite being Stephe's godfather, judged him 'not quite up to Balliol form'. Incapable of academic training, Stephe felt he knew quite enough to convert the heathen and toyed with the dunce's traditional option of taking holy orders. His mother, not rating his ability quite that low, gave Stephe instead his marching orders. She instructed him 'not to be a fool but to go into the Army'. The dictate of the mother, who held all her sons in adoring thraldom, was sound. On their many boating, tramping and camping expeditions Stephe had already proved a dutiful subordinate to his intrepid eldest brother, who 'had a scathing tongue for shirkers and could be a martinet when he liked'. Anyway the army would be no more than an extension of the family and the school, a womb-like institution which yet afforded opportunities for excitement, comradeship, rivalry, fun and 'howling good sport'. Stephe crammed for the examinations, memorizing by means of pelmanism difficult parts of the syllabus without understanding what they meant. Whether this sapient method of learning, or the doltish quality of the other candidates, was responsible for his success it is impossible to say. But succeed he did, coming in the top six and earning himself exemption from a formal military education at Sandhurst. He was at once gazetted into a crack cavalry regiment, being assisted by the family's 'public purse' – the Baden-Powell boys long remained bachelors in order to sustain their formidable mother's system of 'purity and virtue' by which all their money was pooled and drawn only to advance each son's 'special prospects'. So, in 1876, Stephe joined the 13th Hussars, known, from its Colonel's name, as the Baker's Dozen. B-P announced his arrival with a characteristically juvenile piece of clowning, which was also a bravura early display of his skill as a Pied Piper. He led a procession of all the European children he could muster (natives were excluded) through the streets of Lucknow to the strains of 'The Girl I Left Behind Me', played on his ocarina.

III

Thus, before he even entered the barracks, B-P had established himself as a 'card' in the regimental pack, the joker. Such idiosyncratic conduct in a young subaltern would otherwise have been damned as 'putting on side'. More outlandish still, B-P soon took to writing odd articles for the press, and illustrating them himself, an almost unpardonable breach of 'good form' and pukkah sahibdom. 'Nothing,' said a brother officer, 'does a soldier more harm.' But the 13th Hussars, who had taken a front-line part in the Charge of the Light Brigade, plumed themselves on having a keen sense of humour. It was made manifest in their favourite mess amusement, which was to pile all the furniture into a heap and turn somersaults on top of it while proclaiming, 'I am a bounding Brother of the Bosphorus.' The height of comic sophistication reached by the Hussars was to twirl the chandeliers at mess balls and spray the dancers with hot candle wax. In such company the jester could expect much licence, especially the jester whose favourite music-hall 'artistes' were the trick cyclist, the 'fellow with a spring necktie' and the 'champion smasher of plates' (B-P disliked the 'half-stripped lady singer'). Within a short time, therefore, he had won his spurs as a 'delightfully breezy beggar', painting stage scenery with both hands at once, imitating the sounds of musical instruments, singing droll songs, doing facetious recitations, acting waggish parts in and out of the theatre, initiating endless 'rags', here posing as an Italian Count, there impersonating a British General – though he later asserted, 'it is a silly game, that of practical jokes, and I never indulged in it myself.' Laughter, said B-P, was 'a bath for the brain' and it is clear that his brain was washed in the Army as thoroughly as his person. (Cleanliness was always a fetish with him: doubtless because he had, in the words of one biographer, 'the scenting powers of a fox-hound', B-P disapproved heartily of 'niffy' Scouts, recommending that, when unable to manage their ablutions in a more orthodox way, they could, as he did, bath 'quite comfortably in dew-covered grass'.) Anyway, the regiment concluded that B-P was 'a born buffoon, but a devilish clever fellow'.

Naturally, as a professional cavalryman, B-P was preoccupied with more serious matters than entertaining tomfoolery. His most immediate task was to acquire reliable mounts. He realized, of course, that 'like a woman, a horse is subject to moods'. Luckily, though, there was an infallible guide to the selection of both. In a horse, as in a wife, 'blood *will* tell'. B-P bought, broke and trained his own ponies, later remarking that in all India he had 'possessed no better friends'. They were 'as tame as dogs' ('Clown' must have been a maverick for he once 'sadly disgraced himself' by kicking an Indian groom to death) and would go for walks with B-P, 'coming to hand when whistled for, as sensible and as jolly as could be'. With these fine animals the new lieutenant was able to devote himself to the important business of polo and pig-sticking. Polo he valued not simply because it was clean, healthy exercise which encouraged decision and dash in the horseman, but for its 'moral attributes', for teaching young shavers to 'play the game' unselfishly. Pig-sticking became an obsession with him and he wrote an authoritative handbook about it. Being 'a manly and tip-top sport', pig-sticking too fostered 'dash', 'pluck', nerve' and 'keenness'. But it also opened 'the stalker's eye' and provided 'fair and sporting exercise of one's bump of "woodcraft" '. It was difficult to imagine that those rare soldierly qualities, the 'inductive reasoning powers', could be better trained than by 'pugging', tracking pigs via their trotter marks. Moreover, by pursuing the wild boar a bold lancer earned the respect of 'the niggers'. True, they were for the most part 'cringing villains. . . [who] do whatever you tell them'. B-P's bearers actually dressed him and 'if you meet a man in the road and tell him to dust your boots he does it'. On the other hand, some Indians, especially 'the Baboos', were impertinent enough to require 'proof that the Englishman is of a different and superior order of beings', and it was not everyone who could emulate the feat of the Surveyor General of Ordnance in South West Africa. B-P approvingly noted his method of showing the natives that he was 'a born ruler of men': 'with his bare fists he fought and defeated a savage chimpanzee.' The Indians, so B-P argued, would actually benefit from contact with hog-hunters. They would be paid well (though not 'pampered' – their wants were small) and treated well for their pains. It was, in any case, 'fatal to the interests of sport to ill-treat the villagers. . . shouting and cursing at a coolie already dumbfounded at the very sight of a white man is not the way to clear his understanding.' B-P particularly urged that when firing the jungle in order to 'rear' pig, to set them afoot, some care should be taken. One of his own beaters had suffered the misfortune of being roasted alive.

B-P denied that the typical Englishman's waking remark was, 'God damn, it is a fine day. What shall I kill?' But he himself devoted much more time as a soldier to slaughtering animals than to slaying humans. And in his affections the hunting of big game rivalled even the Great Game of spying. B-P killed wolf in Afghanistan, bear in Nepal, bontebok in South Africa, stag in Scotland, impala in Kenya, tiger in India, not to mention assorted lion, ibex, panther, antelope, hyena, buffalo and so on. He used a variety of weapons, butchering black buck with a pistol and assaulting water buck with an assegai. From the Bantu he earned the sobriquet *M'halapanzi*, 'the man-who-lies-down-to-shoot', for scoring a bull's eye in a hippopotamus's eye with a rifle bullet. At his mother's house he proudly displayed the relics of his holocaust, innumerable stuffed heads, mounted tusks, skin rugs and other trophies. Not that B-P was callous about the carnage. He exhibited the hunter's ambivalent feelings towards his prey to a bewildering degree. Sometimes B-P claimed that he killed the thing he loved. 'I hate to see the beautiful eye of a gazelle gently questioning: "What harm have I done that you should shoot me?" ' The execution hurt him more than it hurt his victim but, like most public-school boys, B-P bore the agony with heroic stoicism. Sometimes he asserted that the animals enjoyed the hunt as much as he did and that the 'brutal sport' involved little or no cruelty. The boar, for example, 'rushes whole-heartedly into the scraps' and his 'red-hot rage and desire to kill makes him oblivious to anything in the way of panic or pain'. Sometimes B-P suggested that he only shot for the pot: the sporting dispatch of his hippo was later transformed into an endeavour to feed 'my natives... [who] were almost starving'. Sometimes he seemed almost to anticipate the ideas of his more mystic-minded Scouters, men like John Hargrave, who believed it was salutary for youngsters to 're-act, or recapitulate, the primitive life of the race' in the open air. Boars assisted manfully in this process. B-P observed:

> With us humans, primitive savagery lies close below the surface of our veneer of civilization. When you get the chance of really losing your temper with an adversary and of being able to consummate it by killing him, it is a luxury unknown to those who have never indulged their evil inclinations.

The question of 'savagery' *versus* 'civilization' was a knotty one, except of course that B-P had no difficulty with knots. He could describe the Afghans as brave warriors and 'fine sportsmen' one moment and the next they became 'brutes', their 'hideous' women scurrying about 'aimlessly' under huge burdens, 'just like ants'. He could condemn his own countrymen as effete wasters yet agree with Kipling that 'God has arranged that a clean-run youth of the British middle classes shall in the matter of backbone, brains, and bowels, surpass all other youths.' He could at once exult over the spread of civilization and commerce to 'savage lands' and deplore its squalid, materialistic encroachment on the preserve of Nature. Yet for himself B-P evolved a judicious compromise between barbarism and refinement. He loved the 'flannel-shirt life' of big-game safaris in the jungle, especially when they consisted of ninety-five bearers, seven servants, two hunters, two cooks and an escort of thirty. He adored 'roughing it' in the bush; but a good Scout makes himself comfortable and when camping in India B-P invariably changed into evening dress for dinner. He regarded the Himalayan wilderness as 'a cold tub for the soul'. But he always used scented soap.

Fun and game apart, B-P found regimental life dull. As Colonel Baker Russell contended, the sole duties of the cavalry were 'to look smart in time of peace and to get killed in war'. During B-P's early years as a soldier he met the first obligation, but he longed for a chance to meet the second, or better still to mete out official murder on his own account. This thrilling opportunity arose during one of those periodic bouts of unrest which made the North-West frontier, in B-P's view, a God-given training-ground for the British army. B-P was subsequently to claim that he was 'a pacifist' – in theory if not in practice – and hated war '*worse* than the devil'. But he recorded in his diary for 1880: 'Here's a jolly lark! A telegram came at twelve last night ordering me to get two chargers and go up to Kandahar immediately.' By the time he arrived, however, the revolting Afghans had been suppressed and he did little but draw maps, scout and patrol in the hope of hunting down stragglers. He also mounted three per-formances of *The Pirates of Penzance*, rehearsing on an open stage, the boundaries of which were marked out by swords stuck into the earth because 'there was always the danger of fanatical tribesmen rushing down on us at any moment with their nasty great knives.' Unfortunately this prospect failed to materialize. In the event, the only person B-P managed to shoot during the campaign was himself. He accomplished this while cleaning his pistol for use against marauding horse-thieves. B-P was adept at passing off such trifling vicissitudes with a quip – when a carbine carelessly loaded on one of his pack animals went off he boasted that, while being assassinated by an ass was a common enough hazard, he had nearly been murdered by a mule. So doubtless the Baker's Dozen concluded that potting himself in the leg was just the sort of funny trick the regimental 'card' would play.

IV

Fool in the Hussars' court B-P might have been, but, as he often later insisted, his eleventh commandment read: 'The

Scout is not a fool.' So 'on parade he was', as a trooper reported, 'ON PARADE', smartly doffing the cap and bells of the amateur buffoon for the busby and spurs of the professional dragoon. 'Bathing-Towel', 'Baking-Powder', 'Bread-and-Fowl' – B-P delighted in such plays on the family name, but 'Old Mrs Hyphen' herself was not more proud of it and Stephe was quite as ambitious as his successful brothers to add to its lustre. Moreover, imbued as he was with the conditioned responses and the moral imperatives of a public schoolboy, B-P knew that hierarchies existed for fellows like himself to rise in. Thus he was meticulous about drill and the other martial exercises which fell to his lot in peace-time. And in 1884 he published *Reconnaissance and Scouting*, recommending these crafts as affording the practitioner a uniquely 'good chance of distinguishing himself'. Though his first book sold poorly it was 'a grand advertisement for me'. For B-P sent copies to 'all the boss quartermaster-generals, Wolseleys, etc, asking if they approve of it'. Underlying even B-P's endless theatricals there was, as he subsequently acknowledged, 'a lot of nasty cool calculation'. They earned him the notice of such weighty personages as the Duke of Connaught (to whom he dedicated *Pig-Sticking or Hog-Hunting*) and an entrée into vice-regal society. However, they also attracted the unwelcome attention of what was unchivalrously known as 'the Fishing Fleet', young ladies who sailed to India in the hope of landing a mate. When out for a ride on an elephant with one of these fair anglers he was obliged to warn her that 'if she attempted to make love to me I should immediately get off' and walk home with the chaperone. B-P avoided the distraction of close relationships with men as well as women. He made one significant exception. Before the regiment returned home in 1885 he had formed the most intimate friendship of his life, with a junior officer, Kenneth McLaren, known because of his youthful looks as 'The Boy'. The extent to which this affection was homosexual is difficult to gauge. But it did cause B-P to make a fool of himself at Mafeking. On learning that McLaren lay wounded in the Boer camp, the garrison's commander had to be restrained by his subordinates from rushing to 'The Boy's' bedside.

In 1888 B-P accepted an invitation which he had previously refused, in favour of the delights of polo and pig-sticking, to act as ADC to his uncle, General Henry Smyth, the army commander in South Africa. Regimental life in England was so flat that B-P had sought stimulation from unofficial spying expeditions to observe foreign armies on manoeuvres. He presented *My Adventures as a Spy*, a drama of Buchan-and-water, to a public besotted by fears of espionage during the Great War. To judge by the infantile stereotypes contained in this book (foreign secret agents were men who looked not quite English, spoke with guttural accents and signalled to each other with flash-lamps) and the fact that B-P, with his trimmed moustache and clipped diction, with his clean limbs and upright bearing, was immediately identifiable as a British officer in mufti, it is remarkable that he was arrested but once, in Russia. Such excitements could only be enjoyed on leave and B-P, a Captain by now, was prepared to abandon them for a staff post in which 'you meet with swells whose interest may get you on'. But though he coveted promotion, B-P hankered still more 'to be out in the wilds and away from all this mixture of office and drawing-room; clerk and butler'. He escaped when he could, chivvying foxes or natives as the opportunity arose. On one foray he heard the Zulu chant,

Eengonyama Gonyama! Invooboo!
*Ya boh! Ya boh! Invooboo!**

This luminous incantation was, of course, to become the Boy Scouts' hymn, the anthem of world youth, sage, alert,

---

* He is a lion! Yes, he is better than a lion! He is a hippopotamus!

erect, prepared for...anything. When General Smyth became Governor of Malta in 1890, Major Baden-Powell followed, continuing the 'glorified detective work' of spying all round the Mediterranean. But he still had to play a polite ceremonial role and at tea parties and receptions his mind would suddenly become a blank. A 'single vision' would occupy it, 'lower half yellow, upper half blue – in other words, the yellow veld of South Africa, topped with the blue South African sky.' Such intense longings could scarcely be satisfied by his solitary recreation at Malta – haring to the Governor's country palace in a cart in order to shoot woodcock every time the gardener signified their coming, which he did by hoisting a yellow flag.

At last, in 1895, B-P achieved the kind of fulfilment he desired. With a boy's own 'dodge' on manoeuvres – creating a dust-cloud, and thus a false impression of his squadron's whereabouts, by sending a decoy patrol to drag branches along behind their horses – he attracted the favour of General Wolseley. Releasing him from regular duties, the Commander-in-Chief directed B-P to raise a 'native contingent' on the Gold Coast to prepare a way through the jungle for a punitive expedition against the Ashanti. Their King, known as Prempeh, had broken treaty obligations with the British and, as B-P wrote, he 'stood in the way of civilization, of trade, and of the interests of the people themselves'. B-P recruited his levies from among the friendly Adansis who were, he discovered, 'not far removed from the monkeys they hunted'. Still, the tribe did have royal leaders and it was gratifying to be able to fork monarchs out of hovels 'at the end of a stick'. 'Without undue swank,' B-P confessed, 'there is great joy in cursing a real live king, especially when one is merely in one's pyjamas.' Soon, however, he became incensed by the Adansis' attitude to their work – each one, after all, was paid ninepence a day and given a red fez.

The stupid inertness of the puzzled negro is duller than that of an ox; a dog would grasp your meaning in one-half the time. Men and brothers! They may be brothers but they are certainly not men.

Nevertheless, they did possess a human capacity to resist the tsetsi fly and, not being able to flog donkeys through the bush, B-P relied on them. As for exercising discipline, he forged a characteristic backwoodman's saw to explain his method: 'A smile and a stick will carry you through any difficulty in the world.' Agnes Baden-Powell, who regarded her brother as 'just a fun-loving English boy, full of kindliness and delight in the joys of life's morning', supported Stephe's public assertion that he never actually used the stick. In private B-P admitted to having 'had some experience of flogging' men as well as boys, and his first biographer took a properly robust view of the case. When the smile fails, 'those hard jaws of his lock with a snap, the eyes light up with resistless determination, and *whir-r-r* goes the stick, and – well, it requires a tough head to bear what follows.' Beating native meat to secure results was, of course, a recognized procedure at the time and, as B-P himself said, 'An occasional lick from a whip, is, to an unintelligent savage, but a small matter.' There could surely be nothing sinister in this, for flagellation which did not give much pain to the blacks could hardly give much pleasure to the whites.

None of this meant, B-P explained, that he was 'a regular nigger-hater'. He had many African friends, especially among the Zulus: Jan Grootboom the scout, for instance, who 'proved himself a white man – if in a black skin'. No, B-P merely insisted that

> however good they may be, they must, as a people, be ruled with a hand of iron in a velvet glove, and if they writhe under it, and don't understand the force of it, it is no use to add more padding – you must take off the

glove for a moment and show them the hand. They will understand and obey.

The Ashanti grasped what the iron hand held – Maxim guns, which we had got and they had not. To B-P's dismay they submitted without a struggle and the campaign closed in anti-climax. 'Alas!' he lamented, the drums of Kumasi talked peace. King Prempeh emerged from the palace, 'his somewhat stupid expression rendered,' in B-P's view, 'more idiotic by his sucking a large nut like a fat cigar.' Before being exiled to the Seychelles, he was forced to embrace his conquerors' feet and pay a large tribute in gold. His people had wisely secreted most of their possess-ions in the jungle and the only loot B-P managed to acquire was the ceremonial bowl used for catching blood at human sacrifices and King Prempeh's hat.

B-P had, in fact, a Northcliffean penchant for hats and he later expressed the ambition to acquire President Kruger's topper. To protect his sensitive skin from the solar glare B-P shed the sola topee for the flat-brimmed, indented headgear he was to make famous, thus earning himself another treasured nickname, *Kantankye* – 'He-of-the-big-hat'. King Fever being more of a menace than King Prempeh, B-P took elaborate precautions to keep his 'blood clean and pure'. Doubtless he followed his own advice to Scouts, drinking a nightly pint of hot water and having a daily 'rear'. Certainly he took plenty of exercise, travelling by hammock only when the sun was too hot or the ground too wet. He always tied a spare shirt round his neck so that he could change when the one he was wearing became soaked in sweat, thus once again obviating the perils of suppressed perspiration. Preserved by this remarkable regimen B-P was able, once back in England, to complete his book, *The Downfall of Prempeh*, in just four days. On its cover the author (crowned with an inexplicable helmet which appears to have about it a touch of the tarboosh) grapples with an armed Ashanti warrior. Inside he explains that the volume was written 'to escape the further importunity of his friends'. Actually, as he told an aunt, 'the lucre was offered, my debts stared at me, and I fell.' King Prempeh's own downfall, incidentally, proved to be temporary. He rose again, almost as if to illustrate B-P's point that he was no 'regular nigger-hater'. For Prempeh eventually returned home and became President of the local Boy Scouts Association.

The Matabele proved to be as thrillingly wild as the Ashantis had been disappointingly tame. Their rising in 1896 against the 'white pioneers of civilization', as B-P called them, provided him with the most 'joyous adventure' and the best 'sport' of his career. The land, which had just been expropriated from the Matabele by a typically Rhodesian combination of fraud and force, teemed with 'game. Lion or leopard, boar or buck, nigger or nothing, you never know what is going to turn up.' To this un-cultivated Garden of Eden B-P, now a Lieutenant-Colonel, was sent as Chief of Staff to General Sir Frederick Carrington. They travelled north from the railhead at Mafeking in a 'regular Buffalo-Bill-Wild-West-Dead-wood' coach, through a terrain littered with animals killed by a disastrous outbreak of rinderpest. Sometimes the stench of rotting flesh was so strong that 'one could lean against it', but B-P revelled in the bracing delights of the open-air life. Sleeping under the stars, cooking over the camp-fire, exercising the Englishman's inborn 'talent for woodcraft and the spirit of adventure and independence' – this was the existence for 'the wolf-that-never-sleeps'. Whenever Impeesa was permitted to emerge from his administrative den at Bulawayo he liked to sniff out the enemy for Carrington, who would then 'give the nigger snuff' with howitzers and machine-guns. Clad in an outfit which owed more to stage-craft than to scoutcraft – the characteristic hat, a blazing red shirt with a large neckerchief, knotted at the back, breeches, leather gaiters with a pocket for packing his second pistol – Impeesa ranged over the Matopos, a 'weird jumbled mass of bush and boulders and jagged mountains', where the Matabele lay concealed. His melodramatic appearance naturally attracted their attention:

Didn't my heart go pit-a-pat the first time the Matabele saw me on foot among hill-side boulders. But when I found I could, with my rubber-soled shoes, skip away faster than they could follow, it became a cheerier adventure.

With conspicuous gallantry Impeesa made – was forced to make – many such hair-breadth escapes. He was assisted by an agility acquired from entertaining the mess with skirt-dances. Eventually, persuaded perhaps by the fact that the enemy 'had command of fire over my hat, which I badly wanted', B-P 'came to the conclusion' that it was the 'brilliant red' of his attire which 'caught their eye'. He therefore discarded the vaudeville costume for more sober garb. It was enough that this game of hide-and-seek with the Matabele made his blood fizz and his spirits sparkle. 'A tussle with the niggers' had the same effect on him as tossing off 'a couple of glasses of champagne'.

The root cause of this intoxication lay, surely, in the fact that these were not only licensed hours of aggression but of regression. It was regression to a state appropriate (who could doubt?) for fighting the Matabele, one of child-like barbarism. Thus, for the buoyant B-P at least, the frustrating inhibitions of adulthood dissolved and the hampering restrictions of 'civilized' warfare were abandoned. When, during a skirmish, a Matabele warrior had the effrontery to point his blunderbuss at Impeesa, B-P felt not 'funk' but fury tantamount to a tantrum. When, during an expedition against the 'still unsubdued and cheeky' northern Matabele, their Chief Uwini was captured, court-martialed and shot by B-P, he himself was nearly arrested. The High Commissioner in Cape Town condemned such summary executions. But the subsequent court of inquiry accepted B-P's argument that the 'immediate punishment' of this 'fine old savage' had done 'more than anything else to restore our prestige'. In B-P's eyes the issues, like the combatants, were black and white. Killing 'native "boys"' was the object of the exercise and for killjoys who urged restraint and for spoil-sports who tried to change the rules, B-P had nothing but stiff-lipped resentment and Kiplingesque contempt.

> A man here does not mind carrying his own life in his hand – he likes it, and takes an attack on himself as a good bit of sport; but touch a woman or a child, and he is in a blind fury in a moment – and then he is gently advised to be mild, and to offer clemency to the poor benighted heathen, who is his brother after all. M', yes! And though woman is his first care, and can command his last drop of blood in her defence, woman is the first to assail him on his return, with venom-pointed pen, for his brutality.

No Eve, no serpent, no recherché knowledge of good and evil, entered B-P's Eden. His state of virgin innocence remained sublimely intact. He knew that 'the goodly precepts of the game remain as best of guides: "Keep your place," and "Play, not for yourself, but for your side." ' And if some outsider should question this code, should perhaps ask why it was needful to play the game at all, B-P had an unanswerable reply – *'because it is the game'*. In Matabeleland no one presumed to challenge this axiom. They were boys playing with toys and, as B-P said, they would all continue to play 'with them with as much zest at eighty as at eight... [for] in their company we can never grow old.' Of all his toys Impeesa was proudest of the trophy provided by a warrior whom he had killed. B-P could not, of course, have the native himself stuffed and mounted. But he prized the Matabele's weapon, the seizure of which might be taken to symbolize the tribe's final emasculation, a knobkerrie.

V

Cock-a-hoop from the Elysian simplicities of the Matabele campaign, B-P was soon to be nonplussed by the infernal muddle of the South African conflict. The Boers were no doubt rude, ignorant farmers with a literal faith in the Bible; President Kruger once assured the American circumnavigator, Joshua Slocum, that the world was flat. But B-P could not help admiring these hardy pioneers. They had 'become "gentlemen" by their contact with nature'. But they had certainly not been rendered effete by what he called 'the enervating influences of over-civilization' – before the gold rush in 1886 the Transvaal was so poor that its Postmaster General was paid his salary in stamps. Although the Boers obstructed British colonists who came to mine the gold, although Kruger's Republic blocked British imperial expansion, it seemed unnatural to fight against white frontiersmen in the dark continent. Moreover, B-P never fully grasped what he was supposed to do in South Africa. As new Colonel of the 5th Dragoons he had been once more enjoying life in India, sticking pigs, acting, joking, smartening up his men by training them as scouts, hunting bear in Kashmir and Afghans on the North-West Frontier – 'a pheasant shoot' it was called by his host, General Sir Bindon Blood. Home on leave in July 1899, B-P was unexpectedly summoned by Lord Wolseley. Over innumerable camp-fires he was to spin the famous yarn of his interview with the Commander-in-Chief.

C-in-C: 'I want you to go to South Africa.'
B-P: 'Yes, sir!'

C-in-C: 'Well, can you go on Saturday next?'
B-P: 'No, sir!'
C-in-C: 'Why not?'
B-P: 'There's no ship on Saturday. But I can go on Friday.'

B-P not only kept his 'kit' packed ready for instant departure he also, apparently, memorized the marine time-tables, possibly by pelmanism. Whatever the method it was faulty, for there were in fact two perfectly good ships sailing for South Africa on the Saturday in question. Evidently, then, he received hasty orders while the state of his mind was confused. To judge from the scribbled additions and contradictions in his unpublished account of Mafeking's siege, B-P never did understand why he had spent six months defending that insignificant little railway-siding in the middle of the veldt. Still, perhaps he was no more addle-headed than his military masters; in after years General Kitchener used to explain that Mafeking had been held because the War Office believed 'it was the nearest sea port to Pretoria.'

The most peculiar feature of the siege was Impeesa's docile readiness to be caged in Mafeking at all. B-P's orders were to raise two regiments of mounted infantry (some of them unfortunately had to be picked from South Africa's floating population of 'loafers') with the aim of protecting the Rhodesian frontier. Yet when hostilities began, in October 1899, he at once made that achievement im-possible by sacrificing his own and his force's mobility (though he did give one regiment a roving commission of which its commander, the gloved and eye-glassed Colonel Plumer, took full advantage). B-P apparently regarded it as his duty to keep Mafeking out of Boer hands because it was an 'important centre', of 'strategic value'. Yet these guerilla fighters did not need urban bases and what chiefly made the township a 'prize' was the huge quantity of stores which B-P himself had purchased in preparation for a siege. Having thus invited investment, he later averred that it was essential to his purpose of attracting 'as large a force of Boers as possible' away from Natal and the Cape. Yet he drew few and at the time he expressed the hope that a 'good blow' would drive even these away. Failing that, his men had only to 'sit tight and wait for them to go'. B-P also asserted that the defence of Mafeking was undertaken to 'maintain British prestige'. This was an odd claim from a cavalryman who constantly lauded the offensive spirit and deplored the fact that so many of his countrymen were 'cursed with want of dash'. Yet it was to be marvellously justified. For in this war the Empire appeared uncomfortably to resemble a big (and often worsted) bully, whereas it was clear that at Mafeking a British hero had held out against what *The Times* called 'overwhelming odds', thus demonstrating 'the fundamental grit of the breed'. And, of course, from Corunna to Dunkirk the breed have had a truly alchemical capacity for transmuting averted disaster into glorious triumph. Nevertheless, B-P's willing confinement in Mafeking remains an enigma. As one of his own officers remarked, 'To burrow underground on the very first shot being fired in a campaign, and to commence eating his horses, seemed to me the strangest role ever played by a cavalry leader with his regiment of mounted men.' Could Impeesa, perhaps, have been a sheep in wolf's clothing? Could the Matabele, indeed, have cried Impeesa in jest? It seems certain, at least, that Impeesa found roaming over the veldt less fun when his enemies were equipped with modern Mauser rifles.

However, if B-P lacked the strategist's art he possessed the tactician's craft. Having missed Staff College, he owed this less to his training as a mounted officer than to his instinct as a mountebank. Many a 'joyous little dodge' with which he attempted to outwit the enemy smacked

more of the showman's stage than the theatre of war —
transmitting mock orders through a megaphone, sowing
sham minefields, climbing through imaginary barbed
wire, casting grenades by fishing rod. These expedients
were not altogether effective. Wandering cattle seemed
mysteriously immune to the mines, for example, and
despite the pantomime performed for distant eyes, local
spies must have informed the Boers that B-P had no wire.
Still, such flamboyant tricks were no doubt good for
morale, as was the huffing and puffing of the spectacularly
useless armoured train, which B-P's camouflage rendered
'very invisible'. And luckily for his 1,200 men (not to
mention the 600 white women and children and the 7,500
Africans), surrounded as they were by 6,000 Boers (the
number later shrank to 1,500), B-P had more profitable
stratagems in his repertoire. Unable to give the town
much protection with his few pieces of obsolete artillery,
he deftly extended his chain of fortresses, each one linked
to his headquarters by telephone, until it was six miles in
circumference. With black labour he constructed underground shelters for the whites, who consequently sustained a mere handful of non-combatant casualties from
shell-fire. The blacks, of course, did not need bunkers —
would probably, indeed, have kept coal in them — this
being a 'white man's war'. As a result about three hundred
Africans were killed by shells and more were slain fighting
bravely in the 'Black Watch', a troop of cattle guards and
raiders recruited by B-P. This breach of the unwritten
protocol incensed the Boers. But generally they adhered to
Kruger's mild opinion that Mafeking was not worth fifty
Boer lives. So, after a few tentative thrusts over the open
plain, they feebly resolved to shell and starve the garrison
into submission. Despite their modern 94-pound siege
gun (known as 'Creaky'), which vastly outmatched the
defending batteries, this was a vain endeavour. For, apart
from B-P's stores, Mafeking's most substantial asset was

its very insubstantiality. The town was spaciously laid out and constructed of adobe which crumbled and did not splinter, thus diffusing the force of explosions. The initial Boer bombardment was awaited with trepidation and received with derision. According to *The Times*'s correspondent it was a 'gigantic joke', the most ludicrous episode in the history of modern warfare, the first act in a 'farcical melodrama'. One chicken was killed.

The chief enemy of Mafeking was boredom. More demoralizing even than assaults by hosts of mosquitoes, fleas, flies and ants, the insufferable tedium, the 'endless monotony in which there is absolutely nothing to sustain one's interest', threatened to defeat the garrison. B-P solved this problem with characteristic panache. On Sundays, when a truce was observed and young men's fancies turned, as B-P knew, to thoughts of solitary vice, he organized every sort of entertainment and recreation. There were Beleaguered Bachelors' Balls and beautiful baby competitions, cricket matches and horticultural shows, bicycle races and tea parties, gymkhanas and fêtes worse than death. On Guy Fawkes' Day he mounted a firework display, first having warned the Boers not to be alarmed. At Christmas he presided over a dinner, the menu at which would not have disgraced the Café Royal. He arranged polo fixtures on week-days – when occasional shells added to the game's excitement. Above all he performed as impresario, stage manager and star in a series of hilarious music-hall concerts. Now in a mop of false hair and a falsetto voice, he mimicked Paderewski. Now in a costermonger's suit, cap and muffler, he played a Cockney songster. Now in a white tie and tails, with a clown's hat and a beribboned whip, he impersonated a circus ringmaster. However, as a witness remarked, instantly firing commenced 'the man who had been masquerading as a buffoon was again the commanding officer, stern and alert.' Yet it sometimes seemed that despite this masterly quick-change act the transformation was not quite complete. The flail of 'grousers' (they were in a state of 'funk', said B-P, and should be kicked) trilled choruses from *Cavalleria Rusticana* from cockcrow to nightfall. The scourge of soakers (B-P tried to impose prohibition on Mafeking) rubbed his hands together like a comic opera villain. The upholder of 115 sentences of corporal punishment in 217 days, who dismissed as 'childish' the complaint that a doctor was operating on Africans without anaesthetics, smiled and whistled throughout all difficulties. At times, indeed, it was almost impossible to distinguish between the Colonel in command and the sjambok-wielding merry-andrew.

Nevertheless, the siege was not without its alarms and excursions and B-P did quite enough to deserve his place in the pantheon of school-boy paladins. Of course, he looked the part – the spick-and-span boots (one of the prime pieces of folk-wisdom which B-P passed on to the Scouts was that you could always tell a gentleman by his boots), the immaculate uniform, the penetrating blue eyes, the lithe, vigilant mien, the firm jaw which seemed 'to close every argument with a snap'. True, he was somewhat balder and shorter than the average demigod. But then Kantankye invariably covered his bare pate. And Impeesa's abbreviated size was all the better for prowling with. What is more B-P compensated for small stature by massive modesty, by magnificent lack of ostentation, by an understated bravado which was the quintessence of British pluck. With one breath he would say that the reputation of the siege had been 'exaggerated'. With the next he would refer to the ' "pepperbox" refuge' by the look-out tower over his headquarters 'into which I could retire when bullets came too thickly'. In fact, the town was mostly beyond the range of Boer rifles, though snipers lying in no-man's-land did some damage. Sorties and skirmishes claimed more lives, and in these dangerous tit-for-tats B-P showed that he was a boy's own hero in spirit as well as appearance. An early bayonet raid on a Boer trench, led by Mafeking's Hotspur, Captain Fitzclarence, was bloodily successful though most of the victims proved to be very young, some of them boys. At the end of October the enemy counter-attacked, killing about ten men on Canon Kopje, a small eminence which, though it commanded Mafeking, had not been properly protected.

After a lull, B-P experienced his worst setback. On Boxing Day, 1899, he ordered an assault on a strong-point called Game Tree Fort. The Boers were expecting it and had strengthened their defences. B-P would have dis-discovered that the fort was virtually impregnable had anyone in Mafeking been proficient at the art of... scouting. Consequently the operation was, in the words of the only African diarist to endure the siege, 'regular self-murder', 'a heart-rending burlesque'. The British suffered fifty casualties, the Boers three. However, B-P had his revenge when Kruger's grandson, Sarel Eloff, led the sole serious attack on the township, shortly before the relief, in May 1900. Eloff penetrated the defences and had he been supported by his commanding officer, the inept General Snyman, Mafeking might have fallen. As it was, about forty Boers were killed and 108, including Eloff, were taken prisoner, while British casualties were negligible. B-P treated his captives with knightly courtesy, and the only contretemps occurred when Eloff mistook the 'siege porridge' for soapy water and washed his hands in it.

This incident is one among many which indicates that the investment was far from being, as B-P's modern critics* suggest, a luxurious picnic. Of course, no one now denies that the Africans were reduced to starvation,

* e.g. B. Gardner *Mafeking: A Victorian Legend* (1966); B. Farwell, *The Boer War* (1977).

though then the *Morning Post*'s correspondent did maintain that 'the Kaffir, who has plenty of money, but is only
allowed to purchase a limited amount of meal, browses off
Pâté de Foie Gras, and other similar comestibles.' This
opinion scarcely accords with accounts of emaciated
Africans eating stolen dogs, seizing bones from live dogs,
digging up dead dogs. Famine killed hundreds of blacks,
many of them children. Even so B-P considered their
meagre rations too great a drain on his supplies. He tried
to 'get rid of' as many Africans as possible, notwithstanding the Boers' habit of shooting, or stripping and flogging,
Bantu refugees of both sexes. For those who remained he
instituted a pass system. He also enforced a savage penal
code, executing a black horse-thief while recommending
clemency for a white murderer. This was typical of the
prevailing racial double standard. But the whites did
suffer modest privations of their own. For B-P husbanded
his food stocks, not knowing when he would be relieved.
At the beginning of April one aristocratic lady sent home a
'Kaffirgram' (black runners could always steal in and out
of the loosely invested township) which read: 'Breakfast
today, horse sausages; lunch minced mule, curried locusts.
All well.' And *The Times*'s correspondent, though he
condemned B-P's African policy as being 'altogether at
variance with the dignity of the liberalism which we pro-
fess', acknowledged that 'The garrison is famished; that is,
in reality the kernel of our situation.'

It was a situation which Colonel Baden-Powell could
do little to improve. Improvisation made good other
shortages. Ammunition was manufactured and even a
howitzer, nicknamed 'the Wolf'. (When another gun was
discovered in Mafeking, an old naval cannon made by a
firm called Bailey and Pegg, malicious gossip suggested
that B-P had stamped his own initials on the breech.) A
siege currency was produced. New stamps were issued
featuring B-P's head, a piece of vainglorious lèse-majesté

which delighted him at the time but later proved an embarrassment – he claimed they had been printed without his knowledge. A cadet corps of boy messengers even helped to compensate for the dearth of manpower. B-P later managed to take the credit for this portentous formation but it was actually raised, dressed in khaki uniform, 'smasher' hats and yellow scarves, and trained by his Chief of Staff, Lord Edward Cecil. However, the only manna which the men of Mafeking received was a few locusts and B-P laid provisional plans to evacuate the town, the Boer lines being now but thinly held. The Colonel rubbed his hands together less by this time and was more silent, though the compulsive whistle continued to emerge from under that pursed upper lip. Daily he wrote a letter to the captive 'Boy' McLaren. Nightly he roamed the veldt; to the *Pall Mall Gazette*'s correspondent it seemed as if he never slept. Otherwise, he spent much time in solitary brooding, staring out over the stony wilderness through his binoculars. Luckily the Colonel was not himself much troubled by hunger. His appetite was small. It was a fact on which King Edward passed adverse comment when B-P visited Balmoral in 1901 to receive his Companionship of the Bath:

> I want to speak to you seriously. I have watched you at meals and I notice that you don't eat enough. When working as you are doing you must keep up your system. I am sending you off with some venison to tempt you to eat more. Don't forget – eat more.

Sovereign and subject shared a devotion to smartness, especially in the matter of headgear – Edward once said that Lord Haldane's hat looked as though it had belonged to Goethe. But the stout, self-indulgent monarch apparently did not realize that no hero worthy of the name carried an ounce of superfluous flesh on his body, and that 'eating rich foods' encouraged the evil habit of self-abuse.

At three o'clock in the morning of 17 May, 1900, Impeesa was, for a wonder, asleep in bed. He was roused by his younger brother, called, thanks to 'Old Mrs Hyphen', Baden Baden-Powell, who was a Major in Colonel Mahon's rescue column. After more than seven months Mafeking was relieved. So was the Empire. Soon the British race was 'mafficking', celebrating with such jubilant abandon that a new word was coined to describe it. For days frenzied multitudes surged through bunting-bedecked streets cheering, laughing, dancing, kissing, singing, waving patriotic banners, flourishing portraits of Mafeking's saviour. Such wild saturnalia, though generally good-humoured, shocked the moralists. The Victorian *Times* noticed that 'Well-dressed young women of usually proper demeanour traversed the roadways, arm-in-arm, six abreast, carrying flags and occasionally bursting into song.' Such delirious rejoicings, unprecedented in English history and scarcely to be exceeded on Armistice Day 1918, alarmed the authorities. The Liberal politician Charles Masterman expressed horror that a mob, 'learning to gambol with heavy and grotesque antics', had held the world's richest city in the hollow of its hand. But really these hobbledehoy demonstrations amounted to nothing more sinister than a spontaneous ecstasy of national crowing, a cocky proclamation of imperial virility. As for the legendary British stoicism, it was apparently still to be found among the Baden-Powells. On Mafeking night B-P's mother went to bed leaving instructions that whatever the news she was not to be disturbed. B-P's own conduct was impeccably unassuming. He even professed surprise at all the adulation, though family letters had told him that his piquant 'Kaffirgrams' had been devoured by a vast public, who regarded him as the hero of the hour. In private, however, he could not always contain his exultation. In boisterous boyhood it had pleased him to startle his mother's visitors by uttering loud 'cock-a-doodle-doos'.

While staying at Cecil Rhodes's house in Cape Town, he reverted to his early practice; another of the guests, Dr Jameson, complained that to have B-P crowing like a cock at breakfast-time was 'too much!'

VI

In 1900 Lord Wolseley congratulated B-P on becoming, at forty-three, the youngest General in the British army: 'You now have the ball at your feet, and barring accidents greatness is in front of you.' There were no major accidents, but somehow B-P never succeeded in dribbling his way to the top of his profession. Perhaps, even though Queen Victoria expressed delight over his 'splendid defence', B-P had, as was rumoured, offended his punctilious sovereign by usurping her place on the Mafeking stamps. At any rate, B-P was only given the Bath, an award difficult to justify except as a tribute to his obsession with cleanliness. Certainly Wolseley's successor as Commander-in-Chief, Lord Roberts, had observed B-P's feeble performance after the siege. Impeesa had failed to pursue his prey. Instead, he had ordered his men to fire off 'their guns in the enemy's rear, which, though not within range, perhaps disconcerted them'. In the open at last, he had been out-foxed by Boer commandos. And, seeking a bolt-hole in the town of Rustenberg, he had almost managed to become invested for a second time. So peculiar was his conduct that Lord Edward Cecil wondered if 'the gods were angry with [B-P] and drove him mad'. Yet Roberts himself had interpreted British advances against the Boer forces as triumphs over the Boer people and had left South Africa announcing that victory was at hand. Kitchener agreed, but he discovered that the Boer guerillas were fish swimming in the sea of the population, and it took him two years of filling concentration camps to drain that sea. These and other British commanders had earned their laurels by mowing down knobkerrie-carrying fuzzy-wuzzies with Maxim guns – Kitchener invariably greeted the 9th Lancers with the words, 'Hullo! How are the Ninth? Been killing any more black men?' Compared to such officers B-P was by no means signally incompetent. Winston Churchill was probably correct in stating that the War Office and Whitehall resented the 'disproportionate acclaim which the masses had bestowed on a single man'. Like Gordon, Lawrence of Arabia and Lindbergh, Baden-Powell was an embarrassment to the authorities. The heroic colossus would be less awkward to accommodate if he remained a military manikin.

Accordingly B-P was appointed to supervise what the High Commissioner, Sir Alfred Milner, called 'a sideshow'. He became Inspector General of the South African Constabulary. He was obliged to raise this force, ten thousand strong, partly from 'Stellenbosched' soldiers, fools or knaves relegated to the Cape military base. B-P was touchy about this and wrote to the press denying that there had been a dearth of suitable recruits. His men were all 'first-rate' – except, that is, for the 'hundreds' of loafers and soakers whom he 'weeded out' mercilessly. B-P had no trouble, fortunately, in identifying these pieces of 'waste human material': 'though they thought they looked all right, I knew from their eye or lip or manner.' Presumably, too, those who turned out their toes were eliminated, such people being, as B-P knew, 'generally "liars" '. About two thousand of his policemen were Old Boys of public schools and it was 'possible to put them on their honour'. For the rest B-P tried to engender an appropriate *esprit de corps*. He designed a uniform which anticipated that worn by the Boy Scouts – wide-brimmed hats to ensure cool heads, flannel shirts to guard against suppressed perspiration, breezy shorts to ventilate racial organs. He encouraged initiative by training the men in small troops and patrols. He provided them with that oracular motto, 'Be Prepared'. Joseph Chamberlain, who was conducted on his South African tour in 1903 by B-P, pronounced his Constabulary 'a great civilizing and uniting influence'. Today the words ring with bitter irony, especially when one considers that B-P's contingent was the precursor of the modern South African Police Force – which he was to declare 'a fine body' on its formation. That this peerless organization was initiated by the founder of the Boy Scouts can, of course, lead critics to draw sinister conclusions about the movement which B-P nearly christened 'Young Knights of the Empire'. Some are doubtless justified, but not the most extreme – the Scouts were no imperial equivalent of the Hitler Youth, no germinant Gestapo. For just as B-P's religious opinions were the received orthodoxy of the middle class, so his political views were the accepted clichés of the officer caste. He paid lip-service to both. Yet he remained an eternal Candide, an evergreen innocent. When asked to stand for Parliament he telegraphed this reply: 'Delighted. Which side?' The Constabulary was for B-P simply another great game. It was set in a fair ground and played with bold, plucky adepts of the outdoor life. They regarded B-P as 'an awfully jolly fellow'. He was chiefly concerned about their smartness – dress, after all, was an index of address. When a train carrying a consignment of American 'Boss-of-the-Plains' hats (the initials were a happy coincidence) for his constables was wrecked by the Boers, B-P proclaimed that any unauthorized person found wearing one would be shot.

The War Office evidently considered that a decorative rather than an executive position would best suit B-P. In 1903 he was 'kicked upstairs' to become Inspector-General of Cavalry. This was, as he admitted, a quite inappropriate promotion, for B-P wanted the frolicsome comradeship of the regimental mess and the snug feeling that he was in close touch with his men, preferably in the field. Also he lacked the requisite academic knowledge and 'acted merely from common sense and an appreciation of the methods of Oliver Cromwell'. With such guiding lights he naturally failed to perceive that cavalry had now become obsolete. So, luckily, did the commanders of the German mounted forces, not to mention those of the American, Russian and French, all of whom permitted B-P to observe their horsemen on manoeuvres. What is more, long after the Great War had demonstrated the murderous effects of twentieth-century fire-power, eminent figures like Duff Cooper could be heard maintaining that there would always be a place in modern warfare for the well-bred horse. Thus B-P was not notably unenlightened. Indeed, he established a new training school and a journal, encouraged the employment of scouting methods and improved the lot of troopers (they were 'nowadays', he remarked, 'a better class and do not drink'). Had there been a future for the British cavalry he would have made a modest contribution to it. However, his role, like that destined for the cavalry, was a ceremonial one. He expressed his dissatisfaction with such elevated foppery by frequent trips abroad, by hunting expeditions, by fishing week-ends, by offering to give one lady, whom he met at a garden party, a tracking lesson in the local woods. These escapades, like his adoption of various aliases, also enabled him to avoid being perpetually lionized. Some appreciation, of course, he enjoyed. Most of all he relished the welcome given to him by the boys of Charterhouse. And he was pleased with the house party where he acted as substitute for a delayed conjuror – his trick was to cut up another guest's top hat and invite the professional magician to hey-presto the pieces together again. But the 'recurrent travel fever' which afflicted him was really another symptom of his endemic 'camp sickness'. By 1907, when he was placed high on the military shelf, first as a reserve Lieutenant-General on half-pay and then, for the two years before his retirement in 1910, as commander of the Northumberland Division of the newly formed Territorial Army, he was seeking a remedy for that old ailment. He discovered it, of course, in the Boy Scout Movement, the founding of which not only gave him an opportunity to exploit the 'damnable notoriety I had incurred', but set him at last in his proper sphere – among that lusty 'Brotherhood of Backwoodsmen', that freemasonry of outdoor youth, dedicated one and all to the desire and pursuit of the wholesome.

VII

It was mainly but not merely a faddish enthusiasm for woodcraft and wild life which induced B-P to create his 'jolly fraternity' of Boy Scouts. Like many other Edwardians he was haunted by fears that the race was deteriorating (physically and morally) and that national efficiency and imperial security were jeopardized. Welfare benefits and cinemas were the bread and circuses of a decadent Britain. The flight from the land, the employment of mercenary troops, the growth of luxury, the increase in juvenile delinquency, the habit of tipping, the prevalence of strikes, the 'artificial erection' of class barriers, the difficulty of obtaining dutiful servants, 'the decline of good citizenship and the want of energetic patriotism' – these were the unmistakable signs of incipient degeneration. Another was the deplorable importation from the United States of that molly-coddling slogan, 'Safety First':

> We certainly have the habit of stepping off the kerb without looking round, but this is not so much from blank foolishness as from the feeling that the road

belongs to foot sloggers as much as to any motorist; and if, as a consequence, we get it in the back we merely die asserting our right. That's British.

Most sinister of all was the fact that the sprightly walker had given way to the slovenly sloucher, the 'sickly-minded, sloppy slacker who talks dirt and has no backbone'. Young lads conceived by parents who lacked 'self-restraint' had 'no work and no money'. Alternatively they were earning 'high wages and becoming independent of parental control'. Whatever the case, they not only slobbered over drink and cigarettes, they indulged in 'low and unmanly' acts of onanism, 'loose talk', 'smutty stories', 'lewd pictures', 'filth' and 'loafing with girls' whom they would not care to introduce to their mothers or sisters. This was, of course, a perennial problem for, as B-P said, 'the period of youth is the human "rutting season" '. It might last for a few months or, in exceptional cases, a few years, and it had to be 'got over', like measles. Scouting might not effect a complete cure but it could defer maturity for several years or, in exceptional cases, a life-time. Failing this... well, a Scout was clean in thought, word and deed, and his energies were safely guided into the rut of backwoodmanship, the ideal training, exhaustive and exhausting, for a healthy master race.

In view of all this it is tempting to endorse Saki's opinion that Boy Scouts were 'the Janissaries of the Empire' – in his novel *When William Came*, one of many Edwardian fictions concerning the future invasion of England by Germany, Saki's Scouts saved their grand old country's soul by a staunch refusal to march past the Kaiser. B-P himself toyed with the idea of calling his movement the 'Imperial Scouts'. He asserted that 'every boy should learn how to shoot.' He suggested that Scouts should emigrate and become colonial policemen. He praised the 'plucky self-sacrifice' of Japanese suicide-

The submission of
King Prempeh

B-P overwhelming an
Ashanti warrior

The hero of Mafeking

Mafficking

B-P tells a campfire yarn, 1908

soldiers. And he solemnly cited, and proposed that Scouts should recite, Sir Henry Newbolt's famous imperialist verse, which today reads like a masterpiece of self-parody:

The sand of the desert is sodden red –
Red with the wreck of the square that broke;
The gatling's jammed and the colonel dead,
And the regiment blind with dust and smoke.
The river of death has brimmed its banks,
And England's far and Honour a name,
But the voice of a schoolboy rallies the ranks.
'Play up! Play up! And play the game!'

Moreover many early Scoutmasters arrayed themselves in battlefield trappings, not just Sam Browne belts, gauntlets, khaki tunics, breeches and gaiters, but pistols, swords, bugles, bandoliers, spurs. Others left the movement because of its tendency towards militarism. The most notable defector was John Hargrave, the charismatic but avowedly 'cranky' 'White Fox', who in 1920 founded, at the Pethick-Lawrences' house in Lincoln's Inn, the Kibbo Kift Kindred or 'clan of great strength'. The KKK was 'a body-impulse to get Earth contact in a mechanical age'. It was a quasi-mystical organization consecrated to world unity, social credit and the generation of a new Samurai through the practice of 'campercraft', the performance of pagan ritual, the wearing of hand-made leather belts and cowled jerkins, the roasting of whole oxen. Another splinter group, formed in 1925, was Leslie Paul's Woodcraft Folk, a 'blood-brotherhood of the camp-fire' dedicated to archaic incantation, pacifism, socialism, vegetarianism and naked bathing.

Yet from the first B-P emphasized that '*The Boy Scouts are not military*'. He criticized the Boys' Brigade, started by William Smith in 1883 to advance 'Christ's Kingdom' among young lads by promoting 'habits of Obedience,

Reverence, Discipline, Self-Respect and all that tends towards a True Christian Manliness', because of its rigid reliance on martial exercises such as drill. B-P was, however, strongly influenced by the artist-naturalist Ernest Thompson Seton, whose Woodcraft Indians had since 1900 been satisfying the needs of 'heart-hungry [American] boys tormented with an insatiate instinct for the woods'. Like B-P, Seton admitted to being 'much of a boy myself' and he recognized that 'the boy is a caveman.' Exploiting the primitive propensities of boyhood, especially the gang spirit, Seton taught the members of his tribe to imitate the highest type of savage life, the ideal Indian of Fenimore Cooper – 'physically beautiful, clean, unsordid, high-minded, heroic, picturesque and a Master of Woodcraft'. His boys learnt camping and backwoodsmanship, played tracking and hunting games, took tests and earned badges, conducted Redskin rites before totem poles, wore wampum pouches and scalplocks, adopted names like Hawkeye and Running Bear, uttered watchwords and war-whoops. But Seton specifically abjured military methods in favour of the 'Woodcraft way'. And his first principle was that 'This movement is essentially for recreation'. During its seed-time Scouting was, in fact, powerfully imbued with the romance of the red man; dressed in feathers and moccasins pre-pubertal Scoutmasters would salute each other with the word 'How!' and propose pow-wows for the puffing of peace-pipes. B-P countenanced this, provided it was not taken to extremes, just as he was content to see Esperanto and Morris Dancing included among Scouting activities. For above all the Scouts were devoted to 'fun and jollity' in the open air. An imperial task-force would hardly have assimilated foreigners into its ranks. Even Indian boys eventually became Scouts; at a huge Madras rally in 1921 their leader, Annie Besant, dressed in a green turban, a purple scarf and a sari of khaki-coloured silk with emerald borders, took the oath of loyalty before B-P. A serious para-military organization could scarcely have adopted a creed of international comradeship. Once again P. G. Wodehouse was the voice of common sense; in *The Swoop* (1909) he found the ideal medium to typify soldier-scouting – a farce. His fictional Boy Scout, Clarence MacAndrew Chugwater, managed to save Britain from a fiendish concatenation of invaders – Germans in Essex, Russians at Yarmouth, the Mad Mullah at Portsmouth, the Swiss Navy at Lyme Regis, China at Lgxtpll in Wales, Monaco at Auchtermuchty, Moroccan brigands at Brighton and Bollygolla at Margate.

But if the pretensions and occupations of Scouts appeared ludicrous to Wodehouse and shocking to other Edwardians – knees were barely proper – Scouting itself appealed seriously to the upper classes. Lord Rosebery, for example, said that a nation 'trained in the Boy Scout theory. . . would be the greatest moral force the world has ever known'. For, as a matter of course, B-P infected the movement with his own conservative attitudes. Of these, devotion to the crown was the most potent. In 1910, for example, B-P proposed that Scouts born in the same year as the new heir to the throne might wear a badge of

> Prince of Wales feathers, with the initial of the Prince attached. Wearing this badge would signify willingness to serve as bodyguard to that Prince in case of danger or for ceremonial visits to the district. The object of this is that a number of the rising generation will thus have a material touch of personal loyalty to the Royal Family. It is on the same principle which worked so powerfully with the Zulus. . . The starting of the personal loyal touch will be a good move against socialism.

After making obeisance to the flag, Scouts in camp paid homage to God; B-P insisted that they should not be 'irreligious humbugs', though he was indifferent to which

Deity they worshipped so long as He did not encourage milk-and-watery attitudes, morbid self-consciousness or a 'mysterious and lugubrious' mode of behaviour. Another ideal constantly preached to the Scouts was that of service. B-P was to found Scout training centres where those from distressed areas could learn to be butlers, cooks, gardeners and valets. He recommended that 'members of country families' should, by means of Scouting, 'make good Englishmen' of their villagers' and tenants' lads, 'somewhat on the old feudal lines'. The daily deed of kindness was an earnest of sound citizenship, for though it might upset individuals it did not threaten to upset society.

Modern critics of B-P concentrate on these aspects of Scouting and denounce the movement as a subtle form of (to employ the cant term) 'social control', a method whereby the reactionary ruling classes curbed their upstart inferiors, a means by which adults, while pretending to encourage independence and initiative in youth, imposed conformity to their own standards. There is an obvious element of truth in the charges. Yet though Impeesa often stressed the worth of cunning, B-P was less notable for ingenuity than for ingenuousness. And it is clear from *Scouting for Boys* (1908), probably the most influential youth manual ever published, that B-P was primarily inspired by spontaneous juvenility not by calculating maturity. He wrote dutifully about the spirit of service and the need to hold the Empire against a bullying, 'swaggering ass' of a country. More feeling were his anxious marginalia on genitalia, some of which were suppressed by his publisher. But his most intense enthusiasm was reserved for accounts of heroes of the wild, frontiersmen, pioneers, explorers, Pied Pipers to boys. He waxed almost lyrical about tying knots and seeking 'sign', about first aid and physical jerks, about the useful art of imitating animal noises and the worthwhile craft of distinguishing a 'brutish character' from 'a case of genteel poverty', about camp-fire jollification, 'fair play' (only an 'awful beast' kicks a man when he is down) and the delights of eating iguana – 'when he was boiled and put on the table he looked exactly like a headless baby with his arms and legs and little hands...[he tasted like a baby too], sort of soft chicken flavoured with violet-powder!'

B-P demonstrated the magic appeal of Scouting at his celebrated experimental camp on Brownsea Island in August 1907. Boys of different classes mixed there on terms of equality. They were awakened by a blast on the koodoo horn which B-P had acquired in Matabeleland. They were divided into patrols (Curlews, Ravens, Wolves, Bulls), put on their honour, taught woodcraft, awarded badges. They said daily prayers and were encouraged to perform their daily 'rear'. They swam, competed, cooked, bivouacked. Percy Everett evoked the flavour of the evening entertainments as conducted by B-P.

> I can see him still as he stands in the flickering light of the fire – an alert figure, full of the joy of life, now grave now gay, answering all manner of questions, imitating the call of birds, showing how to stalk a wild animal, flashing out a little story, dancing and singing round the fire, pointing a moral...

Actually, although 'Boy' McLaren was present throughout, Percy Everett seems only to have visited Brownsea for the day. Still, his imagined account is doubtless true in spirit and he must have reported favourably to his employer, the press magnate, Arthur Pearson. For B-P would not rely on the intrinsic enchantment of his programme and he had solicited Pearson's help in giving publicity to Scouting. Pearson's biographer stated that in his subject there was 'a large element of Peter Pan'. Pearson was a devotee of fresh air, an addict of games and practical jokes, a lover of children and outdoor cooking. So while Lord Northcliffe jockeyed him out of *The Times* in 1908,

Pearson scored the minor coup of publishing *Scouting for Boys* and its companion magazine, *The Scout*, which was soon selling over 100,000 copies each week. Thus the Napoleon of Fleet Street (who favoured Scouting itself) undoubtedly considered that 'He-of-the-big-hat' had become 'He-of-the-big-head', and he branded B-P a fraud: 'He is not the inventor of the idea of Boy Scouts.'

Though, like most of Northcliffe's accusations, this one must be taken with a grain of salt, it did also contain a grain of truth, for initially B-P envisaged that existing youth organizations would sponsor his scheme of activities. He assumed direct control of Scouting only when it became a movement, when patrols of Scouts had begun to establish themselves independently. B-P's ambition to attract 'the vast horde of slum boys in the great industrial centres' was doomed; such lads were avid to grow up, despised bare knees as a stigma of immaturity and anyway could not afford the uniform. But the sons of the middle class (or of those aspiring to join it) were, as Leslie Paul wrote, 'electrified' by Scouting. Almost overnight thousands donned the distinctive garb, denuded ironmongers' shops of broomsticks, enrolled Scoutmasters, swore the oath, adopted the left handshake and started to practise Scoutcraft. Soon Scouts were everywhere. They covered pavements with chalked symbols. They littered parks with the remnants of paper-chases. They marooned themselves in belfries. They floated out to sea on rafts. They chopped down trees. They set fire to the countryside. They reported 'foreign-looking' men to the police. They acted as black-legs in strikes. They inflicted good turns on the healthy (one man was informed by an obliging Scout that his wife was committing adultery) and they subjected the sick to the additional hazard of first aid. They poured mugs of cold water, as B-P recommended, down the sleeves of those of their number who were not clean in word. They smiled and whistled — a testing feat when attempted simultaneously – under all difficulties. They enjoyed themselves. The Boy Scouts of England were determined to prove themselves worthy of their founder.

Soon boys all over the world were following their lead and their leader. So, to B-P's surprise and dismay, were girls. Their adhesion would surely make the movement 'sissy'. In 1910, with his sister Agnes, B-P devised a separate female organization. He defined Girl Guides (he disliked the American title, Girl Scouts) as 'jolly people who enjoy themselves. . . a happy sisterhood who do good turns to other people.' Their training was designed to promote mothercraft and home-making. Men did not want 'dolls', still less 'tomboys', as wives. They desired 'comrades', especially those keen on 'camping and the out of doors'. They pined for 'pals' whom they could put 'on a pedestal'. Unfortunately, B-P noted, 'growing girls' were all too often unsuited to this elevation because they were so 'very apt to slouch'. The most frequent exhortations in his *Girl Guiding* were therefore, 'Tuck in Your Back' (TYB) and 'at all times Brace Your Back Muscles' (BYBM). Thus would the future mothers of the sons of the British Empire learn to breed a healthy, upright race. In those benighted areas of the globe which were not painted red on the map, Scouts simply ignored the movement's imperialist patina and concentrated on its essence, on that adventurous game which appealed to the atavistic instincts of youngsters of all ages everywhere.

B-P himself was flabbergasted by, but enthusiastic about, the international spread of Scouting and increasingly stressed its 'non-military, non-sectarian, non-political policy'. For instance, he refused to associate the movement with the British Empire Union because to do so would 'put a stopper on our work':

We are gaining successful touch with elements that are near the edge of disloyalty and by winning their confidence we are able to make effective appeal to their rising generation and so to prevent the growth of sedition.

Despite being an ardent Unionist, B-P offered virtual 'Home Rule' to Irish Scouts. He was also particularly keen on 'piling up friendship with the Boy Scouts of America'. There the organization had been introduced in 1910 as the result of a London Scout's good deed – he guided the Chicago publisher, William D. Boyce, through a 'pea-souper' and refused to accept a tip (a form of bribery in B-P's view). In the bracing frontier atmosphere of the United States Scouting flourished as nowhere else. It combined with Seton's Woodcraft Indians, Dan Beard's Sons of Daniel Boone and other organizations. It secured Theodore Roosevelt as honorary Vice-President. Within three years there were 300,000 American Scouts. Calvin Coolidge was to observe that they helped to fuse the nation together, gave an extra stir to the Melting Pot. At the first world jamboree, in 1920, the Boy Scouts of America placed an Indian war-bonnet on B-P's head and proclaimed him Chief Lone-Pine-on-the-Skyline.

B-P's many tours and inspections increased the membership abroad but at home the 'mushroom growth' of Scouting brought its own problems. Many newly-sprouted troops were in the hands of manifestly 'unsuitable' Scoutmasters, especially drunkards and homosexuals. B-P surely found it even easier to spot buggers than soakers – he doubtless sensed, like John Hargrave, that 'men with high-pitched voices' were 'wrong 'uns'. However, he apparently experienced some trouble in identifying 'duds, idlers and effetes' for he later complained of their presence on the Headquarters Council, whose members he had himself appointed to govern the Scout Movement and its network of local associations. In fact, B-P was to insist on the selection rather than election of the Council because, as he said in 1920,

Scouting was his idea, and it was only in the course of development... He did not think the time was ripe for having men elected to the Council who might not want to see the movement developed in the way he wished.

However the Council was by no means a completely flaccid body and there were occasions when B-P found himself 'raging' at it, especially over the vexed matter of a correct programme for senior Scouts. B-P was convinced that Rovering did much for the young man at a critical time of his life in counteracting the evils of "safety-first", cinemas, women, jazz and idle pleasure'. However, the Rovers were as listless about Arthurian ceremonial and being buffeted on the shoulder as the Wolf Cubs were wild about Mowglian ritual and baying at the moon. B-P never managed to stem the inexorable drift out of the movement. 'Once a Scout always a Scout,' he maintained; but the mature Scout was, apparently, almost a contradiction in terms.

As he grew older himself, B-P seemed disinclined to give a direct lead to his 'Brotherhood of the Open Air and Service' which was, as he remarked, 'a natural growth... an automatic growth'. Rather he acted as the revered Founder, the figurehead at huge jamborees, the focus of uproarious ovations, the patriarch of World Scouting, ever visiting the members of his vast clan. When he stopped B-P became increasingly subject to attacks of 'brain-fag', the only cure for which was more travel or 'a severe course of fishing'. He never lost his verve, though, or his keenness on juvenile practical jokes, a fact which upset more staid Scouters. But by the 1920s and '30s his breezy behaviour seemed as anachronistic as his schoolboy slang. His verdant yarns, endlessly repeated, had become (dared one say it?) a bore. And his puerile pronouncements on the contemporary scene were an embarrassment to the movement. He inveighed against 'crooks and Communists'. He condemned Moscow under its 'German-Jew direction'. He insulted the Indians. He endorsed *apartheid* in South Africa by establishing no fewer than three separate Scouting organizations, white, brown and black – the last, 'adapted to the mentality of the native', B-P wanted to call the 'Adibi', which meant page or squire. He suggested in 1937 that the British Scouts should do 'something to be friendly with the Hitler Youth'. It was perhaps as well that B-P did not devote his full energies to Scouting, that after 1912 he became preoccupied with founding a new family of his own, with playing his private part in averting the deterioration of the race.

VIII

One day, early in 1910, General Baden-Powell's sharp eyes were attracted by a smart young lady with a brown and white spaniel walking near Kensington Barracks. From her gait he at once divined that she possessed 'honesty of purpose and common sense as well as a spirit of adventure'. Two years afterwards B-P met her on board the S.S. *Arcadian*, which was taking him on the first stage of a world tour to inspect Scouts. His first estimation was confirmed and now 'certain characteristics' of her forehead revealed that she had 'so much more sense than I should have guessed'. Olave Soames was the girl's name and she was travelling with her father, a retired brewer whose sole occupation in life was moving from place to place. Olave had received no formal education and confessed to having 'NEVER read a book hardly'. Though beset by 'ineffable longings' to do something useful she had devoted her youth to riding and biking, rowing and skating, hunting and hiking. She had been reluctant to come on the voyage because it meant leaving her horses and dogs. Olave discovered that she was born on the same day as B-P (22

February – later the Guides' 'Thinking Day') but her persistent refusal to notice the thirty-four year difference between their ages made 'the stitches of [his] heart strain'. Soon she was kissing 'the beloved Scout' and blabbing to her diary: 'He sketches away and I talk and we laugh together. Even when we try to be serious the imp of mirth steps in. We feel and think alike about everything. Perfect bliss.' Before the voyage ended they had become secretly engaged. But B-P evinced a strange reluctance to press on with the marriage. Instead of visiting his future bride after his six-month absence he immediately departed again to fish in Norway. No doubt he was nervous about his mother's reaction. Two of her fledglings had already 'left the nest' and she 'rather dreaded' the departure of a third, even though he was now aged fifty-five. Eventually, though, the nuptial knot was securely tied and the couple spent an appropriately energetic honeymoon in Algiers. B-P reported home:

> Olave is a perfect wonder in camp – thoroughly enjoys the life and is as good as a backwoodsman at it. She is a splendid walker, a good scout. . . She looks after me like a mother, absolutely spoils me. You were so right, my dear Ma, when you said one ought to marry a young woman.

Olave was, indeed, the perfect 'pal' for B-P.

B-P's strength had not, it seems, been unduly impaired by the harsh regimen to which he had subjected his person – it included touching his toes twenty-one times a day, uttering at each bend the name of a cavalry regiment. And though, winter and summer, he slept alone on the balcony of Olave's bedroom, his head and feet still exposed to the elements, she apparently sometimes joined him in the middle. For she duly gave birth to three children. B-P rejoiced in their company, though as they grew older the two girls developed what one of them called an 'inferiority complex' because of his ban on the use of nail varnish and lipstick. B-P also discovered the mellow delights of rural domesticity and he developed a passion for weeding, pruning, clipping, sawing, and cutting walking-sticks from hedgerows. Luckily gardeners, servants and secretaries (B-P's was carefully tested to determine whether she was 'capable of addressing the nobility and gentry in the correct manner') enabled the happy couple to give much of their time to the movement. In 1918, after a stiff course in knot-tying, Olave was appointed Chief Guide by... the Chief Scout. Her mother thoroughly disapproved, and whenever a Guide appeared Mrs Soames would run away and hide. In fact, Olave had just the right qualities for the post. She was lady-like: no Guide Jamboree was held in 1922 'owing to the undesirability of having great numbers of girls brought together *en masse* before the public eye'. But she was enthusiastic: camps were 'just divine', tours were 'quite HEAVENLY', rallies were 'absolutely ripping'. Olave's account of their trip to India in 1921, soon after the first Jamboree, at which B-P had been proclaimed Chief Scout of the World, is a characteristic effusion:

> The Chief is so fit and jolly and doing *immense* good. The Scouts are splendid and wildly delighted to see him but the organization and all the separate Scout bodies have tied themselves in tangled knots and we only just came in time. Guiding is all in a comfy-er position, but oh, such a lot to be done, and these dear people do want pushing on and helping... We had a splendid Scout Rally yesterday of about 1100 and in the evening there was a perfectly glorious camp fire... The Taj Mahal is too lovely and of course the absurd camels, camel carts and bullock carts are all too fascinating.

Sometimes, however, the gush ran dry and Olave was overtaken by bouts of seriousness. But her husband could always jolly her out of them by his 'ridiculous acting, comic impersonations and boyish clowning'. In return she transfused some of her blooming vitality into his gnarled frame. For though a boy at heart, B-P was visibly wilting by the 1930s. The twinkle remained in those blue eyes but the bald pate was wrinkled, the leathery skin wizened and the lean figure shrunken. Olave stiffened his failing sinews for every task, from writing his autobiography, *Lessons from the 'Varsity of Life*, to attending Rover Moots; she 'kept his pecker up' through all difficulties.

The Depression did not depress B-P, nor did the lowering political climate dash his perennial high spirits. It was, after all, a duty to 'look on the bright side of things instead of the gloomy one'. In his final message to the Boy Scouts their Founder insisted that 'God put us in this jolly world to be happy and enjoy life'. As for the Girl Guides, by ensuring that their homes were 'bright and cheery' they could reduce the number of public houses and make their future husbands happy. During the ceaseless peregrinations of his latter years, which were spent inspiring rather than inspecting his followers, B-P lived unfailingly by this creed. He was the supreme exponent of an optimism that was not so much fatuous as infantile. In typical bulletins to Percy Everett, Olave would report that 'the Chief...is so PINK! – and rubs his hands in that funny way he has – with delight.' Or, 'The darling is so happy – radiant – beaming – looking and feeling WELL – eating well, sleeping well – all LOVELY.' Of course, B-P had every excuse for his beatific state. His love for Olave was 'glorious'. He had received a British peerage and the Order of Merit and was loaded with decorations from all parts of the globe; only the outbreak of the Second World War, it was said, deprived him of the Nobel Prize for Peace. And in 1938 he retired to what Olave called 'a young Heaven', at Nyeri in Kenya. His gallant offer to return home a year later was refused and he contented himself with urging the Scouts 'to get up comic shows to divert people and take their minds off the bombing'. He was glad enough to spend much of his time in the African sunshine – surely by now he had earned the right – just loafing. And looking back over eight decades he reflected on his

> luck to live in the most interesting evolutionary epoch in the world's history, with its rapid development of motor-cars, aeroplanes, wireless, Tutenkhamen, the Great War, and World convulsion, and so on.

Slowly, carefully, he prepared himself for death. Perhaps he remembered what that bright hope of the movement, Roland Philipps, had written to him shortly before being killed in the trenches: 'the loving Creator who went with me when I bought my first Scout hat and pair of shorts will never take me to another world unless there is Scouting to be done there also.' At any rate, to the end, which occurred on 8 January 1941, B-P's faculties remained intact and alert. He did not enter a second childhood – he had never left his first. Heaven had lain about him since his infancy. And who can doubt that B-P's public-schoolboy soul graduated with honours from the 'Varsity of Life? Who can doubt that the blithe spirit of Impeesa will roam the celestial happy hunting-grounds for ever?

GENERAL BADEN-POWELL

Select Bibliography

R. S. S. Baden-Powell	*Pig-Sticking or Hog-Hunting* (1889)
R. S. S. Baden-Powell	*The Downfall of Prempeh* (1896)
R. S. S. Baden-Powell	*The Matabele Campaign 1896* (1897)
R. S. S. Baden-Powell	*Scouting for Boys* (1908)
R. S. S. Baden-Powell	*Indian Memories* (1915)
R. S. S. Baden-Powell	*Rovering to Success* (1922)
R. S. S. Baden-Powell	*Lessons from the 'Varsity of Life* (1933)
H. Begbie	*The Story of B-P* (1900)
H. Collis (*et al.*)	*B-P's Scouts* (1961)
B. Gardner	*Mafeking* (1960)
J. R. Gillis	*Youth and History* (1974)
W. Hillcourt	*Baden-Powell: The Two Lives of a Hero* (1965)
S. T. Plaatje	*Boer War Diary* (1973)
E. E. Reynolds	*The Scout Movement* (1950)
E. E. Reynolds	*Baden-Powell* (2nd edn., 1957)
J. Springhall	*Youth, Empire and Society* (1977)
E. K. Wade	*Olave Baden-Powell* (1971)
E. K. Wade	*The Chief* (1975)

Original Sources
British Museum: Baden-Powell MSS
Baden-Powell House: Baden-Powell MSS and the records of the Scout Movement